From a transcendental-semiotic point of view

MANCHESTER
UNIVERSITY PRESS

From a transcendental-semiotic point of view

KARL-OTTO APEL

edited by
MARIANNA PAPASTEPHANOU

MANCHESTER UNIVERSITY PRESS
Manchester and New York

distributed exclusively in the USA by St. Martin's Press

Published by Manchester University Press
Oxford Road, Manchester M13 9NR, UK
and Room 400, 175 Fifth Avenue, New York, NY 10010, USA

Distributed exclusively in the USA by
St. Martin's Press, Inc., 175 Fifth Avenue, New York, NY 10010, USA

Distributed exclusively in Canada by
UBC Press, University of British Columbia, 6344 Memorial Road, Vancouver, BC, Canada V6T 1Z2

British Library Cataloguing-in-Publication Data
A catalogue record for this book is available from the British Library

Library of Congress Cataloging-in-Publication Data applied for

ISBN 0 7190 5384 6 *hardback*
     0 7190 5538 5 *paperback*

First published 1998

05 04 03 02 01 00 99 98   10 9 8 7 6 5 4 3 2 1

Typeset by Best-set Typesetter Ltd., Hong Kong
Printed in Great Britain
by Redwood Books, Trowbridge

CONTENTS

AUTHOR'S ACKNOWLEDGEMENTS

I would like to thank all those who made the present collection of essays possible, especially the translators Benjamin Gregg, Christopher Macann, Dale Snow and Rolf Sommermeier, as well as those who contributed in many ways, and also improved my own writing style in English, here and in other cases.

In particular I owe a debt of gratitude to Manchester University Press and Dr Marianna Papastephanou, who first, together with members of the Department of Philosophy at The University of Wales, Cardiff, suggested the project of the present collection and then undertook the editorial work.

Karl-Otto Apel

EDITOR'S ACKNOWLEDGEMENTS

The editor wishes to express her gratitude to Professor Karl-Otto Apel for his guidance, his kind co-operation and the material he supplied me with for this collection as well as for my own writings on the 'Apel–Habermas debate'.

I am grateful to Professor Christopher Norris for his editorial advice and his inexhaustible patience. I would also like to thank the staff and students of the Philosophy Section at The University of Wales, Cardiff, Dr Evy Varsamopoulou in particular, my friends and colleagues at the University of Cyprus, Manchester University Press and all those who contributed in various ways to this volume. A number of these chapters have been published before and therefore it is my pleasure to acknowledge the permission of the publishers to reprint them. Original sources are given at the ends of the chapters. Chapters 1, 2, 9 and 10 are new and previously unpublished. Unless otherwise specified, the chapters have been translated by Karl-Otto Apel. Small changes have been made to some of the previously published material for stylistic reasons or to achieve terminological consistency. Any errors that remain are entirely my fault.

Finally, many thanks to my friends and family for their sustaining encouragement.

Marianna Papastephanou

EDITOR'S INTRODUCTION

Contemporary philosophy is by and large characterized by a shift from the subject–object model of thinking to a more linguistically informed paradigm. From Martin Heidegger's critique of metaphysics, and Martin Buber's questioning of the I–it relation, to Wittgenstein's arguments against the possibility of a private language, down to Lacan's account of the unconscious as structured like a language, the idea of a pre-linguistic origin of reflection has fallen upon hard times.

However, the critique of the notion of a world-constitutive transcendental ego does not necessarily point the way toward a conception of language as truth-yielding in a manner that would favour a correspondence theory of truth or a positivistic prioritization of the referent and the objective world. Current interpretations of the constellation 'subject, object, concept' set up a complex and highly differentiated nexus with far-reaching implications that serve to discourage mere reversals of older binary oppositions like subject versus object, mind versus body, private versus public. Thus the liquidation of the subject often goes along with a rejection of objectivism and scientism but sometimes only turns out to be the flip side of the dated and culture-specific metaphysics it appears to challenge. It is not accidental that many theorists trace residues of positivism in the work of the most prominent detractors of the metaphysics of presence.[1]

This feeling of walking a tightrope one gets when contemplating the giddy talk of paradigm shifts, blanket critique of tradition and reformulations of older concepts should not prevent us from undertaking the task of revisiting, redefining and at times discarding previous worldviews. But it should make us cautious and vigilant as to what we often polemically or prematurely brand as obsolete, logocentric and trapped within the discourse of 'enlightened' or speculative reason. It should also heighten our awareness of the fact that often what we regard as 'trendy' and path-breaking and what we dismiss as outmoded and even tyrannical can very well be secret accomplices. It might also be that alternative interpretations and assessments of past theories that appear to be at odds do in fact converge in respect of some of their deep-seated assumptions. I consider Apel's transformation of Kantian themes to be such an alternative to some postmodern approaches to issues of reason, morality and language.

At first sight, Karl-Otto Apel's interest in epistemology and (post)analytic philosophy and his commitment to transcendentalism would justify us in classifying his work within one major trend of our times – the so-called 'hard-line' philosophy of a return to foundationalism – and in opposition to the other main theoretical tendency – the postmodernist or ironic subversion of time-honoured philosophical ideals. But this foreshortened perspective would not do justice to his endeavour to find a third way between traditional metaphysics and relativism that gives his theory an almost hybrid character; it would also present us once again with a drastic choice between sides, a choice that not only is illusory but also conforms to the bipolar reasoning that postmodernism has been at great pains to condemn.

The complex and multi-dimensional framework which informs Apel's transcendental semiotics and renders it illuminating and useful even for those who would strongly disagree with many of his arguments will become apparent via a brief account of its development. The reconstruction of its 'location' will show indirectly what was indicated above, namely that Apel's philosophy, like Habermas's, shares some objectives with its postmodernist counterpart, thus leaving space for innovative mediations between French and German schools of thought, but also draws from the analytic tradition, and in this way encounters Anglo-American philosophy.

The hermeneutic turn in phenomenology provides one vital component of the architectonics of Apel's project of a transformation of Kantian reason. Heidegger showed that the cognitive aspect of our relation to the world resides always already in the 'contextual structure of being-in-the-world as understanding the coherent significance of the world'. Combined with the cultural anthropology of Erich Rothacker (Apel's mentor) and the Humboldtian conception of language as *Erzeugung*, this Heideggerian conjecture inspired Apel to accommodate in his theory an *a priori* dimension of world disclosure through language. The prioritization of relational ontology over subject-centred rationality entails a departure from Cartesian solipsism and from Husserlian transcendentalism – to the extent that the latter remains committed to the idea of a pre-linguistic philosophical origin. However, this *rapprochement* with Heidegger does not lead Apel to the philosophical dogmas, now well-worn, which trap philosophers of a Heideggerian leaning from both sides of the Atlantic. He endorses neither the Lyotardian or Foucauldian indictment of reason and social order nor the Rortyan suspicion of realism and of concomitant ideals of truth, objective knowledge and emancipation. In the present volume his renegotiation of Heideggerian ideas appears in his 'Meaning constitution and justification of validity: has Heidegger overcome transcendental philosophy by history of being?' (Chapter 5).

On the contrary the shift of interest from consciousness to language and inter-subjectivity brings Apel closer to philosophies of language in the analytic mould. He has been one of the first thinkers to consider seriously and consistently the encounter of two apparently oppositional trends, the continental and the Anglo-American. His preoccupation with the early Wittgenstein has resulted in an astute interpretation which acknowledges, in agreement with Eric Stenius, the linguistic transcendentalism of Wittgenstein's *Tractatus* and its affinities with Kant's Copernican revolution without losing sight of the latter's residual Cartesian dualism of the *res cogitans/res extensa* dichotomy and the former's proneness to efface the subject and resort to behaviourism. His assessment of the *Philosophical Investigations* has led him to make a critical-hermeneutic intervention in the *Erklären/Verstehen* controversy and to adopt a position equidistant from Georg H. von Wright's dualism and Peter Winch's cultural relativism.[2]

By taking issue with the relativistic conclusions drawn from Wittgenstein's concept of life forms Apel seeks its reconstructive import in order to provide a meaningful explanation of inter-subjectivity and communicability. Then again, once freed of relativistic leanings, an interpretation of Wittgenstein aspiring to perform the above task has to part company with the traditional rigid segregation between incommensurable hermeneutic and nomological language games. Hence Apel's overcoming of the divide between traditional hermeneutics and the post-empiricist epistemology of neo-Kantians and Popperians and his partial appropriation of elements from the two thinkers' work. Along the lines of the former school of thought, he emphasizes the peculiar character of communicative or hermeneutic experience; with regard to the latter he feels attracted to 'the normative orientation of the Popperian conception of the hermeneutic reconstruction of the history of science, as it was especially developed by Imre Lakatos'.[3]

Wittgenstein's refutation of the idea of a private language as inadequate to explain rule-following; the phenomenologically inspired critique of logical atomism and formal meta-languages; Morris's turn to pragmatics; Peirce's triadic structure of semiosis; and Austin's and Searle's assertions about the double structure of speech acts – that they involve a performative and a propositional dimension – all these comprise between them the chief developments that mark 'the impact of the broadly analytic or Anglo-American philosophy on Apel's intellectual biography' (to paraphrase the title of one of his essays). Reaching understanding with co-speakers in discourse (*Verständigung über etwas*), the types of validity claims implicitly or explicitly raised in dialogue and the normative presuppositions of argumentation, for example equality and co-responsibility of interlocutors for the outcome of their deliberation, are some of the premises on which transcendental pragmatics (or semiotics, as Apel also terms it) relies and which mirror the boundary-crossing that underpins the theoretical configurations of so-called 'second generation Frankfurt School philosophy'.

The enduring legacy of linguistic analysis would be of limited value for a project that aspires to undo the oppositions between formal logic and grammar, abstract reason and empirical content, nature and culture if not supplemented with a socio-theoretically informed account of communicative competence (context-specific construal of meaning and situated role behaviour) which in turn requires the retrieval of *praxis* chiefly undertaken by thinkers in the 'continental' line of descent. Apel has identified three paradigmatic trends of post-Hegelian philosophy concerning the binary opposition 'theory versus *praxis*': Marxism, existentialism, and American pragmatism.[4] In Marx revolutionary *praxis* dons a historical-dialectic mantle leading to a process of redemption; in Kierkegaard existential *praxis* voices the subject's resistance to totality; and, in keeping with American pragmatism, experimental *praxis* is intertwined with the vision of a democratic human life. Although Apel has never lost sight of those three philosophical tendencies and their significance, his evident indebtedness to Kantianism and his critical retrieval of Peircean themes render his intervention unique and original. It presents a mediatory approach not only to the problem of *praxis* and *theoria* but also to questions of truth, consensus and critique, as becomes obvious from his 'Transcendental semiotics and truth: the relevance of a Peircean consensus theory of truth in the present debate about truth theories' (Chapter 3). His answers to these questions revolve around the idea of certain normative presuppositions of dialogue, necessarily employed by the truth-seeking ideal communication community of all affected by the outcome of a particular discourse.

Now for Apel the presuppositions of argumentation inherent in all discourse (and the fact that by uttering a sentence we automatically raise, implicitly or explicitly, claims to some type of validity) are non-circumventible (*unhintergehbar*) – which in turn means that we cannot sidestep them without performative self-contradiction. To deny that we employ them when taking part in a dialogue amounts to denying that we are arguing or that we are conveying meaning, but the denial itself is evidently an argument with implicit presuppositions and validity claims. His pointing out of the self-disabling aporias produced by discounting or ignoring these implicit validity claims presents a challenge to those sceptics or relativists who do not recognize their language game as discursive and who cast doubt on the primacy of a positive conception of language, that is the communicative aspect of signification. In this way the idea of a performative self-contradiction – which, owing to the linguistic framework of its derivation, differs from previous notions of contradiction – is not easily deconstructible and deserves serious consideration by critical theorists of a post-structuralist persuasion.

However, the idea of the ineluctability of invoking validity claims in our utterances and the priority of communicative over strategic action require, according to Apel, a solid philosophical ground which we attain only if we regard the linguistic-pragmatic justification of articulated speech as an Archimedean point. The implication here is twofold: first, in place of the traditional *prima philosophia* a new grounding has to emerge; second, old foundationalisms have to be unmasked as false or inoperative and replaced with a more plausible claim. As concerns the first point, Apel's essay with the title 'Transcendental semiotics and the paradigms of First Philosophy' (Chapter 2) displays how he tackles the issue of paradigm shifts through a critical overcoming of the specific metaphysical baggage of modern First Philosophy. Regarding the second point, in 'Can an ultimate foundation of knowledge be non-metaphysical?' (Chapter 4) Apel discusses the so-called 'Münchhausen trilemma' – the proposition that extra-linguistic philosophical foundations reduce either to infinite regress or *petitio principii* or dogmatism – and maintains that it does not apply to transcendental-semiotic ultimate justifications.

It should be noted that all theories of regulative ideals (the Habermasian communicative ethics notwithstanding) presuppose a tension between the validity (*Gültigkeit*) and the social currency (*Geltung*) of scientific, social-normative and subjective statements, thus implicitly affirming a surplus of truth or justice unattainable by existing accounts of reality or morality. This introduces fallibilism in a compelling way. All claims are fallible, self-recuperating and subject to revision. But it would be self-defeating for a 'well-founded' philosophy, if consistent, to endorse an unrestricted fallibilism. For, as Apel argues in 'Transcendental semiotics and the paradigms of First Philosophy', the idea of a language game of doubting that does not presuppose some paradigmatic certainties is self-contradictory.

Before ending this brief overview of Apel's philosophy it would be pertinent to make some brief reference to the Apel–Habermas debate. For it is mainly on the issue of foundations that Apel and Habermas disagree. Their divergence on this point has repercussions that can perhaps be felt most strongly in their accounts of the justification of the so-called 'moral point of view'. In short Apel retains the term 'transcendental' for what Habermas terms 'universal' pragmatics in his endeavour to dispense with its idealist and subjectivist connotations. As to foundationalism, Habermas's misgivings regarding the possibility of a linguistic-pragmatic grounding of validity lead him to question the purchase or effectiveness of the idea of performative self-contradiction despite his own use of it as a counter-argument to relativist conclusions; the plausibility of treating the fact that the principle of fallibilism is not self-applicable without contradiction as something more than a 'grammatical' matter; and the proclamation of the necessary presuppositions of discourse as constituting an Archimedean point in philosophy.[5] Transferred to ethics, this mistrust of an ultimate justification leaves room only for weak justifications of morality – like that offered by Strawson[6] for instance – and relegates the question 'why act morally?' to the level of existential choice in order to avoid a moralization of language itself.

In Apel's view, however, Habermas's concessions to anti-transcendentalism weaken the capacity of discourse theory to deal

with problems of science and realism, of the simultaneous imma-
nence and transcendence which characterizes reason, of reflection
and its significance to philosophical method, of the defence of the
primacy of communicative action, and of the binding force of the
normative presuppositions of argumentation. Habermas's socio-
cultural connection of lifeworld and ethics (his *intentio recta* approach
to morality) resembles, as Apel sees it, a naturalistic fallacy. Nevertheless, these divergences aside, Apel and Habermas share many
insights and both are motivated by a common objective: to revisit
Kant via a paradigm that retains the merits of the linguistic turn
while being vigilant enough to avoid its problems and drawbacks.

This commitment to similar ideals often misleads Apel's and
Habermas's critics, those of post-structuralist leanings in particular,
into viewing their theories as interchangeable and subject to the
same criticisms. Given that Apel's work is not as well known to
Anglo-American readers as that of Habermas, the present collection
should hopefully contribute to putting the record straight.
Habermas's universal pragmatics is not foundationalist and Apel's
transcendental pragmatics is not 'logocentric' if by that one means,
as post-structuralists and postmodernists often do, 'in thrall to
Cartesian metaphysics'. Equally, Apel's project is not as open to the
charge of conceding too much to anti-realism or Rortyan pragmatism
as some have argued Habermas's project to be. Those who subscribe
to the most recent trend towards scientific realism and transcendentalism will find this collection of essays a great opportunity
to consider a continental proposal. To those interested in the
Habermas–Apel debate this volume will provide useful information
and background knowledge of one of the parties involved. And to
those who are generally engaged in boundary-crossing philosophical
ventures the essays on Heidegger, Peirce, Husserl and Wittgenstein
will prove exceptionally valuable.

As for the opponents of philosophical pretensions to truth and
reason, they will perhaps be surprised to find that up to a point
Apel is in agreement with their critique of science and formal logic.
Moreover, in his considerable departure from their interpretation of
the linguistic turn, Apel challenges the polemical categorizations and
caricatures which have so far characterized their wholesale rejection
of opposing theories. In this way, the already heated debates around
modernity, postmodernity and their redemptive or counterfactual

possibilities will be furnished with more pertinent critiques. It is to be hoped that this will promote more informed and substantial research on both sides of this supposed epochal shift.

Marianna Papastephanou

Notes

1 For accusations of positivism against Lyotard, see A. Wellmer, *The Persistence of Modernity: Essays on Aesthetics, Ethics, and Postmodenism*, trans. D. Midgley (Cambridge, Mass.: MIT Press, 1991). For similar charges directed against Foucault, see A. Honneth, *Critique and Power: Reflective Stages in Critical Social Theory*, trans. K. Baynes (Cambridge, Mass.: MIT Press, 1991), p. 169.
2 K.-O. Apel, *Understanding and Explanation: A Transcendental-pragmatic Perspective*, trans. G. Warnke (Cambridge, Mass.: MIT Press, 1984).
3 See p. 26 below.
4 See p. 30 below.
5 Here I can only indicate the main issues of the debate. For a more detailed account see M. Papastephanou, 'Communicative Action and Philosophical Foundations: Comments on the Apel–Habermas Debate', *Philosophy and Social Criticism*, 23, 4 (1997), 41–69.
6 J. Habermas, *Moral Consciousness and Communicative Action*, trans. C. Lenhardt and S.W. Nicholsen (Cambridge: Polity Press, 1992).

1

The impact of analytic philosophy on my intellectual biography

The licence of an idiosyncratic perspective in my chapter title will help me, I hope, to cope with a topic that is as vast and full of unsolved problems as it appears to me at first glance. A second aid may be provided by choosing the narrative form of accounting for the variety of my experiences. Finally a certain ideal-typical simplification will be needed for an *ex post* structuring of the dialectics of my long march through the very different camps of so called 'analytic philosophy'.

The linguistic turn

It may have been characteristic of the perspective of my first encounter with analytic philosophy that I used the term 'linguistic turn' (*sprachanalytische Wende*) in order to refer to those directions of twentieth-century philosophy which I first perceived as a challenge in the (late) 1950s. At that time I had already passed the so-called 'hermeneutic' turn of phenomenology: along with Heidegger – and inspired by the cultural anthropology of my philosophical teacher, Erich Rothacker, and the neo-Humboldtism of my linguistic teacher, Leo Weisgerber – I had come to the conclusion that a transformation of the Kantian 'critique of pure reason' had to be considered that would take into account an *a priori* of world disclosure through language. Still I experienced the relationship between this conception of language and that of 'linguistic philosophy' (primarily of Wittgenstein's *Tractatus* and the philosophy of Russell, Tarski and Carnap) as that of an extreme opposition, and I tried to expound this opposition in a history of the modern conception of language as that of the 'transcendental-hermeneutic' conception, on the one hand, and the 'scientific-technological' one, on the other hand.[1] (Still today

I consider this ideal-typical distinction as justified if one associates the term 'linguistic philosophy' with the construction of formalized ('ideal') languages in the service of mathematical logics and exact science.)

The next step in my reception of 'linguistic philosophy' was a three-fold one which has to be explicated in some detail.

First, I realized that Wittgenstein's *Tractatus* should not be understood only as a source of inspiration for logical positivism but also as a kind of transcendental philosophy, namely as a transformation of Kant's critique of pure reason into a 'critique of pure language' (to speak along with Eric Stenius, who thoroughly carried through this particular interpretation).[2] In this transformation of Kant's approach the 'supreme principle of synthetic judgements' (that the conditions of the possibility of experience are at the same time the conditions of the possibility of the objects of experience) was to be replaced by the principle that the conditions of the possibility of describing facts through sentences are at the same time the conditions of the possibility of the facts themselves as 'existing states of affairs' (*bestehende Sachverhalte*) for us. Later it gave me great satisfaction to find out that Wittgenstein himself had explicitly confirmed this interpretation by the following dictum: 'Die Grenze der Sprache zeigt sich in der Unmöglichkeit, die Tatsache zu beschreiben, die einem Satz entspricht . . . , ohne eben den Satz zu wiederholen. (Wir haben es hier mit der Kantischen Lösung des Problems der Philosophie zu tun)'[3] (The limit of language shows itself by the impossibility of describing the fact that corresponds to a sentence . . . , without repeating precisely that sentence. (We are dealing here with the Kantian solution to the problem of philosophy.)).

Second, however, I found my former subsumption of the language conception of the *Tractatus* under the head of the scientific-technological conception of language reconfirmed as well; for I realized that the main difference between the transcendentalism of the *Tractatus* and the classical one, and especially that of my own conception of transcendental hermeneutics, was the fact that in Wittgenstein's *Tractatus* no transcendental subject capable of self-reflection was supposed but instead a kind of absorption of the transcendental *I* by the 'transcendental logical form of language', which at the same time was supposed to be that of the describable world. This feature of a limit case transcendentalism, in which the *I* becomes an 'extensionless point' so that 'solipsism . . . coincides with pure realism' (5.64) obviously corresponded to Russell's logical atomism and to his theory of types, according to which no sign can refer to all signs (nor can any language system be self-referential). Thereby – I would judge today[4] – the philosophical type of discourse rationality, that of a simultaneously communicative and self-reflective structure of thought (Plato's 'voiceless dialogue of the soul with itself'), was subordinate, or even sacrificed, to the rationality of formal (mathematical) logic which had to replace self-reflection of thought (*noesis noeseos*) by the potentially infinite series of meta-languages. This change may perhaps count as the deepest expression of the original claim of the scientific-technological conception of language (Leibniz's *lingua universalis* of the *calculus ratiocinator*), which however, if I see it correctly, has been put into its place by Gödel's insights into the limits of formalization and – simultaneously – by the insight that Russell's (and Tarski's) veto on self-referential uses of language can itself be formulated only by using an (implicitly) self-referential – and hence forbidden – para-language.

Now, to this aporia a thorough correspondence could be found in the deep structure of Wittgenstein's *Tractatus*. For the limit case transcendentalism characterized above led, as far as I could see, to two paradoxical consequences.[5] On the other hand, the absorption of the transcendental *I* by the logical form of language, which precluded transcendental self-reflection of thought, made it impossible for Wittgenstein, from the outset, to acknowledge as meaningful his own philosophical language, which he used in talking about the relationship between the form of the language and the form of the world. He veiled this aporia of the para-language by the distinction between what 'can be said' and what can only 'show itself' and by the literally effective metaphor of the ladder (language) which after its indispensable use has to be thrown away (cf. 6.54).

Third, Wittgenstein could not suppose the existence of an *I* as a subject of intentions (and of intentional meanings of words or sentences) within the describable world either (cf. 5.631); for the describable facts of which the world consists had to be either atomic facts, that is existing *Sachverhalte* to be depicted by atomic sentences, or objects of complex sentences that can be conceived as truth functions of atomic sentences. Now, since intentional sentences like 'A believes that *p*' or 'A says that *p*' can be understood neither as pictures of *Sachverhalte* (i.e., configurations of things) nor as truth functions of atomic sentences, Wittgenstein decided that their true meaning is that of semantical sentences, namely of ' "p" says p' (cf. 5.542). By this move, however, the entire language of communicatively understanding other people and hence of hermeneutic *Geisteswissenschaften* was excluded from the meaningful language of world representation. This latter was restricted to that of the 'natural sciences' (4.11). Wittgenstein thereby reduced the problem of inter-subjective understanding (*Verständigung*) about the linguistic world interpretation (from Humboldt to Heidegger) to that of information transfer under the presupposition of one meaningful language (or, at best, one deep structure of meaningful languages) of a correct world representation; and, at the same time, he suggested a physicalistic – for example behaviouristic – thematization of all kinds of meaningful actions or cultural institutions within the world of empirical facts. In both respects he reinforced the technically oriented language philosophy of logical positivism and its reductionist programme of a 'logic of unified science'.

Nevertheless, the programme of critical analysis of language (*Sprachkritik*) which could also be derived from the *Tractatus* and indeed was carried through by Carnap and others in the way of constructing different syntactico-semantical frameworks of possible scientific languages testified to the possibility and undeniable necessity of communicative (inter-subjective) understanding (*Verständigung*) about the 'logical form of language' on the meta-level, so to speak, of all physicalistic-scientific descriptions of the world, including the social world. This fact was in a way taken into account by Carnap himself, in his consideration of the 'pragmatic' dimension of language, that is the use of natural language as an ultimate meta-language for all construction of syntactico-semantical frameworks. By this terminological architectonics, Carnap followed the foundation of semiotics by Charles Morris,[6] who, by supplementing the syntactic and the semantic dimension of 'semiosis' with the pragmatic one (i.e., that of sign use by the interpreter), wanted to reconfirm and apply Charles Peirce's insight into the in-principle-triadic structure of 'semiosis' as the function of mediating human cognition and actions through signs. But Carnap, like Morris himself, who tried to integrate his pragmatism into the programme of a unified science, did not really account for the triadicity of the sign function. For the fact that the pragmatic dimension of language construction concerns a subjective–inter-subjective presupposition (in Kantian terminology, 'condition of the possibility'), of all possible reference of semantical frameworks and hence of scientific descriptions of mundane facts, and thus far cannot be adequately thematized as an object of empirical scientific description, was considered by Carnap only in so far as he spoke in this respect of an 'external' problem of constructive semantics which was to be solved not by philosophical theory but by practical decisions.[7] At the same time, like Morris, he suggested a description and explanation of the 'formative' use of language construction as part of the subject matter of empirical (behaviouristic) pragmatics.[8] Thus far the transcendental function of the 'logical form' of language (in the sense of the *Tractatus*) was not accounted for, as it would be expected, through the introduction of the pragmatic dimension of 'semiosis'. (This situation remained the same even when Morris, Carnap, Martin and Montague projected a 'pure' or 'formal' pragmatics that, by constructing a theoretical meta-language for the object language of empirical pragmatics, provided a 'semantization', so to speak, of pragmatics.)[9] In brief: a genuine transcendental reflection on the semiotic place and epistemological function of communicative (inter-subjective) understanding remained taboo even after the recognition of the 'pragmatic dimension of semiosis'. I considered this fact as being the most characteristic, nay even paradigmatic, feature of the first phase or stage of linguistic philosophy, a feature that could be explained in a sense by the superseding of philosophical discourse rationality (as I would call it today)[10] through the rationality of mathematical logic.

At this juncture I came to outline a heuristic, as it were, with regard to my study of the development of linguistic philosophy in its second phase: that of so-called 'ordinary language philosophy'. But, being fascinated by Morris's and Carnap's talk of pragmatics, which soon became the key word for all unsolved rest or limit problems in the neo-positivistic logic of science – broadly displayed in Germany by Stegmüller[11] – I soon began to include also American pragmatism, especially the work of Charles Peirce, into my study of Anglo-Saxon analytic philosophy. Corresponding to what I have suggested above, my heuristic comprised the following two main perspectives. First, there was the remaining interest in the question of a language-analytical transformation of the Kantian programme of transcendental philosophy. Second, there was my interest in a critical examination of the analytic philosophy of science (in a wide sense comprising the neo-positivist logic of science as well as Popperianism and, later, the so-called post-empiricist history of science) under the point of view of looking and even waiting for the reappearance of the problems of intentional actions and hermeneutic understanding within the frame of history and the social sciences after the complete failure of physicalistic reductionism (e.g. behaviourism) had become obvious.

With regard to both perspectives of my interest in analytic philosophy, my heuristic was steered, I may say, by some ideas that directly resulted from my critical view of the first phase of linguistic philosophy. First, there was my very early conviction that transcendental reflection on the subjective–inter-subjective conditions of the possibility of valid thought and cognition must not be dropped along with the critique of 'meaningless' (or 'nonsensical') questions of traditional metaphysics but rather belongs together with the meaning-critical (*sinnkritische*) refoundation of transcendental philosophy after the 'linguistic turn' of First Philosophy. Later I would even consider the test of the performative self-contradiction to be the very core of meaning critique as well as of an ultimate foundation of transcendental philosophy.[12] This viewpoint of my heuristic was first subsumed under my concept of 'transcendental hermeneutics', where it was to supplement somehow the older conception of world-meaning-disclosure by language, inspired by Humboldt and Heidegger. Later (from around 1970) I opted for the term 'transcendental pragmatics of language' for the dimension of meaning critique and reflective ultimate foundation of the conditions of the possibility of valid thought. The term 'transcendental pragmatics of language' points also to a second main viewpoint in the background of both perspectives of my heuristic. For 'transcendental pragmatics' could be considered to be the right term for a programme of reflection on the third place within the relation of semiosis (that of the 'interpreter' qua subject of sign-mediated action and cognition), a programme that would thoroughly overcome the 'abstractive fallacy' that, on my account, was entailed in all tendencies to reduce the triadicity of semiosis through replacing transcendental reflection on the third place by some kind of semantization strategy, either directly by empirical (e.g. behaviouristic) pragmatics or by formal pragmatics as a meta-language of empirical pragmatics.[13]

With regard to the first, transcendental, perspective of my heuristic of studying the second phase of language-analytical philosophy, I first focused on the later philosophy of Wittgenstein. In the *Philosophical Investigations*, which I studied under the viewpoint of a thoroughgoing comparison with the quasi-transcendental architectonics of the *Tractatus*,[14] I found not only a novel – thoroughly pragmatic – conception of language and its meaning but also, together with the continuation of the programme of *Sprachkritik*, a transformation of the quasi-transcendental architectonics of the *Tractatus*. Considering the idea of grammar, or of the grammatical deep structure of language games, as parallel to the transcendental logical form of language in the *Tractatus*, one could ascertain that the quasi-Kantian problem of the conditions of the possibility of world description (or world interpretation) underwent a diversification according to the different – possibly even incommensurable – deep structures (including extra-linguistic *Muster*, criteria or paradigms) of the language use in different language games, belonging to different forms of life. Now, this diversification of the *a priori* of linguistic world interpretation was apt to open up also, second, a new perspective to the problem of hermeneutic understanding, which in the *Tractatus* was rather dissolved or made to disappear by (or in favour of) the dichotomy of *Sachverhalte* (as objects of the natural sciences) and the one logical form of world representation. It seemed to be possible then to conceive of *Verstehen* not as *Einfühlung* into specific kinds of (behavioural) *Sachverhalte*, as it was suggested by the neo-positivists,[15] but rather as the capacity of participating in a specific language game and thereby in a form of life *praxis* and world interpretation. The presupposition, though, of this conception of hermeneutic understanding seemed to me that it was considered to be not so much a type or method of empirical cognition but rather a competence of rule-following that (belonging to a language game as a form of life) had to be presupposed by any successful act of factual understanding, either on the pre-scientific level of communication and interaction or on the level of 'understanding social sciences'. These latter, to that extent, had almost to be equated to a philosophy concerned with studying different socio-cultural forms of life as being the ultimate – non-transcendible – transcendental-logical preconditions of world interpretation and communicative understanding of other people.

This at least was the perspective of interpreting Wittgenstein's later philosophy that was opened up by Peter Winch in his book *The Idea of a Social Science*.[16] I was fascinated by this book because it did not, as was usual even in the circles of ordinary language philosophy, interpret Wittgenstein's *Philosophical Investigations* (especially his polemics against the hypostatizations of meaning intentions as psychical states) in a behaviouristic spirit but, inversely, understood even the given facts of human behaviour from the point of view of (intelligible and justifiable) rule-following. Thereby Winch, so to speak, redeemed my postulate, set up already in face of the first phase of linguistic philosophy, that the obvious contradiction between its method – that is of language analysis – and its scientific-physicalistic methodology with regard to given phenomena of linguistic meaning had to be overcome in favour of connecting the problem of language analysis (or of constructing semantical frameworks) with that of (transcendental) hermeneutics.[17] On the other hand, however, through comparing and confronting Winch's conception of a hermeneutic social science – and, in its light, the work of the later Wittgenstein – with the German tradition of hermeneutics (from Schleiermacher and Dilthey to Gadamer), I arrived at the final result that the novel view of analytical hermeneutics had to pay too high a price for its undeniable achievements. For there were two polar-opposite but corresponding deficits or aporias resulting, it seemed to me, from the Wittgensteinian approach.

First, it was not possible to account for the fact that hermeneutic understanding of the *Geisteswissenschaften* was capable, and in charge, not only of interpreting particular phenomena of human culture in the light of already understood rules of language games and forms of life but also, inversely, of understanding and interpreting particular phenomena (especially texts or works of art, but also single actions) in such a way as to disclose gradually novel rules of language games and strange forms of life. Here the abstract distinction between rules and cases of their application had to be replaced, it appeared to me, by a more dialectical relationship between form and content of understanding, as suggested, for example, through the 'hermeneutic circle' (Dilthey, Heidegger, Gadamer) or the conception of a historical 'fusion of the horizons' of world interpretation (Gadamer). On the other hand, it was a consequence of Wittgenstein's or Winch's diversification of the quasi-transcendental rule conditions of world interpretation and communicative understanding that it became unintelligible how the sociologist or social philosopher might understand a form of life that was not always already his or her own. Winch seemed to draw upon himself at least half of the conse-

quences of this difficulty by denying the possibility not of understanding but of critically evaluating the paradigmatic rule conditions
(e.g. witchcraft oracles) of a primitive form of life.[18] I later had to take
issue again and again with the relativistic impact of the reception of
Wittgenstein's conception of *Lebensformen* (i.e. the interwovenness
of language games, forms of actions or institutions and evaluative
modes of world interpretation) in cultural anthropology (e.g.
Geertz), post-empiristic philosophy of science (e.g. Thomas Kuhn's
thesis of the incommensurability of paradigms), and communitarian
types of ethics (e.g. MacIntyre, Winch, Rorty and many others).[19]
Indeed, the brilliant arguments of Wittgenstein's *Philosophical
Investigations* against the possibility of private rule-following or a
'private language' which I considered a main support to my own
efforts towards overcoming methodological solipsism (the paradigm
of modern philosophy of consciousness from Descartes to Husserl)
seemed to be internally connected with the suggestion (to my mind
unacceptable) that there are no conceptual criteria of correct rule-
following, say in mathematics or in ethics, independent from factual
customs (*Gepflogenheiten*) or institutions of socio-cultural forms of
life. Should it not be possible to set up novel rules or norms that are
to change (e.g. to revolutionize) the customs and institutions of a
factual form of life?

In this context the most puzzling feature, from the point of
view of a consistent transformation of Kantian transcendental
epistemology into a transcendental critique of language or meaning,
appeared to me to be the fact that Wittgenstein, in all his verdicts
against the 'idle running' or the self-misunderstandings of the philosophical language games, did not find it necessary to answer the
question, by what kind of sound language game he himself could be
enabled to carry through his critical analysis, that is, to suggest the
philosophical point of his questions and examples by talking about
language games in general and their relationship to activities
and forms of life, in order to cure the philosophical sickness.
In this respect I finally allowed myself to assign a positive, that is a
transcendental-pragmatic, interpretation to Wittgenstein's last work,
Über Gewissheit (*On Certainty*), which appeared in 1969.[20]

In this book Wittgenstein takes up G.E. Moore's examples of
unarguable commonsense certainties and suggests that they owe
their status to the specific role they play within a language game,
here specifically in a 'system' of arguing. Their role for Wittgenstein

seems to be that of 'paradigmatic evidence' (my term) because their certainty is presupposed by all possible evidence and counter-evidence one could appeal to within the system of a certain language game (cf. e.g. 672, 3, 83, 105, 114 f., 126, 185, 188, 196, 247 ff., 341, 432, 657, 672). In this context Wittgenstein even offers some summaries that appear very principled, like the following:

> Wer an allem zweifeln wollte, der würde auch nicht bis zum Zweifeln kommen. Das Spiel des Zweifelns selbst setzt schon die Gewissheit voraus. (114)

> (If you are not certain of any fact, you cannot be certain of the meaning of your words either.) (114)

and:

> Alle Prüfung, alles Bekräften und Entkräften einer Annahme geschieht schon innerhalb eines Systems. Und zwar ist dies System nicht ein mehr oder weniger willkürlicher und zweifelhafter Anfangspunkt aller unsere Argumente, sondern es gehört zum Wesen dessen, was wir ein Argument nennen. Das System ist nicht so sehr der Ausgangspunkt als das Lebenselement der Argumente. (105)

> (All testing, all confirmation and disconfirmation of a hypothesis takes place already within a system. And this system is not a more or less arbitrary and doubtful point of departure for all our arguments: no, it belongs to the essence of what we call an argument. The system is not so much the point of departure, as the element in which arguments have their life.) (105)

Now, I took up this summary as a quasi-transcendental argument to be used against the thesis of the so-called 'consistent', that is even 'self-applicable', fallibilism which was suggested by some proponents of Karl Popper's critical rationalism, such as W.W. Bartley, Hans Albert and Gerhard Radnitzky.[21] For this purpose, however, it was necessary to distinguish the philosophical language game, which is used for example by Wittgenstein in his summaries, from all other language games or systems of arguing. For Wittgenstein himself did not deny that the language games or systems about whose paradigmatic evidences he was talking could change under the influence of novel experiences (cf. 63, 65, 16 ff., 256, 291). To this extent Hans Albert was right, as well as in claiming that, even if there might be paradigmatic evidence or certainties constitutive for the activity of doubting within a particular language game, it is still possible, in principle, for critical rationalists to question virtually all language games together with their specific paradigmatic grounds of evidence. This generalized doubt on the meta-level of fallibilistic reflection seemed to me to be indeed characteristic of the enlightening power of critical philosophy; but the story of critical reflection was not finished at this point, for it was possible to ask for the paradigmatic evidence of precisely that critical philosophical language game in which – by questioning all other language games – the universal principle of fallibilism could be formulated. I called it the 'transcendental language game' of philosophical discourse.

The normative presuppositions of argumentation

Thus far I was reclaiming, as it were, the Wittgensteinian strategy of argument on the meta-level of 'pancritical' (Bartley) reflection. But, as it appears to me now, my argument was different from Wittgenstein's strategy as well; for I did not think that for the paradigmatic evidence of the 'transcendental language game' no ultimate foundation could be provided, as Wittgenstein indeed suggested with regard to all paradigmatic certainties (cf. e.g. 110, 112, 131, 144, 148, 166, 175, 185, 192). It seems to me that Peter Strawson has recently – after abandoning his belief in transcendental arguments – taken up and renewed this Wittgensteinian position under the heading of 'soft-naturalism'.[22] Contrary to this, I thought that in the case of the transcendental language game, which is constituted by the virtually universal doubt of philosophical fallibilism, we are not contingently dependent, as Wittgenstein suggests, on the 'natural history' of the development of language games, but can orient our search for paradigmatic evidence by asking the quasi-Kantian question as regards the conditions of the possibility of the validity of the meaning claim of phrases like 'all philosophical theses are fallible . . . are dubitable . . . may be falsified, etc.'

This orientation directs our search for the paradigmatic evidence for the transcendental language game to the necessary presuppositions of meaningful arguing, as for example to the fact that we must have universal validity claims and must suppose that they can and should be tested by arguments only and eventually confirmed or refuted by the universal consensus of an unlimited discourse community. Furthermore, from the paradigmatic relationship of the search for paradigmatic evidence to the meaning claim of the principle of virtually universal fallibilism we can even derive a formal criterion for the possible validity of that evidence that cannot be doubted in principle and thus can be considered to be ultimately justified or grounded. Validity claims have to fulfil the following two conditions.

First, every attempt at disputing the relevant validity claims must lead to a performative self-contradiction, and second, at the same time, it must be impossible to ground them by deduction without committing a *petitio principii*.[23] It should be noted that this transcendental-pragmatic criterion cannot be invalidated by Rorty's argument 'to end all transcendental arguments', namely by the thesis that transcendental arguments concerning 'categorial schemes' can at best have an *ad hoc* validity with regard to certain sceptical doubts that are parasitic upon them, or, more radically, by the thesis that 'the very idea of a categorial scheme' that could be separated from its content can no longer be tenable.[24] For these arguments, which may indeed be valid with regard to most of the transcendental arguments that were proposed by Strawson and his followers, cannot pertain to those undeniable presuppositions of arguing that are implied in the performative part of all – even Rorty's – philosophical arguments. Thus I have indeed been led through an over-interpretation of Wittgenstein's last work into the research programme of a transcendental pragmatics of argumentative discourse[25] which I have pursued in the last few decades, in particular with regard to an ultimate foundation of discourse ethics.[26]

I may supplement this report about my transcendental-pragmatic interpretation of the later Wittgenstein's work with a reference to my parallel study of Austin's and Searle's theory of speech acts in the 1970s.[27] Here, as in my study of Chomsky's generative linguistics,[28] I could go along with and share a great deal of Jürgen Habermas's interpretation of the same theories in his conception of a 'universal' – or later 'formal' – pragmatics.[29] This holds in particular with regard to the following aspects.

First, with regard to the performative-propositional double structure (*Doppelstruktur*) of all speech acts, and even of all sentences that have been made explicit with regard to their deep structure, so to speak, I was especially fascinated by the self-referential meaning of explicit performative phrases, such as 'I hereby tell you, promise you, order you' etc., which on the level of discourse can even be transformed by any competent arguer into propositional knowledge by a kind of public reflection that belongs to the language game itself. I see here the possibility of renewing the problematic of philosophical (transcendental) self-reflection of thought in a non-psychological way. By contrast Habermas has recently appeared to consider any renewal of the problematic of reflection with the aid of language pragmatics as a relapse into the obsolete paradigm of the transcendental philosophy of consciousness.[30]

Second, I could almost fully endorse Habermas's architectonics of the three or four validity claims that belong to speech acts or to their world relationships (*Weltbezüge*), as there are the claims to sharable meaning, truth, veracity and (morally relevant) rightness, and his tenet that to understand the meaning of a speech act (or explicit sentence) means not only to know the 'truth conditions', or even the 'fulfilment' or 'satisfaction conditions' (Strawson and Searle), but also to know the 'acceptability conditions' with regard to the good or bad reasons for all the implicit or explicit validity claims. Nevertheless, in my reception of this interpretation and expansion of speech act theory, I also stuck to my own transcendental-pragmatic frame of interpretation.

Thus, concerning, for instance, Searle's recent turn to the priority of mental 'representation' and 'intentionality' over communication by language, I came to advance a critique quite similar to that of Habermas,[31] but, at the same time, I could not completely agree with Habermas and his dealing with a problem that he himself had exposed through his further development of speech act theory in his *Theory of Communicative Action*. I am referring to the problem of the difference between 'consensus-oriented' (*verständigungsorientiertem*) and 'strategic-oriented' (*erfolgsorientiertem*) use of language.[32] I cannot agree that the priority of the former over the latter, if it is not implicitly admitted by the speaker (as in the case of lying or rhetorical manipulation) but openly disregarded (as in the case of restricting the dialogue to offers and threats in negotiations), can be demonstrated by any – say, linguistic or sociological – argument except the transcendental one that consists in showing that, on the level of philosophical discourse, any arguer who denies the priority of the consensus-oriented use of language in favour of the strategic-oriented must commit a performative self-contradiction.[33]

From this anticipation of some final results of my study of the second phase of linguistic philosophy from the heuristic vantage point of a linguistic transformation of transcendental philosophy, let me once again return to the second perspective of my heuristics, namely an expected convergence of linguistic and hermeneutic philosophy. In this regard two focal points of the recent discussion seemed significant: on the one hand, the so-called 'New Dualism'[34] of the neo-Wittgensteinian approach to the old question of the relationship between causal (nomological) explanation and hermeneutic (e.g. intentional or teleological) understanding; and, on the other hand, the obvious convergence of hermeneutic perspectives (e.g. those of Heidegger and Gadamer) and the later Wittgenstein's conception of different paradigms of language games or forms of life in the so called post-empiricist philosophy of science.

With regard to the first focal point of the recent discussion, I was stimulated by G.H. von Wright's book *Explanation and Understanding*[35] into a comprehensive thematization of the old topic of the explanation-versus-understanding controversy,[36] which was familiar to me from the tradition of hermeneutics and the Diltheyan project of providing a foundation for the *Geisteswissenschaften*.[37] Already von Wright himself had emphasized that in his book he had tried to apply a teleological (or intentionalist) action theory, which was a result of the anti-positivist tendency within analytical philosophy, to the methodological controversy about *Verstehen* and *Erklären* which in Germany was initiated in the nineteenth century. However, he stressed the possibility of a teleological *ex post* explanation of action as a historical fact which he understood as an Aristotelian alternative to the causal and nomological explanation of action qua behaviour event, characteristic of the Galilean style of modern science. By contrast, I considered the main alternative to consist in the difference between causal and nomological explanation of behaviour events (so far going along with von Wright) and pure understanding of the possible – good or bad – reasons for actions (which is hermeneutically relevant even in cases where it cannot be applied to an adequate (*ex post*) explanation of behaviour events, say, because the actions were only planned but not executed, or because the bad reasons for the executed actions made it necessary to provide an external causal explanation of the actions taken as behaviour events).

One of the main reasons for this shift in understanding the 'New Dualism' of the different language games that underlies the explanation-versus-understanding controversy was given by my background assumption that a profound difference – and at the same time a complementarity – of cognitive interests is constitutive for the difference between the 'why' questions in case of either causal explanation or understanding of reasons. What is meant here could even be illustrated by the 'experimentalist' or 'interventionist' theory of causality (very plausible, in my opinion) defended by von Wright.[38] For, if the possibility of a causal explanation of an event *e* by the preceding *e* conceptually presupposes the possibility of our 'bringing about' *e* by 'doing' (something that corresponds to) *e*, then we find here an example of the irreducible difference and, at the same time, complementarity of our cognitive interests in causal-nomological explanation of behaviour events and pure understanding of the reasons of intentional actions. (The conception of complementarity is further illustrated by the fact that not only does the notion of causal necessity presuppose that of understandable free action but also the inverse holds; for when we say 'we *can do* this' (e.g. climb a mountain, or swim a lake) we suppose as well that the possibilities of our free actions are restricted by causal laws.)

Through my (transcendental-pragmatic) account of the 'new dualism' of understanding and explanation by the supposition of a profound difference of cognitive interests (which could be considered to be constitutive for the different meanings of our 'why' questions and thus for the different language games) I was led to consider the examples of intentional or teleological explanation, which by von Wright and other analytic philosophers are opposed to causal-nomological explanation, as being rather cases of a dialectical mediation between the cognitive interests of pure hermeneutic understanding and causal explanation. In this respect, though, there were again very different types of mediation to be considered, on my account.[39] For it is possible, for instance, to put understanding of reasons as a heuristic means in the service of causal explanation (and thereby of prediction), as is done in the so called 'behavioural sciences', which are guided by a social-technological interest (this is a case always considered by the neo-positivists like Hempel, Abel and others); but it is also possible to go the other way around and mediate deep understanding of human motives through quasi-causally explanatory phases of inquiry, as is done in psychoanalysis or sociological critique of ideology (both of them searching for motives that, being virtually understandable but unconscious to the agents, may exert compulsive effects on them).

Under this perspective von Wright's paradigm case of teleological explanation turned out to be a novel type of mediation; for his preferred example of *ex post* explanation in history does, on my account, presuppose a hermeneutic understanding of a good reason and the belief in the causal effectiveness of that reason (warranted by the fact that the action, which was well understood *ex post factum*, has in fact happened); but it does not presuppose any knowledge of a causal law.[40] Thus it is a mediating event explanation through hermeneutic understanding; but, in contradistinction to the relevant cases of 'behavioural science', it does not lend itself to social-technological predictions. (This may be considered as a confirmation as well as a correction of Karl Popper's criticism of the prediction claims of 'historicism'; for it affects Karl Marx but not Hegel, who claimed only *ex post* explanations of historical necessity.)

The second focus of the recent discussion in analytic philosophy that brings together hermeneutic and Wittgensteinian motives of thought is represented by the so-called 'post-empiricist philosophy of science'. I found that interesting, especially in connection to Thomas Kuhn's *The Structure of Scientific Revolutions* (1962) and the debates following its publication.[41] What struck me, from the beginning, with regard to Kuhn's book was the convergence of Wittgenstein's notions of language-game paradigms and Heideggerian (and Gadamerian) notions about epochal (or epoch-making) groundings of our pre-understanding of the world by world disclosures (uncoverings) of meaning and truth. (But also themes from American pragmatism, to which I shall come back later, seemed to be influential in the background.)

Now, as concerns the convergence of hermeneutic and Wittgensteinian ideas, I was well prepared to accept, and even welcome, many insights that helped to surmount the methodological solipsism and the overlooking of the *a priori* of linguistically and socio-historically impregnated world interpretation which characterized the traditional – positivistic and mentalistic-transcendental – epistemology and philosophy of science. Yet, on the other hand, there were also tendencies that I had already criticized in the later Wittgenstein (and Winch, as mentioned above) and in Heidegger's and Gadamer's philosophies, which I now found especially irritating in the context of a philosophy of science. After what I have already intimated, my resistance to certain tendencies of Kuhnian (and post-Kuhnian) philosophy of science may here perhaps be signalled provisionally by noticing that my opposition to scientism in the light of hermeneutics did not mean to my mind a questioning of the rationality of science and its progress; and my opposition to transcendental mentalism and methodological solipsism did not commit me to a rejection of the universalism of transcendental philosophy altogether in favour of a relativistic historicism. From this general point of view I tried to defend – as already in the case of Gadamer's *Truth and Method* – the normative-methodological implications of a differentiated philosophy of science (according to different cognitive interests which themselves have a normative underpinning) against the tendency to replace the idea of a possible scientific progress toward the truth (in different normative dimensions) by the conception of a history of truth happenings or mere paradigm changes.

The post-Kuhnian philosophy of science

Here I shall mention only two points of my encounter with the post-Kuhnian philosophy of science. A minor point of challenge was presented to me by the tendency (or rather fashion) – to be found especially in the Anglo-American scene – to propagate a novel version, as it were, of the ideal of a unified science, but this time in the name of pan-hermeneutics. All the subtle criteriological achievements of three or more phases of the explanation-versus-understanding controversy were swept aside by the strange argument (advanced by people who probably did not even know the older history of hermeneutics) that the natural sciences have a hermeneutic character too because their history has indeed shown that they are always dependent on a historically impregnated pre-understanding of the lifeworld. Against this conclusion at least the following arguments should be put forward.

First, the socio-historical pre-understanding of the world is primarily thematized not by natural science itself but by history of science, which, of course, always was and still is a hermeneutic *Geisteswissenschaft* (even more so than the quasi-nomological sciences of social behaviour).

Second, the natural sciences must try to separate methodologically over and again their subject matter – nature objectified as epitome of nomic structures – from the (different!) pre-understandings of the lifeworld from which they indeed have to depart. For they must try to establish – also linguistically – a new pre-understanding of their object: a pre-understanding to be shared with all members of the scientific community but not – as at least virtually in the case of the hermeneutic social sciences – with the very objects of their cognition. This leads to the third and most important argument.

Third, the specific object of the natural sciences does not contain or imply any understanding of the world, or hence any meaning intentions that could express themselves through symbols but only signs of the character of indices or symptoms. Hence it could be rightly said that, if the natural sciences are considered hermeneutic because of their own presupposed pre-understanding of the world, then the social sciences presuppose a 'double hermeneutics'.[42] But I would prefer to say that the methodological point of the hermeneutic sciences is constituted precisely by the need of mediating through communication between their own pre-understanding of the world and that of their subject-objects.[43]

A second, more important reason for taking issue with post-empiricist philosophy of science was the grounds of the debate between Thomas Kuhn and Karl Popper and his followers. One of the most striking results of this confrontation was the fact that the Popperians – who previously had defended (in loose alliance with the neo-positivists) a rather scientistic-reductionist view of the social sciences – came to discover, all of a sudden, the genuine problems of hermeneutics and the *Geisteswissenschaften*, as they are indeed mirrored in the topics of history of science. Confronted with these topics, they not only tried to develop their own conception of 'third-world hermeneutics',[44] which is not so very different from that of the neo-Kantians, especially that of Heinrich Rickert, but in fact even developed a conception of the hermeneutic reconstruction of history[45] that amounted to establishing a non-value-free type of critical social science (in contradistinction to Max Weber's stance on this question which had always been defended by the Popperians). Now, trying to find my ground with regard to the debate between Kuhn and the Popperians, I was in a peculiar and somewhat ambivalent position. On the one hand, I felt obliged to defend traditional hermeneutics, and partly also Gadamer and Kuhn, against the neo-Kantian and Popperian 'third-world hermeneutics'. On the other hand, however, I felt strongly attracted also by the normative orientation of the Popperian conception of the hermeneutic reconstruction of the history of science, as it was especially developed by Imre Lakatos.

With regard to my first concern, I tried to elucidate – along with Dilthey, but also with the aid of a Peircean semiotics – the peculiar character of hermeneutic or communicative experience, already on the basic level of the meaning-expressive sense-data, and to play off this function against Popper's approach, which – similarly to Rickert in his polemics against Dilthey – relied only upon the conceptualization of the possible meanings as it is represented through the quasi-Platonic 'third world' of 'objective knowledge', including, on Popper's account, even problems and problem situations. Thus, to take an example of Popper's,[46] it is possible that Popper is right in supposing that Galileo had good reasons (according to a Popperian methodology) to stick to his theory of the tides against Kepler's better theory because his theory was simpler and not yet refuted. But the given textual evidence of hermeneutic experience, which Popper does not take into account at all, might after all provide testimonies to the fact that, contrary to Popper's hypothesis, those interpreters are right who suppose that Galileo refused Kepler's proposals out of jealousy or similar motives.

This point, I think, may be generalized into the tenet that not only empathetic understanding, as Popper supposes – still along with Hempel – but third-world projections of objective structures of problems and solutions as well can have a heuristic function only within the whole methodological procedure of hermeneutic understanding, which is rather regulated through the principle of the 'hermeneutic circle'.[47]

Nevertheless, with regard to the problem of a hermeneutic reconstruction of the whole process of the history of science, it may very well be derived from the Popperian conception that the hypothetical construction (again and again to be renewed) of an ideal history of progressive science (i.e. a history of creative moves of thought to be understood and evaluated as having been motivated by good reasons) must be given priority over all attempts – not at learning from the given texts by the hermeneutic experience but – at explaining the particular decisions of scientists by supposing causally effective 'external motives', as for example interests or passions. This was, roughly put, Lakatos's proposal for the reconstruction of the history of science in his distinction between 'internal and external history'.[48] Without this distinction and the pertinent methodological maxim of maximizing as much as possible the scope of the 'internal history', it would indeed be possible neither to identify selectively the relevant facts (about persons and events) of the history of science from the whole of human history nor to learn from the history of science something relevant for the actual progress of science.

Now, in my reception of Lakatos's understanding of the history of science, I came to ask the following question, obviously inspired by my interest in generalizing this approach: what about the transition from understanding facts of the internal history to explaining facts of the external history? Is it allowed, in the case of motives that have to be considered as bad reasons in the light of even the maximized construction of the internal history of good science, to switch over immediately to looking to external motives that can be considered only as causally effective factors, such as hidden interests or passions?

The answer to this question must obviously be no; for the history of what can be understood and evaluated as done for good reasons is wider than only the most comprehensive internal history of science. If, for instance, Newton's motive for introducing the concept of 'absolute space' into his philosophical theory (namely the supposition that space is the *sensorium dei*) cannot be evaluated to be a good reason within a maximized internal history of physics, it may nevertheless be understood and even evaluated as a good reason within the frame of a maximized internal history of religious ideas (which indeed has to be supposed by someone who wants to understand the bulk of Newton's life work hermeneutically). Starting out from this consideration, I tried to generalize Lakatos's conception into that of a maximized internal history of human cultural evolution. The ideal limit of this conception would be marked by those facts of human behaviour that cannot be hermeneutically understood from good reasons at all but can merely be causally explained (and possibly understood – by deep psychology or critique of ideology – from reasons that have to be evaluated as bad from all normative perspectives of a hermeneutic reconstruction of human history or, on the other hand, cultural evolution).

However, it should have become clear from these last remarks that the generalization of Lakatos's conception is possible only if we can utilize an expanded conception of the normative yardsticks that can be presupposed in the process of evaluative reconstruction. That is to say, the normative foundation of cultural hermeneutics had to go beyond the normativism of the late Popper and Lakatos which always remained limited by the ideas of, respectively, truth or progress towards truth in science. Now, the conception of those normative conditions of the possibility of arguing that we cannot deny without committing a performative self-contradiction may, I suggest, provide the bridge to the enlarged conception of normative yardsticks of evaluation and thus to a foundation of the hermeneutics of historical reconstruction.[49]

On account of my reception of the post-empiricist philosophy of (the history of) science, my narrative reconstruction of 'the impact of analytic philosophy' on my intellectual biography could be considered to have been concluded. But I have already mentioned that I consider my study of American pragmatism – especially of Charles S. Peirce's work – as almost an integral part of my taking issue with analytic philosophy. Therefore, in what follows, I will argue, through a brief reconstruction of my own experience, that the intertwining of the problematic of pragmatism with that of analytic philosophy is not only an interesting topic seen from the perspective of my intellectual biography but probably also for objective reasons that have to do with the character of pragmatic philosophy and its function in the intellectual history of this century.

A historical interpretation of the intertwining of analytic philosophy and pragmatism in this century from my own point of view, in so far as it might be representative, may start out from at least three problem perspectives. First, it may take up that part of the history of semiotics that through the co-operation of Morris with Carnap was integrated in the history of linguistic philosophy, as well as of neo-positivistic logic of science. Second, it may conceive of the whole development of ordinary language philosophy and of post-empiricist philosophy of science as part of that 'pragmatic turn' of analytic philosophy that already announced itself in the days of Morris and Carnap. Third, it may concentrate on single persons and specific movements of thought that make up the impact of pragmatism or neo-pragmatism in the present scene of philosophical discussion.

I think that I have already, at least implicitly, given an account of the first two stages or aspects of the impact of pragmatism from my perspective. Therefore I will now proceed according to the third possibility. But I will concentrate on my reception of the work of Peirce and on my effort to show why Peirce's direction of pragmatism (his 'pragmaticism') is more relevant than many other directions of pragmatism, and neo-pragmatism, within the context of a critical assessment and selective reception of analytic philosophy in the broadest sense.

Peirce and pragmatism

In my first study of American pragmatism in the 1960s my interest was not yet focused on the links between pragmatism and analytic philosophy but on the – very general – post-Hegelian problem of a future-directed philosophy of the mediation of theory and *praxis*.[50] From this point of view I came to distinguish between three paradigmatic trends of post-Hegelian philosophy: Marxism, existentialism (first represented by Kierkegaard) and American pragmatism. Each of these trends, I suggested, has given an answer to the above-mentioned problem. Marx's answer to Hegel was directed towards the *praxis* of social revolution within the frame of a dialectical conception of the necessary course of history. Kierkegaard's answer to Hegel was directed toward the existential *praxis* of the incommensurable decision of the single person on the basis of belief. Finally American pragmatism was a – somewhat delayed – answer to Hegel that was oriented towards the experimental coping with the *praxis* of human life. But with regard to this third answer, one could state furthermore that it again allowed for an ideal-typical differentiation into three main directions, two of which, namely that of James and that of Dewey, could be co-ordinate, in a sense, with Kierkegaard and Marx, respectively; although the experimentalist – and that means also the undogmatic – character of pragmatism united James and Dewey as against Kierkegaard and Marx. The third direction of American pragmatism, however, that of C.S. Peirce, could not be related, primarily, to a subjective-psychological (or existentialist) or a socio-historical (or political) perspective of life-*praxis*, but rather to the perspective of logic (in a narrow and in a wide sense of a transcendental-semiotical, epistemologically relevant, logic of science) and its function for the evolution of rationality through human *praxis*. Thus far Peirce's pragmatism (or 'pragmaticism') was an answer not primarily to Hegel but rather to Kant, and, to that extent, an early rival, so to speak, of analytic philosophy, one that comprised all its topics (logic of science as well as language analysis and meaning critique) within a much broader horizon of experimentalist speculation.

It was for these last-mentioned reasons that I concentrated my study on American pragmatism and Peirce's philosophy, and that I studied it over and again by drawing comparisons with the different phases and strands of linguistic philosophy. In what follows I will deal only with those aspects of Peirce studies that led me to discover novel, alternative answers to the main problems of analytic philosophy, some of them appearing to me even superior to those of analytic philosophy.

As in the case of my Wittgenstein studies, so in the case of my Peirce studies I employed the heuristics of inquiring on its relationship to Kant's 'transcendental logic'. In the first case this was justified by Wittgenstein himself in the *Tractatus* and in the *Philosophical Investigations*; in Peirce's case there is a similar authorization to be found, from his early work on a 'New List of Categories' (1864) through the 'Logic of Inquiry' (1870) down to the 'Normative, Semiotic Logic' in 1902. But there is not only an analogy but also a remarkable difference between Wittgenstein's linguistic transformation of Kant's transcendental logic and Peirce's transformation of Kant's approach into that of a 'semiotic logic of inquiry'. From the *ex post* perspective of my study of both thinkers I would characterize the affinities and the differences in the following overview.

In both cases there is a shift from mentalism to a philosophy of language, and that means also from transcendental methodical solipsism of Cartesian provenance towards a recognition of the quasi-transcendental function of the community of sign interpretation qua world interpretation. This parallel goes along – in both cases – with a critique of (metaphysical) meaning as well; and with the later Wittgenstein we find even a strong 'pragmatic turn' and a certain equivalent to Peirce's 'pragmatic maxim' of meaning explication. To that extent one could talk about two versions of language-oriented pragmatism. But to these analogies the following differences may be opposed: whereas Wittgenstein's 'linguistic turn' is focused first on one ideal system of world depiction, and later – more realistically – on language games as parts of life forms, Peirce's philosophy of language is from the beginning a part of semiotics. This means that, corresponding to the three Peircean fundamental categories – 'firstness', 'secondness' and 'thirdness' – there are, even within language, three main types of signs functioning, namely 'icons', 'indices' and 'symbols'. From these three types of signs only the conventional 'symbols' (of concepts) are peculiar functions of language, whereas 'icons' and 'indices' are functions of natural signs as well as co-functions, as it were, of linguistic symbols, as for example 'indexical signs' like 'this', 'there', 'now' etc. Already this basic difference between the 'linguistic' and the 'semiotic turn' opens up epistemological possibilities for Peirce's semiotic logic that are missing in the twentieth century's analytic philosophy. First, the non-conceptual – and that means non-interpretation – functions of icons and indices, that is functions in the sense of presenting relation-free suchness (firstness) and pointing to causally affective existent beings (secondness in the sense of the encounter between the *I* and the non-*I*), establish a connection between language and reality that is at least not fully accounted for by mainstream analytic philosophy. Thus the function of presenting relation-free suchness of icons, which are co-functioning with indices and interpretative symbols in the use of language (e.g. through the exemplary introduction of predicators within the context of a situation), shows that it is in fact possible to rehabilitate Husserl's evidence phenomenology to a certain extent within a transcendental semiotics of world interpretation.[51] This latter has of course to combine an account of the pre-interpretative function of presenting suchness (which was absolutized in Husserl's eidetic phenomenology) with its account for the conceptually interpretative function of the symbols which is indispensable for the constitution of true or false cognition. Within linguistic philosophy – which in its semantical phase (e.g. with Carnap and Tarski, as with Popper) considered evidence not to be a reason (i.e. a non-sufficient criterion) for the legitimization of true knowledge but only as a causally effective psychological feeling – it was only Kripke's and Putnam's so called 'realistic semantics',[52] especially the theory of the 'original baptism' of individuals and natural kinds by 'rigid designators', that accounted for the epistemological function of the indexical and – implicitly – of the iconic sign-functions of language. Still these achievements of 'realistic semantics' have to be integrated into a transcendental semiotics of Peircean provenance, I would suggest.[53] This holds especially with regard to the relationship between the (transcendental) 'semiotic logic of inquiry' and the (empirical-hypothetical) 'metaphysics of natural evolution' which, on Peirce's account, can be established by a semiotic analysis of the co-function of natural and conventional signs (e.g. in perceptual judgements or in mathematical diagrams).[54]

Also with regard to the overcoming of methodical solipsism (from Descartes through Husserl) by a recognition of the quasi-transcendental function of the community of language use or sign interpretation, there is an important difference between the Wittgensteinian and the Peircean version. With Wittgenstein the point of the overcoming of methodical solipsism is represented by the famous arguments against the possibility of 'private rule-following' or a 'private language'. I have already mentioned that I can readily consider these arguments as critical ones but cannot follow Wittgenstein's – at least intimated – affirmative answer to the question of the criteria of correct rule-following, for this answer seems to make all correct rule-following, and thus even the concept of a rule, dependent on the factual usage (and so far the life form) of a factual (and so far limited) community. Now, with Peirce there may be found different but complementary arguments against the Cartesian mentalism and methodical solipsism, arguments in favour of the supposition of an indefinite trans-individual process of thought qua inference and sign interpretation. From the vantage point of the possible progress of this trans-individual process of sign-bound thought the insistence on individual mental evidence by Peirce is reduced to the insistence on idiosyncrasy and thus on error. However, the subject of the trans-individual process of sign interpre-tation, on Peirce's account, cannot be any factual finite community that would be bound to a specific socio-cultural form of life: for such a restriction for Peirce would also amount to a fixation to idiosyn-crasy and hence the blocking of the possible progress toward the truth. This latter, however, according to Peirce can be defined only by the regulative idea of the consensus (i.e. the 'ultimate opinion') – never completely reached – of the indefinite community of investigators.[55]

I must confess that I always preferred this Peircean account of the semiotic process and its subject to the Wittgensteinian (or post-Wittgensteinian) account at least with regard to epistemology and philosophy of science, but partly with regard to the problematic of ethics and politics as well, although here a mediation between universalism and particularistic communitarianism has to be accom-plished.[56] At least the Peircean account opens up a perspective of acknowledging, along with Wittgenstein, the public and community-bound character of any rule-following without falling a victim to intolerable relativism and ethnocentrism. In what follows I will briefly outline some particular problem dimensions in which I followed Peircean inspirations rather than those of mainstream analytic philosophy.

I touched above upon the internal connection, in the Peircean philosophy, between the notions of the indefinite process of inference and sign interpretation, the indefinite community of investigators and interpreters, and the idea of explicating the meaning of truth with the aid of the counterfactual supposition and regulative idea of the ultimate consensus of the indefinite community. With Peirce this explication of the meaning of truth is in fact only an application of the 'pragmatic maxim' of explicating all conceptual meanings by 'mellonization', that is by asking for the possible consequences with regard to our actions and experiences in the future. Thus far there is common ground in the theories of Peirce and of James[57] – as now again Rorty – allowed for, or even suggested, an explication of the idea of truth in terms of the fruitful or useful consequences of a personal belief just within the context of a finite life and its striving for happiness. Contrary to this 'humanism' (or existentialism), Peirce insisted from the beginning on the strictly universal, inter-subjective validity that is bound up with the idea of truth. Hence he had to restrict the possible 'mellonization' with regard to the concept of truth to the context of experimentation and argumentative discourse of the indefinite community of those who search for consensus. Starting out from this conception as well, and combining it with 'realistic semantics' within the context of a transcendental semiotics, I attempted to outline a consensus theory of truth that would be criteriologically relevant (in contradistinction to the metaphysical and the logico-semantical correspondence theory) by its capability of taking into account (by critical weighing up against each other within the horizon of a striven-for synthesis of interpretation) all available truth criteria – for example evidence, coherence, prospective fruitfulness – which, taken for themselves, are never sufficient.[58]

The conception of progress towards the truth just outlined, on my account, stands in close connection to the peculiar mode of Peirce's transformation of Kant's transcendental logic into a normative semiotical logic in inquiry. In this regard Peirce's residual transcendentalism is quite different not only from Wittgenstein's but also from that of the so-called 'transcendental arguments' discussed by Strawson, Bennett and many of their followers. The main difference

seems to be that the latter focused on the problems of the 'constitution' of the structure of possible experience, whereas Peirce focused,
from the beginning, on the regulative principles that (together with
the empirical reference of signs) would make up the conditions of
the possibility of reaching the truth in the long run.

Thus Strawson and his followers set out to reconstruct meaning critically, that is by eliminating the conception of unknowable
'things in themselves' and the pertinent conception of transcendental idealism – Kant's transcendental analytic – and thereby to save
the function of the 'categorical schemes' and the *a priori* validity of
the 'principles of intellect' (*Grundsätze des Verstandes*) by 'transcendental arguments'. In this context they completely neglected Kant's
'transcendental dialectics' and its problematic of 'principles of reason' for the completion of the whole process of cognition in the long
run. Therefore they had to give up transcendentalism altogether,
when it turned out that transcendental arguments for 'categorical
schemes' are no longer tenable.

By contrast, Peirce, who first reduced the fundamental categories to the three elements of semiotic representation of the world
(namely presentation of suchness, encounter between I and non-I,
and conceptual mediation or interpretation), had neither to care for
transcendental idealism nor for the *a priori* validity of 'principles'
because for him all prepositional sentences – synthetic judgements
a priori as well as perceptual judgements – were only sedimented,
and hence provisional results of a continuous process of – mostly
unconscious – 'synthetic inferences' ('inductive' and 'abductive'
ones) and sign interpretations. Hence, for Peirce the problem of a
residual transcendentalism was from the beginning reduced to the
question of the conditions of the possibility of the validity of synthetic inferences and sign interpretation in the long run. Peirce gave
the definite answer to this question in his normative semiotic logic of
inquiry. There he would concentrate on those regulative principles
that – like the pragmatic maxim of meaning explication and the idea
of truth as ultimate consensus, which itself follows from the pragmatic maxim – are required as procedural norms for guiding the
research process. Through this shift from 'constitutive' to 'regulative
principles', I suggest, Peirce has in fact reached a solution of the
problem of a transcendental logic that is immune to the recent
critique of 'transcendental arguments', for even the holistic
critique of 'the very idea of a categorical scheme' does not affect the

'regulative ideas' that are *a priori* related to the whole of a meaningful process of inference and discursive interpretation.

In this context a final remark has to be made about the Peircean theory of meaning as it is implied in the pragmatic maxim and the relevant concept of sign interpretation as compared with the explication of meaning in terms of use as they are characteristic of the pragmatic turn of linguistic philosophy, especially that of the later Wittgenstein. I touched upon this topic already when I mentioned that I refused the affirmative criteria of a correct rule-following to be found in Wittgenstein's *Philosophical Investigations*. These criteria appear to me to be in line with Wittgenstein's suggested definition of linguistic meaning in terms of the – factual – use. Now, in order to understand the meaning of words, it is of course useful to look for the use, and for a linguist or a sociologist this may even exhaust the problem if he or she needs a realistic corrective against the semantical fictions suggested by the system of language. But for Peirce the problem of meaning explication dealt with in the pragmatic maxim, and later in his semiotic logic, was a different one from the outset. His problem was primarily a normative one, which he later isolated semiotically by distinguishing the 'logical interpretant' of a sign from the 'immediate' and the 'dynamical' ones. His main examples were those of the hardness of a diamond and heaviness in the sense of physical gravity, and he suggested from the beginning that, in order to apply the pragmatic maxim, one has to look not for the factual use but for the possible use of words in the context of thought experiments that try to relate experimental operations to possible experiences. This method of clarification of meanings was obviously intended not for linguists (or behaviouristic semioticians like Morris) but for philosophers and scientific researchers who know from the outset that observation of people's behaviour (or even empirical-hermeneutic understanding of their factual use of language) finally could not help them because the factual use of the words simply does not provide an adequate elucidation of their problematic deep meaning. (This does not mean however that the pragmatically oriented explication of meaning had to be given up in favour of a return to pure mentalism – say of a dialectics of concepts – but it means that an explication of the deep structure of meaning has to go beyond all factual use towards the possible use by future-oriented imagination, by 'mellonization' in Peirce's sense.)

A good example of a meaning explication along the lines of Peirce's pragmatic maxim was delivered by Einstein's special theory of relativity, which essentially consists of thought experiments in order to find out how the meaning of the concept 'simultaneity of two events' could be clarified by possible measurements. It is well known that the outcome of Einstein's meaning explications through imagined measurements delivered quite novel definitions of the physical terms 'time', 'space' and 'simultaneity': definitions that were quite different even from the former common use of the physicists. I think however that this method of meaning explication through thought experiments is by no means restricted to the natural sciences. For another good example of its application is delivered by John Rawls's constructive explication of the meaning of justice through imagining the 'original position' of establishing a just social order by a social contract that would be based on consenting rational decisions in that situation.[59]

In order to illustrate the significance of the difference between the mainstream pragmatic explication of meaning in terms of use, on the one hand, and Peirce's pragmaticist method, on the other, I point to another result of analytic philosophy in recent times that has strongly impressed me. John Searle, in his book *Intentionality* (1983),[60] has written a fascinating chapter on 'the background' of our understanding linguistic utterances or making understandable utterances. The 'background' comprises presuppositions in the sense of 'knowing how to act' and 'knowing how things are' that make the application of our understanding of linguistic meaning to the lifeworld possible, but cannot be made, in principle, completely controllable, that is representable by propositional sentences. To that extent Searle's conception of the 'background' is closely related to Heidegger's and Gadamer's concept of the (existential pre-structure of) the 'pre-understanding' of the lifeworld, but even more so to Wittgenstein's conception of the contingent paradigmatic certainties that must be presupposed in a functioning language game. Like Wittgenstein and the latest Strawson, Searle suggests that all the background presuppositions of our meaningful speech or understanding linguistic meaning are not transcendental but contingent in the sense of a soft naturalism.

Now, I will only mention here that I could question the last tenet, as I did above, by pointing to that part of the 'pre-structure' of our understanding meaning that cannot be disputed in serious arguing without committing a performative self-contradiction. What I want to stress here is that the pragmatic meaning theories of Wittgenstein on the one hand, and Peirce on the other, stand in very different relationship to Searle's theory of the 'background'. For it is the equation of meaning with the factual use, that is the usual application of our understanding of linguistic meaning, that completely confirms Searle's tenet that our understanding meaning cannot win control, in principle, over the background of our being able to apply the understanding of linguistic meaning to the lifeworld. By contrast, Peirce's theory of meaning explication shows that it is at least possible – in principle – to expand our control progressively over the contingent 'background' of our understanding linguistic meaning with regard to its possible application to the lifeworld.

A final comment on my encounter with Wittgenstein's (as well as Strawson's and Searle's) and Peirce's pragmatic theories of meaning and understanding may perhaps serve as an example for making understandable – at the end of the present retrospective – that and why through my long parallel study of linguistic philosophy (in the narrower sense) and pragmaticist semiotics (in Peirce's sense) I came to the conclusion that the latter approach (which can also be conceived of as a supplementation of analytic philosophy in the twentieth century) had, after all, the greater impact on my philosophizing. It provided, so it seems, a wider horizon for my transcendentalist ambitions which, notwithstanding all my attempts at a radical transformation, are deeply rooted in the Kantian tradition and hence cannot so quickly comply with the programme of a thorough 'detranscendentalization' (Rorty), which, as it appears to many, stands at the end of the pragmatic turn of analytic philosophy. I have to stop short of trying to outline my own conceptions of transcendental semiotics and transcendental pragmatics, for example in a conception of the three paradigms of First Philosophy (to be derived from the triadicity of semiosis)[61] and of discourse ethics.[62] These conceptions, no doubt, are rather remote in their spirit from analytic philosophy. But I hope that they, nevertheless, have preserved and show up what I have learned from that whole movement of critical thought.

Notes

1 K.-O. Apel, *Die Idee der Sprache in der Tradition des Humanismus von Dante bis Vico* (Bonn: Bouvier, 1963, 1980).

2 E. Stenius, *Wittgenstein's 'Tractatus': A Critical Exposition of its Main Lines of Thought* (Oxford: Blackwell, 1960). Parenthetical references are given in the

text to L. Wittgenstein, *Tractatus Logico-philosophicus*, trans. D.F. Pears and B.R. McGuiness (London: Routledge and Kegan Paul, 1961).

3 L. Wittgenstein, *Vermischte Bemerkungen* (Frankfurt a. M.: Suhrkamp, 1977).

4 Apel, 'Rationalitätskriterien und Rationalitätstypen: Versuch einer transzendentalpragmatischen Rekonstruktion des Unterschieds zwischen Verstand und Vernunft', in G. Meggle and A. Wüstehube (eds), *Pragmatische Rationalitätstheorien* (Würzburg: Königshausen & Neumann, 1995).

5 Apel, 'Die Entfaltung der "sprachanalytischen" Philosophie und das Problem der "Geisteswissenschaften"', in Apel, *Transformation der Philosophie*, 2 vols (Frankfurt a. M.: Suhrkamp, 1973), vol. 2, 28–95; English translation: *Analytic Philosophy of Language and the 'Geisteswissenschaften'* (Dordrecht: Reidel, 1967); repr. in Apel, *Towards a Transcendental Semiotics* (Atlantic Highlands, N.J.: Humanities Press, 1994), 1–50.

6 C.W. Morris, *Foundations of the Theory of Signs: International Encyclopedia of Unified Science*, vol. 1, no. 2 (Chicago: University of Chicago Press, 1938).

7 R. Carnap, 'Empiricism, Semantics, and Ontology', in *Revue Internationale de Philosophy* (1950), 20–40; repr. in Carnap, *Meaning and Necessity* (Chicago: University of Chicago Press, 1956).

8 C.W. Morris, *Signs, Language and Behaviour* (New York: Braziller, 1946). Cf. my critical introduction to the German translation, *Zeichen, Sprache und Verhalten* (Düsseldorf: Schwamm, 1973), 9–66; repr. in A. Eschbach (ed.), *Zeichen über Zeichen über Zeichen: 15 Studien über C.W. Morris* (Tübingen: G. Narr, 1981), 25–82.

9 R. Carnap, 'On Some Concepts of Pragmatics', *Philosophical Studies*, 6 (1955), repr. in Carnap, *Meaning and Necessity*; R.M. Martin, *Toward a Systematic Pragmatics* (Amsterdam: North-Holland, 1959); R. Montague, *Formal Philosophy*, ed. and introduced by R.H. Thomason (New Haven: Yale University Press, 1974).

10 See note 4.

11 W. Stegmüller, *Probleme und Resultate der Wissenschaftstheorie* (Berlin: De Gruyter, 1969).

12 Apel, 'Das Problem der philosophischen Letztbegründung im Lichte einer transzendentalen Sprachpragmatik: Versuch einer Metakritik des "Kritischen Rationalismus"', in B. Kanitschneider (ed.), *Sprache und Erkenntnis* (Innsbruck, 1976), 55–82; English translation in *Man and World*, 8, 3 (1975), 239–75: repr. under the title: 'The Problem of Philosophical Fundamental Grounding in Light of a Transcendental-Pragmatic of Language', in K. Baynes, J. Bohman and T.A. McCarthy (eds), *After Philosophy: End or Transformation?* (Cambridge, Mass.: MIT Press, 1987), 250–90.

13 In particular Apel, *Towards a Transcendental Semiotics*.

14 Essays on Wittgenstein in Apel, *Transformation der Philosophie*.

15 C.G. Hempel, 'Explanation in Science and History', in W. Dray (ed.), *Philosophical Analysis and History* (New York: Harper & Row, 1966); and T. Abel, 'The Operation called "Verstehen"', in H. Feigl and M. Brodbeck (eds), *Readings in the Philosophy of Science*.

16 P. Winch, *The Idea of a Social Science and its Relation to Philosophy* (London: Routledge & Kegan Paul, 1958).

17 Apel, 'Die Entfaltung'.

18 P. Winch, 'Understanding a Primitive Society', *American Philosophical Quarterly*, 1 (1964), 307–24.

19 See e.g. Apel, 'Universal Principles and Particular (Incommensurable?) Decisions and Forms of Life – A Problem of Ethics that is both post-Kantian and post-Wittgensteinian', in R. Gaita (ed.), *Value and Understanding: Essays for Peter Winch* (London: Routledge, 1990), 72–101; and Apel, 'Wittgenstein und Heidegger: kritische Wiederholung eines Vergleiches', in J. Habermas (ed.), *Der Löwe spricht … und wir können ihn nicht verstehen* (Frankfurt a. M.: Suhrkamp, 1991); English translation in C. Macann (ed.), *Martin Heidegger: Critical Assessments* (London and New York: Routledge, 1992); and Apel, 'Das Anliegen des anglo-amerikanischen "Kommunitarismus" in der Sicht der (transzendentalpragmatischen) Diskursethik. Worin liegen die Kommunitären Bedingungen der persönlichen Identität?', in M. Brumlik and H. Brunkhorst (eds), *Gemeinschaft und Gerechtigkeit* (Frankfurt a. M.: Fischer, 1992), 149–72.

20 L. Wittgenstein, *Über Gewissheit (On Certainty)*, ed. G.E.M. Anscombe and G.H. von Wright (Oxford: Basil Blackwell, 1969).

21 H. Albert, *Traktat über kritische Vernunft* (Tübingen, 1986); and G. Radnitzky, 'In Defense of Self-applicable Critical Rationalism', in International Cultural Foundation (ed.), *Absolute Values and the Creation of the New World* (New York: International Cultural Foundation Press, 1983), vol. 3, 1025–69. For my critique of these positions see note 12 and also Apel, 'Fallibilismus, Konsenstheorie der Wahrheit und Letztbegründung', in Forum für Philosophie Bad Homburg (eds), *Philosophie und Begründung* (Frankfurt a. M.: Suhrkamp, 1987), 116–211.

22 P. Strawson, *Scepticism and Naturalism: Some Varieties*, The Woodbridge Lectures (London: Methuen, 1985).

23 See Apel, 'Das Problem der philosophischen Letztbegründung'.

24 R. Rorty, 'Verificationism and Transcendental Arguments', *Nous*, 5 (1971); Rorty, 'Criteria and Necessity', *Nous*, 7 (1973); Rorty, 'Epistemological Behaviorism and the De-transcendentalization of Analytic Philosophy', *Neue Hefte für Philosophie*, 14 (1987); Rorty, 'Transcendental Arguments, Self-reference, and Pragmatism', in P. Bieri *et al.* (eds), *Transcendental Arguments and Science* (Dordrecht: Kluwer, 1979), 77–103. For a critical comment on Rorty's arguments see M. Niquet, *Transzendentale Argumente: Kant, Strawson und die Aporetik der Detranszendentalisierung* (Frankfurt a. M.: Suhrkamp, 1991), 536 ff.

25 With regard to this programme see the references in note 21, and also Apel (ed.), *Sprachpragmatik und Philosophie* (Frankfurt a. M.: Suhrkamp, 1976); W. Kuhlmann and D. Bohler (eds), *Kommunikation und Reflexion* (Frankfurt a. M.: Suhrkamp, 1982); W. Kuhlmann, *Reflexive Letztbegründung: Untersuchungen zur Transzendentalpragmatik* (Freiburg and Munich: Alber, 1985); A. Dorschel, M. Kettner, W. Kuhlmann and M. Niquet (eds), *Transzendentalpragmatik* (Frankfurt a. M.: Suhrkamp, 1993).

26 See in particular Apel, 'Das Apriori der Kommunikationsgemeinschaft und die Grundlagen der Ethik', in *Transformation der Philosophie*, vol. 2; also Apel, *Diskurs und Verantwortung* (Frankfurt a. M.: Suhrkamp, 1988) (English translation forthcoming.

27 Apel, 'Sprechakttheorie und transzendentale Sprachpragmatik zur Frage ethischer Normen', in Apel (ed.), *Sprachpragmatik und Philosophie*, 10–173; Apel, 'Die Logosauszeichnung der menschlichen Sprache: die philosophische Relevanz der Sprechakttheorie', in H.-G. Bosshardt (ed.), *Perspektiven auf*

Sprache (Berlin and New York: De Gruyter, 1986), 45–87; also 'Is Intentionality more Basic than Linguistic Meaning?', in E. Lepore and R. van Gulick (eds), *John Searle and his Critics* (Cambridge, Mass.: Blackwell, 1991), 31–55.

28 Apel, 'Noam Chomskys Sprachtheorie und die Philosophie der Gegenwart', in Apel, *Transformation der Philosophie*, vol. 2, 264–310.

29 J. Habermas, 'Was heisst Universalpragmatik?', in Apel (ed.), *Sprachpragmatik und Philosophie*, 174–272; Habermas, *Theorie des Kommunikativen Handelns*, 2 vols (Frankfurt a. M.: Suhrkamp, 1981), vol. 1, 3: 'Erste Zwischenbetrachtung'.

30 J. Habermas, *Moralbewusstsein und kommunikatives Handeln* (Frankfurt a. M.: Suhrkamp, 1983), 106 ff.

31 See Habermas's and my contributions to E. Lepore and R. van Gulick (eds), *John Searle and his Critics*.

32 J. Habermas, *Theorie des kommunikativen Handelns*, vol. 1.

33 In particular Apel, 'Sprachliche Bedeutung, Wahrheit und normative Gültigkeit', *Archivio di Filosofia*, 55 (1987), 51–88; and Apel, 'Das Problem des offen strategischen Sprachgebrauchs in transzendentalpragmatischer Sicht', in H. Burckhardt (ed.), *Diskurs über Sprache* (Würzburg: Königshausen & Neumann, 1994).

34 C. Landesmann, 'The New Dualism in the Philosophy of Mind', *Review of Metaphysics*, 19 (1965/66), 329–49.

35 G.H. von Wright, *Explanation and Understanding* (Ithaca, N.Y.: Cornell University Press, 1971).

36 See Apel, *Die Erklären/Verstehen-Kontroverse in transzendentalpragmatischer Sicht* (Frankfurt a. M.: Suhrkamp, 1979); English translation: *Understanding and Explanation: A Transcendental-pragmatic Perspective*, trans. G. Warnke (Cambridge, Mass.: MIT Press, 1984).

37 Apel, 'Das "Verstehen" (eine Begriffsgeschichte als Problemgeschichte)', *Archiv für Begriffsgeschichte*, 1 (Bonn: Bouvier, 1955), 142–99: and most recently Apel, 'Diltheys Unterscheidung von "Erklären" und "Verstehen" im Lichte der Ergebnisse der modernen Wissenschaftstheorie', in E.W. Orth (ed.), *Dilthey und die Philosophie der Gegenwart* (Freiburg im Breisgau: Alber, 1985), 285–347; selective English translation: 'Dilthey's Distinction between "Explanation" and "Understanding" and the Possibility of its "Mediation"', *Journal of the History of Philosophy*, 25, 1 (1987), 131–50.

38 G.H. von Wright, *Explanation and Understanding*, ch. 2.

39 Apel, 'Types of Social Science in the Light of Human Cognitive Interests', *Social Research*, 44, 3 (1977), 425–70, repr. in S. Brown (ed.), *Philosophical Disputes in the Social Sciences* (Brighton: Harvester Press, 1979), 3–50.

40 G.H. von Wright, *Explanation and Understanding*, ch. 3, especially p. 117. Cf. Apel, *Die Erklären/Verstehen-Kontroverse*.

41 T. Kuhn, *The Structure of Scientific Revolutions* (Chicago: Chicago University Press, 1962); I. Lakatos and A. Musgrave, *Criticism and the Growth of Knowledge* (Cambridge: Cambridge University Press, 1970); W. Diederich (ed.), *Theorien der Wissenschaftsgeschichte* (Frankfurt a. M.: Suhrkamp, 1974); K. Popper, *Objective Knowledge: An Evolutionary Approach* (Oxford: Clarendon Press, 1972).

42 A. Giddens, *Studies in Social and Political Theory* (New York: Routledge, 1977), 12.

43 Apel, 'Diltheys Unterscheidung'; Apel, 'The Hermeneutic Dimension of

Social Science and its Normative Foundations', *Man and World*, 25, 3/4 (1992), 247–70.

44 See K. Popper, *Objective Knowledge*, ch. 43.

45 See especially I. Lakatos, 'Zur Geschichte der Wissenschaft und ihrer Rationalen Rekonstruktionen', in W. Diederich (ed.), *Theorien der Wissenschaftsgeschichte* (Frankfurt a. M.: Suhrkamp, 1974), 55–119.

46 K. Popper, *Objective Knowledge*, 170 ff.

47 Apel, 'History of Science as a Problem of Hermeneutics: An Argument with Karl Popper's Third-world Hermeneutics', Chapter 9 below.

48 I. Lakatos, 'Zur Geschichte der Wissenschaft'.

49 Apel, 'The Hermeneutic Dimension'.

50 Apel, *Der Denkweg von Charles Sanders Peirce: eine Einführung in den amerikanischen Pragmatismus* (Frankfurt a. M.: Suhrkamp, 1975), 11 ff.; English translation: *Charles S. Peirce: From Pragmatism to Pragmaticism* (Amherst: University of Massachusetts Press, 1981), 1 ff.

51 Apel, 'Das Problem der phänomenologischen Evidenz im Lichte einer transzendentalen Semiotik', in M. Benedikt and R. Burger (eds), *Die Krise der Phänomenologie und die Pragmatik des Wissenschaftsfortschritts* (Vienna: Staatsdruckerei, 1986), 78–99.

52 S. Kripke, *Naming and Necessity* (Oxford: Basil Blackwell, 1980); and H. Putnam, *Mind, Language and Reality* (Cambridge: Cambridge University Press, 1975), ch. 12.

53 Apel, 'The "Pragmatic Turn" and Transcendental Semiotics', in *Towards a Transcendental Semiotics*, 132–74.

54 Apel, 'Transcendental Semiotics and Hypothetical Metaphysics of Evolution', in *ibid.*, 207–30.

55 In particular Apel, 'Peirce and Post-Tarskian Truth', in *ibid.*, 175–226; also, 'Fallibilismus, Konsenstheorie der Wahrheit und Letztbegründung'; and 'Transcendental Semiotics and Truth', in M.A. Bonfantini and A. Martone (eds), *Peirce in Italia* (Naples: Liguori, 1993), 191–208.

56 See Apel, 'Das Anliegen des anglo-amerikanischen "Kommunitarismus"'.

57 W. James, *The Will to Believe, and other Essays in Popular Philosophy* (New York: Longmans, Green & Co., 1887); James, 'Pragmatism' (Longmans, Green & Co., 1907); and James, *The Meaning of Truth* (Longmans, Green & Co., 1909).

58 See the works cited in note 55.

59 J. Rawls, *A Theory of Justice* (Cambridge, Mass.: Harvard University Press, 1971), chs 1, 4.

60 J. Searle, *Intentionality* (Cambridge: Cambridge University Press, 1983), ch. 5.

61 Apel, 'Transcendental Semiotics as First Philosophy', in *Towards a Transcendental Semiotics*, 112–31; and 'Kann es in der Gegenwart ein postmetaphysisches Paradigma der Ersten Philosophie geben?', in H. Schnädelbach and G. Keil (eds), *Philosophie der Gegenwart – Gegenwart der Philosophie* (Homburg: Junius, 1993), 41–70.

62 For my relevant works, see note 26.

2

Transcendental semiotics and the paradigms of First Philosophy

Introduction: derivation of the three paradigms of First Philosophy from the triadic sign-relation

The term 'First Philosophy' was used by Aristotle to designate the science of the being as being (*on he on*) which later – in the seventeenth century – was called 'ontology'; but the same fundamental science was also called 'metaphysics' already by the commentators of Aristotle. Now, I do not intend to deal with different paradigms of ontological metaphysics, say the Aristotelian and the Platonic, or materialistic and idealistic ones, or ancient, medieval and modern ones. By contrast I intend to deal with ontological metaphysics and two other competing paradigms of First Philosophy, that is of a philosophy that might take over the methodological role of First Philosophy in replacing Aristotle's paradigm. For I think that, precisely in respect of the methodological role, the paradigm of First Philosophy has changed in modern times, and again in the twentieth century. This does not mean that in modern times, or in the twentieth century, there *is* no longer ontology or even ontological metaphysics, but it does mean that in modern times, say from Descartes to Husserl, the paradigm of First Philosophy has been taken over by philosophy of consciousness, especially of consciousness as the transcendental subject of knowledge in the Kantian sense; and in the twentieth century the methodological paradigm of First Philosophy has come to be taken over by transcendental semiotics, including transcendental hermeneutics and transcendental pragmatics of language.

My main thesis is that the suggested sequence of three paradigms of First Philosophy – ontological metaphysics, (transcendental) philosophy of consciousness and transcendental semiotics – is not just a contingent succession of – perhaps incommensurable –

paradigms, as Thomas Kuhn[1] suggested with regard to the paradigms emerging in the history of science. Rather, the sequence of the three paradigms of First Philosophy can be accounted for in a systematical way, I suggest, at least *ex post factum* of our occidental history of philosophy; and the systematic account I have in mind can be derived from a schema that in my opinion constitutes the core or centre of the third paradigm, namely the triadic relation of the sign function or semiosis. The diagrammatical scheme of this relation is presented as in Figure 1.

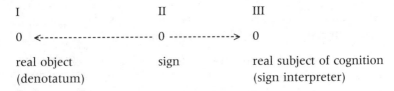

I	II	III
0 ←---------------------- 0 -------------→ 0		
real object (denotatum)	sign	real subject of cognition (sign interpreter)

Figure 1

The schema may be interpreted by the definition of the sign, as it was given by Charles S. Peirce, whom I consider the most important inspirator of the conception of transcendental semiotics. The definition reads: 'A sign, or representamen, is something which stands to somebody for something in some respect or capacity', or: 'A sign is a conjoint relation to the thing denoted and to the mind'.[2]

If one assumes that the structure of the sign-relation is at the same time the structure of sign-mediated cognition of the real (and this constitutes a distinctive mark of transcendental semiotics), then one is able to derive our three paradigms of First Philosophy from the triadic sign-relation according to a logic of abstraction, so to speak. For the three paradigms may be distinguished according to whether the foundation of First Philosophy takes into consideration only the first position, or else the first and the third, or else all three positions of the triadic sign-relation. The thematizing of objectivized being in the sense of the first position of the triad is characteristic of metaphysics qua ontology; that of the first and the third position in the sense of the subject–object relation as a transcendental condition of the possibility of knowledge is characteristic of classical transcendental philosophy of consciousness, say Kant or Husserl; and thematizing all three positions in the sense of the function of sign-mediated world interpretation is characteristic of transcendental semiotics.

To be sure, there are still four other possibilities of combination implied in the triadic structure of the sign-relation. We could also thematize the first position in combination with the second (I/II), that is being and the sign as such, or the second in combination with the third (III), that is the consciousness. And it can be shown that these four possibilities of combination can also be co-ordinated to philosophical positions which in fact have been defended in the course of history, positions that can be understood as sub-paradigms in connection with the three main paradigms of First Philosophy.[3] But I will concentrate on the three main paradigms and show the following with regard to them.

From the vantage point of the third paradigm, which takes into account all three places of the triadic sign-relation in order to account for the idea of First Philosophy, the two other paradigms, namely ontological metaphysics and (transcendental) philosophy of consciousness, can be considered as being based on abstractive or reductive fallacies with regard to the conditions of possibility for knowledge or thought, so that from these abstractive fallacies the characteristic aporias of these deficient paradigms of First Philosophy can be derived in a certain manner.

But I do not pretend to develop this aporetics in a purely systematic way, that is by abstraction from the process of history. Rather I will try to show that the sequence of the three main paradigms of First Philosophy can be understood as a historically plausible succession that was brought about through an intrinsic tendency of philosophical reflection towards overcoming scepticism with regard to the conditions of the possibility of philosophizing.

In what follows I have to restrict my account of the history of First Philosophy to a very rough and simplified reconstruction, focusing on some characteristic features of the successive paradigms in order to illustrate my approach. I can only assert but not substantiate that the heuristic of the three (or seven) possible paradigms of First Philosophy can be pursued and implemented even with regard to the details of the history of philosophy that I have tried out in recent years.

The first paradigm of First Philosophy: ontological metaphysics

Let us start off then with a rough characterization of the first paradigm, ontological metaphysics. This paradigm, as I see it, was dominant in different versions from the beginning of philosophy in Greece and throughout the Middle Ages, and even in modern times it continued in a complicated struggle with the novel paradigm of the philosophy of consciousness.

Claiming that the first paradigm took into account only being but not the consciousness or the signs of language, in order to account for the idea of the First Philosophy, I am not implying that within the frame of ontological metaphysics there was or is no place for epistemology or philosophy of language. This would obviously be false. But the point is that, during the epoch of the first dominant paradigm, epistemology and/or philosophy of language could not take the role or function of First Philosophy but were thematized just as a kind or region of being. The reason for this, I suggest, is the fact that ontological metaphysics as paradigm of First Philosophy is conceived as a topic – the most general one – of the *intentio recta*, in the same way that all intramundane kinds of being were thematized and are still today thematized by the empirical sciences. This may be elucidated by many striking examples.

Thus it would be completely misleading in the context of ancient Greek epistemology to speak of the subject of knowledge or the subject–object relation as a condition of the possibility of knowledge. For within the first paradigm of First Philosophy there is no need for transcendental or quasi-transcendental reflection on the conditions of the possibility of objectivizing being. For Aristotle the subject of cognition is just the soul (*psyche, anima*), and instead of dealing with the subject–object relation of cognition, in *De Anima* he deals with an intramundane relationship of adequation (*homoiosis*), between the soul (more precisely, its highest part or layer: the *nous*) and other beings in the world. And if Aristotle says 'the soul is somehow everything' (*psyche pos esti panta*) this is not a proposition of transcendental phenomenology of consciousness but an ontological proposition concerning the soul's capacity of adequation with regard to the form of all beings.

The difference between the first and the second paradigm may be illuminated by the following comparison. Both Plato and the fifteenth-century philosopher Nicolaus Cusanus dealt with the famous proposition of Protagoras 'Man is the measure of all things.' But for Plato, as presumably for Protagoras himself, the proposition was meant as a plea for an anthropological, that is ontological, relativism that precluded the possibility of universally valid truth.

For Cusanus, on the other hand, who was himself a Christian Platonist, the proposition of Protagoras can be interpreted in a quasi-transcendental way, so that it points to the condition of the possibility of universally valid truth, for example in mathematics. The reason why Cusanus can afford this switch to a quasi-Kantian approach is provided by his Christian doctrine of the human mind as a living image of the divine mind, in particular of God's intellectual creativity. Thus the mathematician, according to Cusanus, is capable of 'precise' knowledge because he is a *secundus deus*, constructing his objects as God creates the real things.

But why is ontological metaphysics a deficient paradigm of First Philosophy, so that it had to be replaced by, or transformed into, the second paradigm according to an internal tendency of philosophical reflection? Christian Platonism, from Augustine through Cusanus, with its central conception of the *intellectus divinus* who recognizes the world by creating it, may have been an important historical catalyst for the 'Copernican turn' in First Philosophy, according to which Man's (*sic*) mind or consciousness (as *imago dei*) became the transcendental subject of constructive and thus a priori valid knowledge. Nevertheless, we need an intra-philosophical argument in order to realize that the ontological conceptualization of epistemological problems is misleading and has to be replaced, or at least supplemented, by answering the transcendental question as to the conditions of the possibility and inter-subjective validity of knowledge.

I think that the aporetics of the first paradigm of First Philosophy can be clearly demonstrated by a short analysis of the difficulties of the strong ontological version of the correspondence theory of truth. In trying to provide this analysis I take it for granted that a weak version of the correspondence theory of truth is indispensable as a starting point for every possible truth theory, but that at the same time it is completely irrelevant criteriologically. At the centre of ontological metaphysics, however, there is a strong correspondence or adequation theory of truth, which was developed from Aristotle through Thomas Aquinas. According to this theory, as I have already intimated, the truth of knowledge is conceived as adequation of the mind to other beings with regard to their form. Now, this strong version of the correspondence theory, which is meant to be criteriologically relevant, cannot fulfil its promise; for it leads to the following alternative aporias.

The process of *homoiosis* has to be considered as an intra-mundane process, taking place between two things, which can be studied by a kind of natural science. This view was pursued already by Aristotle in *De Anima* (*Peri Psyches*), and it consequently leads to what is nowadays called 'cognitive science', in terms of which there cannot be a difference between truth and falsehood. This difference cannot, in principle, be found to be something in the world of possible objects of science. It must rather belong to the subject–object relation of cognition which is a transcendental condition of the possibility of cognition.

Now, if the difference between truth and falsehood belongs to the subject–object relation of cognition, then adequation of the mind to things (*adequatio intellectus ad res*) must be something to be recognized only from a standpoint outside the subject–object relation of cognition, that is from a divine perspective, as it were. Now this view could best be taken up by a metaphysician and theologian like Aquinas. But, even in this case, it remains criteriologically irrelevant. For we, human beings, cannot examine the subject–object relation of cognition from outside.

Precisely this is the main argument that was directed against the strong version of the correspondence theory of truth by the representative thinkers of the second paradigm of First Philosophy, for example by Kant,[4] by Franz Brentano[5] and, in the most radical way, by Gottlieb Frege.[6] Today, for example with Hilary Putnam,[7] it has become the main argument against the so called 'external' version of realism. For the 'external' version of realism is only another name for the first paradigm of First Philosophy which can conceive of the function of true knowledge only in ontological terms, that is either as a relation between intramundane objects to be studied by some kind of natural science, or as a relation between the human subject and things in themselves which could be checked only from God's view.

The second paradigm of First Philosophy: transcendental philosophy of consciousness

It is interesting to see how Kant, who in a sense is the classic representative of the second paradigm, dealt with the problem of true knowledge. On the one hand, he clearly recognized that our knowledge cannot be compared to 'things in themselves' but only to other knowledge (and this again to other knowledge, and so forth *ad infinitum*); and with regard to *a priori* valid knowledge, which Kant considered to be the condition of the possibility of inter-subjectively valid knowledge in general, he abandoned the conception of *adequatio intellectus ad res* altogether and instead of it proposed the 'Copernican turn' towards a constructive version of 'transcendental idealism'. Nevertheless Kant did not succeed in thoroughly breaking with the ontological-metaphysical paradigm of the correspondence theory of truth and hence of the first paradigm of First Philosophy. For, since he wanted to avoid absolute idealism, he could not avoid ascribing the material or empirical truth of our knowledge somehow to the affect of our senses by the things in themselves.

Thus it turns out that the famous aporia of the Kantian system – the fact that he simultaneously had to suppose and to disclaim the possibility of a categorically schematized knowledge about the things in themselves – is identical with the fact that his transition from the first to the second paradigm of First Philosophy (namely transcendental philosophy of consciousness) was incomplete, so to speak. For it seems clear that Kant's presupposition of the causal affect of our senses by the (allegedly unknowable) things in themselves must be considered a residual piece of the first paradigm of First Philosophy. But at this point the question arises whether a completed and at the same time consistent version of the second paradigm of First Philosophy is possible at all.

The reasons why I do not think that this question was successfully answered by the philosophy of German Idealism I leave to one side. Instead, I shall show that (and why) Husserl, the last classic of the second paradigm of First Philosophy, could not prove the sufficiency of the second paradigm of First Philosophy, although he provided an ingenious answer to the problem of truth theory from the point of view of his transcendental phenomenology of consciousness. Husserl's theory of truth was no longer an ontological-metaphysical one, but it was for the first time a criteriologically relevant answer to the problem of truth. It may be called, I suggest, the theory of 'evidence of correspondence' between the mind and the mundane phenomena. That is to say, Husserl conceived of correspondence not as an ontological relation between beings in the world, but as a relation of fulfilment of our noematic intentions by the self-givenness of the phenomena to be stated by reflection on our acts of intention and cognition.

By doing this, Husserl avoided the aporias of the ontological adequation theory which cannot become criteriologically relevant;

and at the same time he also avoided Kant's aporia of the un-knowable thing in itself, for his reference to the 'self-givenness' of the phenomena deals only with the world of 'empirical realism', to speak along with Kant. So what deficiency can be found in his theory?

I do not think that the fact that the fulfilment of our noematic intentions has to be stated by reflection on our acts of cognition generates a novel version of the problematic adequacy relation that leads to a *regressus ad infinitum*, as has been objected against Husserl. For in the context of the 'lifeworld' – to speak along with Husserl – it is sufficiently clear that when I say 'behind my back there is a cat on a mat', I can turn around and state that the noematic intention of my judgement is, or is not, fulfilled. Thus, one could say, I suggest, that Husserl has indeed shown what the criteriologically relevant meaning of truth as correspondence in ordinary life can be. But precisely at this point the paradigmatic aporia of Husserl's approach can be brought to bear.

For Husserl's theory of correspondence as the intuitively grasped fulfilment of our noematic intentions by the self-givenness of the phenomena does indeed function only in the lifeworld, that is it functions as long as we can suppose, as a matter of course, that the people involved share a common linguistic interpretation of the world. This can be supposed even in those cases where the transla-tion between different languages is unproblematic, as in the case of the English 'it is raining', the French 'il pleut', and the German 'es regnet'. But in the case of scientific observations, which are im-pregnated by theories, or in cases of encounters between different cultures, which are distinguished by different linguistic world inter-pretations, the tacit presupposition of Husserl's postulate that the linguistic world interpretation is unproblematic is no longer fulfilled. Here, all of a sudden, the problem of true cognition, even of true perception, is shifted from intuitively grasping the fulfilment of one's noematic intentions, hence the evidence of correspondence, to the problem of adequate linguistic interpretation of the phenomena, that is of interpreting something as something, to adopt Heidegger's idiom.

This aporia of the Husserlian evidence theory of truth is the best example I know for illustrating the necessity of the transition from the second paradigm of First Philosophy to a third one that came about in the course of the twentieth century.

The third paradigm of First Philosophy:
transcendental semiotics

The transition to a third paradigm of First Philosophy in the twentieth century is represented, I suggest, by the turn from Husserlian phenomenology to hermeneutic phenomenology as well as through the rise of linguistic philosophy, from the early to the later Wittgenstein and the schools of ordinary language philosophy, as well as through the development of semiotics in its structuralist and its Peircean version. All of these movements, which are very different from each other and, in my opinion, are only – at best – on the way towards the fully fledged paradigm of transcendental semiotics – all these movements of the twentieth century have realized the fact that intuitive evidence for my consciousness, a central concern of modern philosophy from Descartes to Husserl, is not adequate to account for the possibility of the constitution of a common world of meaning and for the possibility of truth as inter-subjective validity of knowledge.

In stating this I do not mean to say that Husserlian evidence by intuition is not a necessary ingredient of truth, as was suggested by Carnap and Popper, who wrongly identified evidence with the psychological feeling of evidence. In the meantime these simplifications of early analytic philosophy have been replaced by much more sophisticated views that can do justice to phenomenology as well as semiotics.[8] But there is no return to a pre-linguistic or pre-semiotic type of evidence phenomenology. That is to say, we may very well insist on the capacity of our consciousness of intuitively identifying and re-identifying (for example by memory) certain qualities of the self-givenness of the phenomena we are or were confronted with; but this evidence for our consciousness is not the same as inter-subjectively valid knowledge, which can be ensured only by a discursive agreement about sign-mediated interpretation of the phenomena.

In saying this I am not speaking only about those phenomena that – within the second paradigm of First Philosophy – are considered to be objects of the transcendental subject or consciousness. I am also speaking about the phenomenon or, alternatively, the conception of the *I* (ego) or consciousness itself, which was considered the basic fact of apodictic evidence by the second paradigm of First Philosophy. I would admit, on the one hand, that one is acquainted with oneself by introspection in such a way that one is able to re-identify oneself, for example by looking into a mirror. A child of two years is already able to pass this test, and thereby he or she shows that a certain evidence of self-acquaintance must indeed precede all kinds of self-understanding in the light of linguistic interpretation. But this evidence of self-acquaintance from self-familiarity does not prove that the self-understanding as being somebody or as an *I* is independent from interpretation by language in general, and in particular from the reciprocity of symbolic interaction (in the sense of G.H. Mead).[9]

In short, Husserl's deep conviction of the methodological autarchy of transcendental solipsism – a conviction that he shared with all representative thinkers of the second paradigm – is untenable. When Descartes or Husserl insisted on the apodictic evidence of the *ego cogito* they were not wrong, but they completely overlooked the fact that – even as empirically solitary thinkers – they were already arguing, that is using public language and participating in an argumentative discourse. Hence, the uncircumventible fact for a philosopher is not the *ego cogito*, taken in the sense of methodical or transcendental solipsism, but the *I argue* within the context of our argumentative discourse and hence my being a member of an argumentation community.

This necessary overcoming of transcendental solipsism does not amount to the 'death of the subject', as it was sometimes suggested from the point of view of linguistic and post-linguistic structuralism. It rather amounts to *a priori* conceiving of the subject of thought and knowledge as an inter-subject, that is as a member of a communication community.[10]

At this point of our reconstruction of the transition from the second to the third paradigm of First Philosophy we are already in a position to supplement the diagrammatic schema of the sign-relation or semiosis from which we started in order to derive systematically the three possible paradigms of First Philosophy. For we can now see that the third paradigm of First Philosophy – that of transcendental semiotics – not only takes into account all three places or positions of the triadic sign-relation, in contradistinction to the two preceding paradigms, but also transforms the third position, that of the transcendental subject, if we compare it with classical transcendentalism. It integrates the position of the transcendental subject of thought or cognition into that of the transcendental communication community. Thus transcendental philosophy of consciousness transforms itself into transcendental pragmatics of language. We can represent this diagrammatically, I suggest, as in Figure 2. And, if we want to get a better diagrammatical representation of what it means that our thought and cognition is *a priori* mediated through language, we may even supplement Figure 2 by Figure 3.

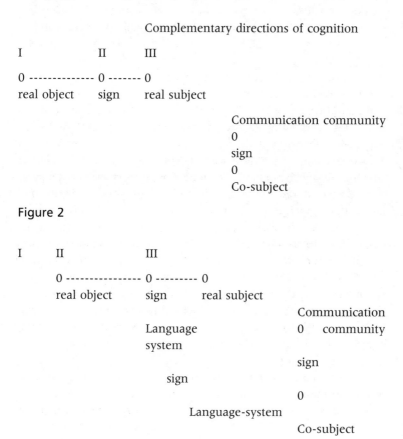

Figure 2

Figure 3

Now, having so far introduced some characteristic features of the third paradigm of First Philosophy, we should try to continue our elucidation of the different potentials of the three paradigms by discussing the problem of grounding a criteriologically relevant theory of truth. We have already shown that and why the ontological-metaphysical correspondence theory of truth is criteriologically irrelevant and that Husserl's correspondence-based evidential theory of truth, which represents the fully fledged second paradigm, is criteriologically relevant, but only in a very restricted sense. It does not reflect on the fact that cognitive evidence as meaningful evidence is always already mediated through interpretation in the light of language.

At this point the question arises, how to take into account this fact of semiotic or linguistic mediation of the meaning of cognition by a criteriologically relevant theory of truth. Is there already such a theory of truth available in the twentieth century?

The first and most famous answer to the problem of an adequate explication of the meaning of truth given in the twentieth century by language-analytical philosophy was provided by A. Tarski in his 'semantical theory of truth'.[11] If we compare his truth theory with Husserl's, we end up with polar-opposite models that represent the advantages and the deficiencies of pre-linguistic phenomenology as the last stage of transcendental philosophy consciousness, on the one hand, and logical semantics as an early stage of semiotical philosophy, on the other. Husserl's aporia – the unsolved problem of the variety and indeterminacy of the linguistic interpretation of phenomena – is completely avoided by Tarski's approach. For Tarski, from the outset, deals only with the meaning of true sentences of a specific constructed language or semantic system. Through the so-called 'truth rules', which provide a semantical interpretation of the language system, a so far precise meaning is co-ordinated to all the sentences of the language with one stroke, so to speak. And by these 'truth rules' the referential meanings of all sentences of a language system are interpreted by their truth conditions, that is by their possible correspondence to facts.

But this means that the relationship of correspondence between the true sentences of a language L and reality is only suggested by the 'convention T', that is by the rule of equivalence between a sentence 'p' and the fact that is designated by this very sentence. Can we thereby reach a rehabilitation of the realistic correspondence theory of truth in an ontologically and/or epistemologically relevant sense? Popper held this opinion,[12] but Tarski himself explicitly stated that his theory was ontologically and epistemologically neutral. Precisely by virtue of this neutrality it could serve as a semantic foundation for the logical conception of truth and truth-preserving statements as distinct from mere syntactical implication. What does this mean with regard to our problem of a criteriologically relevant theory of truth?

I think that the semantical truth theory as such is criteriologically irrelevant, since it abstracts from the question of whether a constructed semantical system can be pragmatically interpreted as a possible reconstruction of the language of science that is already in use. However, if a constructed semantical system can be pragmatically interpreted in the way indicated, then the semantical truth theory for that system may indeed – indirectly – gain a criteriological relevance, in so far as it provides a logico-semantical improvement of the language of science. But even in this case everything depends of course on the possibility of a successful application of the language of science to the phenomena. But at this point the problem of the adequate linguistic interpretation of the phenomena that was overlooked by Husserl reappears. Thus the question arises: isn't there a gap left between the Husserlian and the logico-semantical theory of truth, such that we need a general and criteriologically relevant answer to the question what it means that a linguistic interpretation of the phenomena can be considered to be true?

Carnap tried to avoid this difficulty by suggesting that the philosophical problem of explicating the meaning of truth was solved by Tarski whereas the remaining problems are those of verification that have to be solved by the empirical sciences. But I do not think that this suggestion can bridge the gap between Tarski's theory and the question of the true interpretation of phenomena. For we want to know precisely which philosophical conception of truth the empirical sciences must presuppose as a regulative idea for searching for the truth through taking into account all relevant criteria of truth, such as perceptual evidence, logico-semantical consistency and coherence, instrumental fruitfulness and the like.

At this point we should reflect on the fact that, by introducing Tarski's logico-semantic theory of truth, we have not yet utilized a fully fledged transcendental-semiotic theory in the sense of the third paradigm of First Philosophy; for the transcendental-pragmatic dimension of the sign-relation or semiosis – the dimension of the subject of sign interpretation as a member of a communication community – is still completely lacking in Tarski's (and in Carnap's) version of linguistic philosophy. I think indeed that logical semantics is only a sub-paradigm or initial stage of transcendental semiotics, a position that wrongly abstracted from the transcendental-pragmatic or subjective/inter-subjective presuppositions of cognition and the use of language.

By abstracting from the transcendental-pragmatic presuppositions of the cognitive use of language, the truth theory of logical semantics cannot deal for instance with that part of natural language through which real phenomena can be identified. For this cannot be immediately achieved by the terms of a semantical system, but only through indexical terms that are actually used by some interpreter within the context of a discourse. Now, it seems clear that only by such an identification of given phenomena with the aid of indexical terms can qualitative features of reality be taken into account as belonging to the facts to which our perceptual judgement has to correspond.

These facts, which we can identify through stating, for example, 'Over there, under the large tree, there is a swan swimming which is black', are quite different from those that belong to so-called logical space, as for example that it is the case that there are black swans or that Caesar was murdered in the Roman senate. The latter facts cannot be seen, as Strawson has stated quite correctly, but neither can they be something to which our perceptual judgements – say our experimental observations – should correspond in a Husserlian sense. But they are precisely those facts that can be taken into account by the semantical theory of truth. This shows again that the semantical theory of truth is criteriologically irrelevant. By contrast, those phenomenal facts that can be identified by a real interpreter with the aid of indexical terms may very well provide perceptual evidence for the truth of our pertinent perceptual judgements.

This shows that only the pragmatic use of the indexical terms of natural language in the context of an actual discourse about the phenomena of perception can definitively bridge the gap between the semantic theory of truth and the phenomenological evidence theory of truth. But, in this pragmatic context, it may even be demonstrated that the synthesis of phenomenal evidence and linguistic interpretation, which obviously has to be postulated as a presupposition of a criteriologically relevant theory of truth, is not a matter of course in the context of our searching for the truth.

For the phenomenal facts, which our interpretations should fit in order to make our perceptual judgements true, may even provide perceptual evidence of qualitative features of things that previously were not covered by the intensional meaning of our concepts. This may have been the case, for example, when for the first time black swans were encountered. This proves already that the evidence of the phenomena in a sense can correct the intensional meanings of our concepts from the point of view of the real extensions of the concepts and can thereby lead to a correction of our linguistic-conceptual interpretation of the phenomena.[13]

But the disparity between phenomenal evidence and linguistic-conceptual interpretation may be even more profound. For it may happen that we perceive things – individuals or natural kinds – whose qualitative properties we cannot subsume under a concept at all, so that we are confronted with phenomenal evidence for which we have almost no linguistic interpretation. Even in this case we can give a name to the strange thing with the aid of an indexical definition, as Kripke has shown.[14] And we can connect this name of the unknown thing with a description, or perhaps with a photo, in order to make a re-identification possible. Then, one good day, we may succeed in subsuming the strange thing under a concept that perhaps gives rise to a novel scientific theory. Only now has the process of perceptual cognition been completed, so that we are now in a position to form a perceptual judgement concerning the strange thing that may be true or false. Thus we have now succeeded in uniting the intuitive evidence concerning certain qualitative criteria and the conceptual interpretation into a synthesis of true or false cognition.

But it seems clear that in the course of scientific research the weight of the different truth criteria that are represented by phenomenal evidence, on the one hand, and linguistic interpretation, on the other, can be very different from case to case. The reason for this is primarily the fact that the linguistic interpretation, especially within the context of a methodical search for the truth, brings to bear the truth criteria of logical consistency and theoretical coherence as a counterweight to perceptual evidence – as a counterweight that tends to grow during the course of history. Thus the question arises: what are we searching for when we are searching for the truth, given the fact that the metaphysical conception of correspondence to reality is criteriologically irrelevant and that the truth criteria which we indeed have to take into account – for example phenomenal evidence, logical consistency and theoretical coherence – are never self-sufficient but rather competing with each other?

At this point, I suggest, we have to remember that in searching for the truth – as scientists and as philosophers – we have always already entered into the context of an argumentative discourse which is indeed the non-circumventible fact for the paradigm of transcendental semiotics or transcendental pragmatics, as I have already pointed out. Now, in this context, we must always already presuppose that we have a claim to truth in such a way that we are trying to show that our propositions are inter-subjectively valid, that is capable of a consensus by all possible members of an unlimited ideal argumentation community which we counterfactually antici- pate in addressing our real discourse partners. Now, this proves, I contend, that we are always already in possession of a regulative idea of truth that does not contradict the idea of correspondence to reality but, in contradistinction to this ontological-metaphysical idea, is criteriologically relevant. It is the idea of truth as ultimate consensus of an ideal unlimited argumentation community which was first envisaged by Peirce who, in my opinion, is also the initiator of transcendental semiotics, including transcendental pragmatics.[15]

In applying the transcendental-semiotic consensus theory of truth, I think, everything depends on conceiving of and using it as a regulative idea (in the sense of Kant and the late Peirce). That is to say, it is not itself a criterion, since it can never be given in space and time. But precisely in virtue of this negative property, in conjunction with the claim about reaching consent through argumentation, the idea of the ultimate consensus can take over the pragmatic function of directing or steering our search for the truth by taking into ac- count all possible truth criteria, that is all indices that may support or speak against our truth claims within the context of argumentative discourse. In a certain weak sense, even the factual consensus 'of all, or most, or the wise people', as Aristotle said, can function as a truth criterion, but this pre-Peircean meaning of consensus, which is close to an appeal to authority, can at best be integrated into a transcendental-semiotic consensus theory of truth. For, when we are following the regulative idea of the ultimate consensus, we will try hard, it is true, to reach a factual consensus that takes into account all available criteria; and, in the event that we cannot surmount factual dissensus, we will at least try to reach factual consensus concerning the reasons of our dissensus – for example the fact of different paradigms of thought – but, even if, or when, we succeed in reaching factual consensus on the basis of all available criteria, the regulative idea of the ultimate consensus compels us to try to transcend it by looking for further criteria that are not yet covered by the factual consensus.

I think indeed that the example of the consensus theory of truth can show how the aporetics of previous truth theories can be surmounted, partly even by integrating the contributions of older, more abstractive truth theories into the architectonical framework of transcendental semiotics. Thus it can also illustrate the superior potential of the third paradigm of First Philosophy as compared with the first and the second. But I want to emphasize that the same can be illustrated by other examples of basic philosophical problems as well.

Thus it may be shown that the problem of an ultimate foundation of the principles of theoretical and practical philosophy finds a different treatment according to the three different paradigms of First Philosophy.

According to the first paradigm, philosophical grounding had to be equated to deriving something from something else, for example deduction. Taken in this sense, the problem of ultimate foundation must lead to a trilemma, as Hans Albert demonstrated in the name of Critical Rationalism;[16] for it must lead either to a *regressus ad infinitum* in the search for the last principle from which to deduce, or to a logical circle in so far as we must presuppose by the deduction what has to be grounded, or, finally, to a dogmatization of some axiom as being evident apodictically.

Now, according to the second paradigm, deduction from something else is, in the case of ultimate foundation, replaced by reflection on what cannot be circumvented by reflection in the case of radical doubting. This leads to the Cartesian *ego cogito*, or more precisely, to that of Husserl. The idea of ultimate grounding through self-reflection of thought, I think, is a decisive step in the right direction, if reflection is understood in a transcendental sense.

Still there remains the problem of an adequate interpretation or explication of *cogito*. Now, this problem, I suggest, can be solved, according to the third paradigm of First Philosophy, by starting off from the language game of doubting; that is to say: one has to start off not from one of the many language games of doubting about something specific, but from the philosophical language game of doubting about everything. But even this is still ambiguous. For the Wittgensteinian thesis[17] that every meaningful doubt within the context of a language game presupposes some (paradigmatic) certainty, may first be de-dramatized by the argument that, of course, one cannot doubt about everything simultaneously but that one can doubt virtually everything together with the pertinent language game. But then the philosophical language game of doubting everything may be conceived of as that language game, in which the phrase 'virtually everything can be doubted, or is fallible' has its place.

Now in this case we can realize immediately that precisely this language game is inconsistent since, in order to be meaningful, it must itself presuppose indubitable certainties, for example that there is a language game of argumentative discourse, that in arguing one has a claim to truth, that it is possible, in principle, to come to a decision about the truth or falsehood of our truth claims by arguments etc. If these presuppositions of the language game of argumentative discourse are not taken for certain, the philosophical verdict about doubting everything, or unrestricted fallibilism, makes no sense; but if it does make sense, given its paradigmatic presuppositions of certainties, it cannot be true, according to the Wittgensteinian insight that every meaningful language game of doubting must presuppose paradigmatic certainties. Hence the language game of unrestricted fallibilism is self-contradictory.

It should be noted that in this argument the remaining problem of explicating the meaning of the undoubtable presuppositions of doubting is rather irrelevant.[18] For there is the frame of the transcendental language game or discourse, in which the presuppositions of meaningful doubting can be identified as those presuppositions of arguing that cannot be denied without rendering the language game meaningless. Hence a test procedure becomes possible for the ultimate transcendental pragmatic foundation of principles, which I have indicated by the following formula: 'All those principles can be considered to be grounded ultimately [*letztbegründet*] that cannot be denied without committing a performative self-contradiction of arguing and, precisely for that reason, cannot be grounded by deduction without committing a "*petitio principii*".'[19]

To conclude, I can only affirm that there are also discourse-ethical presuppositions of arguing that can be grounded in accordance with the test procedure of transcendental pragmatic ultimate foundation. This ultimate foundation of discourse ethics is possible for the third paradigm of First Philosophy, because we can reflect on the fact that as interlocutors, we are members of a real communication community and, at the same time, in addressing our discourse partners, must counterfactually anticipate an ideal communication community and its norms of communication and interaction.[20]

These transcendental presuppositions of arguing were not available for the second paradigm of First Philosophy, because that one was based on the presupposition of the transcendental solipsism of the *ego cogito*. Therefore Kant had to introduce *ad hoc* the metaphysical presupposition of a 'realm of purposes', that is of an ideal community of intelligible reasonable beings (*Vernunftwesen*) in order to initiate his foundation of ethics in his *Groundwork of the Metaphysics of Morals*. And within the frame of the first paradigm of First Philosophy, that is ontological metaphysics, there was only the possibility of dogmatically deriving *ought* from *being*. (Plato, it is true, asserted that the 'idea of the good' has its place 'beyond all present being' (*epekeina tes ousias*). But this in the light of Aristotle's ontology was conceived of as the divine *telos* of being.)

Thus it appears that only the third paradigm of First Philosophy can redeem the promise of grounding ethics by the self-reflection of reason (which was anticipated by Plato and Aristotle as God's *noesis noeseos* and by Kant as *Selbsteinstimmigkeit der Vernunft*). However, it must be clear that this grounding of principles of self-reflection of reason cannot integrate the whole scope of substantial (historical) knowledge as Hegel suggested through his monological speculation, which belonged to the second paradigm of First Philosophy. Ultimate foundation according to the third paradigm of First Philosophy can only mean to provide regulative principles for seeking the truth by unlimited theoretical discourses and for the procedures of grounding material moral norms through practical discourses of those affected by a norm or, if necessary, their advocates.[21]

Notes

1 T.S. Kuhn, *The Structure of Scientific Revolutions* (Chicago: University of Chicago Press, 1962).

2 C.S. Peirce, *Collected Papers*, ed. C. Hartshorne and P. Weiss (Cambridge, Mass.: Harvard University Press, 1931–35), vol. 2, p. 228; vol. 3, p. 360.

3 K.-O. Apel, *Selected Essays*, vol. 1, *Towards a Transcendental Semiotics* (Atlantic Highlands, N.J.: Humanities Press, 1994), 120 ff.

4 I. Kant, *Logik*, ed. G.B. Jasche (Königsberg: F. Nicolovius, 1800), 50.

5 F. Brentano, *Wahrheit und Evidenz* (Leipzig: Meiner, 1930).

6 G. Frege, 'Über Sinn und Bedeutung', *Zeitschrift für Philosophie und Philosophische Kritik*, new series 100 (1892), 195–205, repr. in Frege, *Funktion, Begriff, Bedeutung*, ed. G. Patzig (Göttingen, 1986); and Frege, 'Logik' (1897), repr. in *Schriften zur Logik und Sprachphilosophie*, ed. G. Gabriel (Hamburg, 1990).

7 H. Putnam, *Realism and Reason* (Cambridge, London and New York: Cambridge University Press, 1983).

8 Apel, 'Das Problem der phänomenologischen Evidenz im Lichte einer transzendentalen Semiotik', in M. Benedikt and R. Burger (eds), *Die Krise der Phänomenologie und die Pragmatik des Wissenschaftsfortschritts* (Vienna: Österreichische Staatsdruckerei, 1986), 78–99.

9 G.H. Mead, *Mind, Self and Society* (Chicago: Chicago University Press, 1934).

10 Cf. M. Niquet, 'Transzendentale Intersubjektivität', in A. Dorschel and M. Niquet (eds), *Transzendentalpragmatik* (Frankfurt a. M.: Suhrkamp, 1993), 148–66.

11 A. Tarski, 'Der Wahrheitsbegriff in den formalisierten Sprachen', in K. Berka and L. Kreiser (eds), *Logik-Texte* (Berlin: De Gruyter, 1971), 447–550; and Tarski, 'Die semantische Konzeption der Wahrheit in die Grundlagen der Semantik', in J. Sinnreich (ed.), *Zur Philosophie der idealen Sprache* (Munich: DTV, 1972), 5–100.

12 K.R. Popper, *Objective Knowledge: An Evolutionary Approach* (Oxford: Clarendon Press, 1972), 319 ff.

13 H. Putnam, *Mind, Language and Reality* (Cambridge: Cambridge University Press, 1975), chapter 12; Apel, *Selected Essays*, vol. 1.

14 S. Kripke, *Naming and Necessity* (Oxford: Basil Blackwell, 1980).

15 Apel, *Der Denkweg von Charles Sanders Peirce: eine Einführung in den amerikanischen Pragmatismus* (Frankfurt a. M.: Suhrkamp, 1975), English translation: *Charles S. Peirce: From Pragmatism to Pragmaticism* (Amherst: University of Massachusetts Press, 1981; repr. by Humanities Press, Atlantic Highlands, N.J., 1995); Apel, 'C.S. Peirce and the Post-Tarskian Problem of an Adequate Explanation of the Meaning of Truth: Towards a Transcendental-pragmatic Theory of Truth', in E. Freeman (ed.), *The Relevance of Charles Peirce* (La Salle, Ill.: Hegeler Institute, 1983), 189–223, repr. in Apel, *Selected Essays*; Apel, 'Fallibilismus, Konsenstheorie der Wahrheit und Letztbegründung', in Forum für Philosophie Bad Homburg (ed.), *Philosophie und Begründung* (Frankfurt a. M.: Suhrkamp, 1987), 116–211; Apel, 'Transcendental Semiotics and Truth', in M.A. Bonfantini and A. Martone (eds), *Peirce in Italia* (Naples: Liguori, 1993), 191–208.

16 H. Albert, *Traktat über kritische Vernunft* (Tübingen: Mohr, 1968).

17 L. Wittgenstein, *Über Gewissheit* (Frankfurt a. M.: Suhrkamp, 1970), 39.

18 See Apel, 'Fallibilismus'.

19 See Apel, 'Das Problem der philosophischen Letztbegründung im Lichte einer Transzendentalen Sprachpragmatik', in B. Kanitschneider (ed.), *Sprache und Erkenntnis* (Innsbruck, 1976), 55–82, English translation: 'The Problem of Philosophical Fundamental Grounding in Light of a Transcendental-Pragmatic of Language', *Man and World*, 8 (1975), 239–75, repr. in K. Baynes, J. Bohman and T.A. McCarthy (eds), *After Philosophy: End or Transformation?* (Cambridge, Mass.: MIT Press, 1987), 250–90; W. Kuhlmann, *Reflexive Letztbegründung: Untersuchungen zur Transzendentalpragmatik* (Freiburg and Munich: Alber, 1985).

20 Apel, 'Das Apriori der Kommunikationsgemeinschaft und die Grundlagen der Ethik', in Apel, *Transformation der Philosophie* (Frankfurt a. M.: Suhrkamp, 1973), vol. 2, 358–436, English translation: 'The *A Priori* of the Communication Community and the Foundations of Ethcs', in Apel, *Towards a Transformation of Philosophy*, trans. G. Adey and D. Frishy (London: Routledge & Kegan Paul, 1980), repr. in Apel, *Selected Essays*, vol. 2, *Ethics and the Theory of Rationality* (Atlantic Highlands, N.J.: Humanities Press, 1996); Apel, *Diskurs und Verantwortung* (Frankfurt a. M.: Suhrkamp, 1988).

21 Apel, *Diskurs und Verantwortung.*

3

Transcendental semiotics and truth: the relevance of a Peircean consensus theory of truth in the present debate about truth theories

Introduction

It is not my primary aim to contribute to the hermeneutic interpretation of Peirce's theory of truth. I undertook this task elsewhere.[1] In what follows I will consider the relation between Peirce's conception of truth and certain prominent truth theories of our century, such as the phenomenological evidence theory of truth, the logico-semantical theory of truth and the coherence theory of truth. I attempt to demonstrate the following three points.

First, all the prominent truth theories just mentioned have their specific merits in comparison with an ontological-metaphysical correspondence theory of truth which is criteriologically irrelevant. Moreover, they are capable of partly supplementing one another in the context of a dialectical discourse. This is due to the fact that these different truth theories cluster around different truth criteria.

Second, nevertheless, since none of these truth criteria is sufficient in itself, and since none of the truth theories I mentioned covers all necessary truth criteria, there are shortcomings and aporias remaining with regard to all of them. These shortcomings call for a further supplementation, integration or *Aufhebung* (in the Hegelian sense of this word), within the framework of a more comprehensive theory of truth. This postulated comprehensive truth theory should be capable *a priori*, that is through its fundamental conception as a regulative idea of settling truth claims by empirical inquiry and argumentative discourse, of taking into account all possible truth criteria and, furthermore, of weighing them against one another and bringing them to a synthesis in the long run. (This postulate, of course, will have to become more specific.)

My third contention is that Peirce's conception of truth – or perhaps rather a transcendental-semiotic consensus theory of truth that is strongly inspired by Peirce – can fulfil precisely the task outlined so far. It can provide the regulative principle of collecting, weighing and integrating all relevant truth criteria in the long run.

The aporias of the ontologico-metaphysical correspondence theory of truth

Let me start out with some remarks on the ontological correspondence theory of truth whose classical *topos* reads as follows: 'to say of the being that it is not, and to say of the non-being that it is, is false; but to say of the non-being that it is not and of the being that it is, is true'.[2]

In my opinion there is a very weak version of this correspondence theory that expresses a correct and indispensable intuition – an intuition that is presupposed and must be taken into account by any plausible truth theory. I shall later try to corroborate and elucidate this point. However, there is also a stronger version of the correspondence theory which is at the centre of ontological metaphysics, for example in Aristotle's conception of *homoiosis* and in Aquinas's conception of *adequatio rei et intellectus*.[3] This strong version of the correspondence theory, I claim, is obsolete for a post-Kantian type of critical philosophy. And so is the whole paradigm of ontological metaphysics.

The reason for this verdict does not lie in its realism taken as a commonsense intuition. Rather it lies in the fact that it conceives of the relevant relationship between the mind or consciousness and the things as objects of cognition as a relationship between two things in the world, that is, between two objects. This conception entails either that the relation of true cognition and its difference from falsehood is something like a natural relationship to be detected by natural science; or that we, humans, are capable of standing outside of the subject–object relation of our actual cognition and observing it, so to speak, from outside, such as a relationship between the mind and the things in themselves.

I regard both of these paradigmatic presuppositions as characteristic implications of ontological metaphysics in the pre-Kantian sense. The first presupposition, that is the quasi-naturalistic conception of true cognition as *homoiosis*, namely adequation of the soul to the things outside, is especially testified to by Aristotle's treatment of these problems in *De Anima*; the second presupposition is rather characteristic of Aquinas who, so to speak, looks upon the relationship of *adequatio intellectus et rei* in the light of God's extramundane standpoint.

Now, in both cases we cannot, in principle, arrive at an explication of the meaning of truth that would be criteriologically relevant. For in the first case, which was later continued by natural science, we can never detect such a thing as the difference between truth and falsehood. For natural processes or relations are completely indifferent with regard to this distinction. In the second case, however, we would have to look behind the mirror of the given phenomena, which is impossible for us, since we are under the spell of the subject–object relation of actual cognition.

Therefore Kant, Brentano and other modern philosophers have claimed that every attempt to compare our judgements with the things in themselves must lead to a *regressus ad infinitum*, since we can only compare our judgements with other judgements about the phenomena, which, in turn, would have to be compared with the things in themselves, and so on *ad infinitum*.[4]

Kant nevertheless upheld the metaphysical presupposition that our empirically true knowledge has to be traced back to the affect of our senses by the unknowable things in themselves. Thereby he ran into an unsolvable aporia of his truth theory. For owing to his supposition of the existence and causal efficacy of unknowable things in themselves, Kant stuck to the metaphysical solution of the problem of correspondence whose central difficulty he himself had exposed. This very problem, however, was solved in a post-metaphysical sense by the phenomenological evidence theory of truth as proposed by Husserl.

Merits and shortcomings of the phenomenological evidence theory of truth

This theory is distinguished, in my view, by the fact that it completely dispenses with the old metaphysical presupposition of conceiving of the subject–object relation of cognition as a kind of object–object relation that could be looked upon, as it were, from an external position. Thus Husserl dispenses with the problem of the unknowable things in themselves as well. He construes the relationship of truth (i.e. of true cognition) strictly as cognition and its self-reflection. From this vantage point he defines truth, as distinct from falsehood, as fulfilment of the subject's noematic intentions by the self-givenness of the phenomena.[5]

Thus, to offer an example, the asserted proposition 'behind my back there is a cat that lies on a mat' would be true if, and only if, after turning round, I could ascertain by a perceptual judgement that the *noema* of my propositional intention is in fact fulfilled by the self-givenness of the phenomenon that there is a cat lying on a mat.

I think indeed that by this phenomenological analysis of the fulfilment relation of evidence Husserl has succeeded in explicating – without presupposing an ontological objectification of the subject–object relation – the natural intuition that lies at the ground of the common sense-notion of truth as correspondence between our judgements and the facts.

There is, however, one serious deficiency in this phenomenological evidence theory of truth. It is satisfactory only as long as we can presuppose as a matter of course that all people involved in the settling of truth claims are sharing a common linguistic interpretation of the given phenomena. Now, precisely this can indeed be supposed in ordinary communication, that is in the lifeworld in Husserl's sense, thus for instance in the case of statements like 'it is raining' or 'the cat is on the mat'. The fact that all phenomena that can be grasped as something, that is being significant, must already be mediated by a linguistic world interpretation, can simply be neglected in the case of everyday communication.

This does not mean, however, that a philosophical truth theory may ignore that fact. For the situation changes completely, once we come to scientific statements about experimental phenomena, or when we encounter communication between different cultures and their different linguistic world interpretations. In these cases the tacitly presupposed linguistic world interpretation becomes conspicuous or surprising, so to speak. The ascertainment of the truth of a proposition is, in such cases, no longer simply a matter of perceptual evidence for a solitary subject with regard to its subject–object relation of cognition. Rather, such cases show that every true or false judgement about something is also a matter of hermeneutic communication, that is of coming to a consensus with others about the correct interpretation of the phenomena taken as signs. (In the case of science this could mean that the given phenomena, in order to be grasped as something, call for novel theories or even language games that are based on novel 'paradigms' of research.[6] In the case of an encounter with foreign cultures it could mean that one has to learn a language in the light of which even the lifeworld of ordinary communication has to be largely re-interpreted.) Already at this point I could introduce a Peircean conception of sign interpretation and consensus-formation on sign interpretation in the long run, in order to suggest an integration of Husserl's transcendental-phenomenological evidence theory of truth into a transcendental-semiotic consensus theory of truth. Before this step, however, I will first consider two other prominent truth theories which may also claim to correct, by taking into account the necessity or even priority of linguistic world interpretation, the phenomenological recourse to immediate evidence.

Tarski's abstract linguistic turn alternative to Husserl's phenomenological evidence theory truth

Compared with Husserl's phenomenological evidence theory, Tarski's logico-semantical theory of truth[7] is the polar-opposite conception which provides a one-sided but instructive supplantation of the former theory. The relationship between the theories could be characterized in the following way. Whereas Husserl is the last classic of a pre-linguistic or pre-semiotic type of transcendental philosophy of consciousness, Tarski is an early classic of linguistic philosophy, that is a classic of its semanticist phase prior to the pragmatic turn of its orientation towards ideal-construct(ed) languages prior to the turn to the analysis of ordinary language. This difference between Husserl and Tarski has the following implications with regard to their respective theories of truth.

Whereas Husserl does not reflect at all on the linguistic pre-interpretation of what he calls phenomenological evidence, Tarski from the outset restricts his analysis of the meaning of truth to the explication of the meaning of the predicate 'is true' with regard to the sentences of a certain constructed formalized language or semantic system. Thus Tarski, in contrast to Husserl, apparently has no problem with the indefiniteness or ambiguity of linguistic world interpretation, since he relies from the outset on the definiteness of the meanings of signs within a formalizable semantical system. Through his definition of 'true in L' (e.g. a certain language), so to speak, all sentences of L get their definite meaning, since they are equipped with their truth conditions through truth rules.[8] But the price for this advantage lies in the abstraction of the semantical systems. By his explication of the truth of sentences in L, Tarski must exclude all situation-bound meanings of natural language as pragmatically applicable languages, for example the meanings of 'indexical terms'; hence he cannot reach the given phenomena of the real world at all.

To put it in other words: in his convention $T^9 - x$ is true if and only if p or, in another version: 'p' is true if and only if p – Tarski tries indeed to reconstruct the point of the Aristotelian correspondence theory of truth as does Husserl. By the second p – the p without quotation marks – Tarski is indeed pointing to the real world in the light of the meaning of a sentence of the 'object language'. However, by the restriction of his explication to the meaning of sentences of a semantical system he also wishes to avoid all ontological or epistemological implications of his theory. The theory is to be both metaphysically neutral and free of any implications with regard to the problem of verification (as Tarski himself emphasizes).[10]

The price for this abstractive semanticist restriction of Tarski's theory of truth is, again, that it does not reach the phenomena of the real world; and that means, as Tarski himself confirms, that the theory has no criteriological relevance for epistemology. It accounts only for a necessary semantic precondition of the concept of conclusiveness, that is of truth-transfer in a semantic system in distinction to the merely syntactical concept of implication. But this supplementation of logical syntax by logical semantics by no means warrants that the constricted semantic system can be applied to the actual world – say, as a reconstruction of scientific language.

In order to assure contact with the actual world, it must be presupposed – at least tacitly – that the whole semantic system – together with the pertinent (recursive) definition of its true sentences – can be pragmatically interpreted. But this can be done only with the aid of a natural language, as it is used even by the scientists. Natural language, which also contains indexical signs, is the ultimate pragmatic meta-language of all abstract hierarchies of semantic language system.

It is therefore false to suppose – with Tarski and Carnap – that the logico-semantic definition of truth is a sufficient basis or precondition for the explication of the meaning of truth, such that, under this precondition, the problem of verification could be solved by the empirical sciences themselves. Contrary to this supposition, I would claim that the solution of the problem of verification – or of confirmation and falsification – presupposes an explication of the meaning of truth with regard to natural language as the ultimate pragmatic meta-language, with the aid of which every constructed semantic system must be interpreted in order to be applicable to the phenomena of the actual world.

Now, if this analysis is correct, it follows that all those problems of linguistic world interpretation – that is of the ambiguity or indeterminacy of linguistic meanings – that are connected with the primordial perception of the given phenomena will appear when it comes to the question whether a construed semantic system can be pragmatically applied.

Briefly put: a gap remains between Husserl's phenomenological evidence theory, which does not consider at all the linguistic interpretation of the phenomena, and Tarski's abstract semantical truth theory, which neglects the pragmatic interpretation of its construed language systems. Neither of these opposite conceptions deals with the problems of the linguistic interpretation of the given phenomena by the human (co-)subjects of communication, and hence with the inter-subjective dimension of true cognition as publicly valid cognition. For in Husserl's conception of the fulfilment of noematic intentions only the 'transcendental-solipsistic' aspect of the subject–object relation of true cognition is taken into account without any reflection on its mediation by inter-subjectively valid meanings of linguistic signs. In Tarski's conception, on the other hand, only the prefixed meanings of a semantic system and their reference to the possible *designata* of the abstract system are taken into account, whereas the possibility of applying the semantic system through communicative understanding (*Verständigung*) and through the identification of real *denotata* (in space and time) must be tacitly presupposed.[11]

At this point the question obviously arises what kind of truth theory can close the gap between the perceptual evidence of the given phenomena and the abstract logico-semantic explication of truth as is presupposed in a consistent system of truth-preserving statements. Should not the coherence theory of truth fulfil this function? After all, the coherence theory of truth has always been taken to be able to deal with the conceptual, and to that extent linguistic, interpretation of all possible phenomena of theoretical cognition.

Merits and shortcomings of the coherence theory of truth: Hegel's case

Hegel, still the most influential representative of a coherence theory of truth, praised 'language' as the 'more truthful' in comparison to the immediate 'sense certainty' (*Sinnliche Gewissheit*) which he called 'the untrue' (*das Unwahre*). He did so in the famous first chapter of the *Phenomenology of the Spirit*.[12] And in his 'Science of Logic' he tried to show that (and how) the *a priori* coherent development of our concepts can display the whole of what we can and must understand as being the truth of things in God's intellect.

In his chapter on 'sense certainty' Hegel has indeed shown that those indexical words of language that represent our sense certainty – words like 'this', 'here' and 'now' – if taken in isolation, that is separated from the meaning of the conceptual words of language, have no referential meaning and no relevance for the truth of our world representation. 'The This' or 'the Here' or 'the Now', as Hegel caricatures the hypostatization of sense certainty, cannot represent any definite object of cognition at all.

However, Hegel suggests by these examples that only the conceptual words of our language can through their coherence constitute the truth of our linguistic world representation. He does not see or take into account that the indexical words by their situation-bound meanings can and must provide some specific and indispensable contribution to our knowledge if and when they are used as parts of perceptual judgements, as for example in the context of experimental protocols. In these cases indexical words, through their directing our attention – in a way that is still conceptionally determined – to the given phenomena, provide exactly that kind of evidence that is needed by the empirical sciences in so far as they are distinct from the type of conceptual philosophical science that Hegel, like Plato, favoured as providing the coherent truth of the whole. In other words: within the context of perceptual judgements, indexical words, in pointing to qualities of suchness, provide precisely the kind of knowledge that makes it possible for us to distinguish between the real world of experience and all merely possible worlds that may fulfil criterial conditions of a coherence theory of truth.

My critical comments on Hegel should not be taken to suggest that we turn back to the phenomenological evidence theory of truth and simply set pre-linguistic intuition over against the truth of conceptual coherence. (Ludwig Feuerbach's critique of Hegel can be interpreted as a regression to the evidence of pre-linguistic intuition.)[13] Rather, I am suggesting that Hegel, in appealing to the 'truth of language', failed to understand the linguistic function of the indexical words and thus the whole possible truth of the linguistic world interpretation. The point of the perceptual judgements as compared with mere assertive propositions rests precisely on the fact that the former through the function of indexical signs are capable of integrating novel empirical informations into the conceptual-linguisitic interpretation of the world. They extend the extensional and hence also the intensional meaning of terms, for example the meaning of the term 'swan' by stating (that) 'this over there is a black swan'.[14]

Only Charles Peirce distinguished semiotically between different types of (linguistic and non-linguistic) signs, namely 'symbols', 'indices' and 'icons', and assigned to these different types of signs three fundamental categories: 'thirdness','secondness' and 'firstness'. Peirce thus made it possible to understand the interaction and synthesis of phenomenological or 'phaneroscopic' evidence and conceptual coherence within the context of linguistic world interpretation. For him pre-linguistic evidence of the given phenomena of suchness was not nothing as for Hegel and the twentieth-century semanticists; but neither was it already the truth of cognition, as it was for Husserl. On Peirce's account, phenomenological evidence provides indeed a necessary ingredient of truth on the level of firstness and secondness that enters into those abductive inferences that underlie perceptual judgements. But only by the conceptual-symbolic interpretation, which on the level of thirdness completes the abductive inferences, can the cognitive result of the perceptual judgements and hence their truth or falsehood emerge.

Clearly, our assessment of the truth or falsehood of perceptual judgements must depend also on their coherence (or non-coherence) with the whole body of our well-confirmed knowledge. Yet this postulate should not be taken to mean that truth or falsehood of perceptual judgements depends merely on their coherence with some possible coherent systems of propositions. The selection of systems as candidates for the postulated coherence between propositions (or between whole theories) must in turn be constrained by the very possibility of justifying truth claims of propositions (or of whole theories) by the confirmatory powers of perceptual judgements that are based on the evidence of given phenomena.[15]

Thus the relationship between perceptual evidence and conceptual or propositional coherence is one of competing and complementary truth criteria which again and again must be weighed and brought to a provisory reflective equilibrium by means of consensus formation in the community of researchers. This synthetic consensus formation cannot be construed as a matter of deducing consensus from the criteria of evidence and coherence. Nor can it be construed as an appeal to consensus as an additional truth criterion. Instead, we should think of it as a process that results uncoerced from all kinds of inference processes (deduction, induction and abduction) and sign interpretations that lead to plausible arguments in the community of discourse.

Integration of truth criteria within a Peircean consensus theory of truth

The preceding sections already reveal my contention that a transcendental-semiotic and transcendental-pragmatic consensus theory in the vein of Peirce's philosophy can integrate all truth criteria that are taken into account by the three modern truth theories that I have outlined.

First, from a (transcendental-)semiotic point of view, it can be seen that Peirce's theory of sign interpretation covers precisely the so-called pragmatic dimension of semiosis. That pragmatic dimension, as Charles Morris recognized,[16] must be presupposed in order to make use of the modern apparatus of syntactical and semantic constructions of ideal formalizable languages of science. Peirce's theory is based on the triadic structure of the sign-relation or semiosis. This means that, in contradistinction to formal semantics, it does not abstract from the place and function of the sign interpreter or – in traditional terms – of the subject of cognition and his or her truth claims. Peirce's theory shows that this function has to be integrated into that of an indefinite community of interpretation and consensus formation about truth claims because non-mediated cognition depends on a semiotic process of sign interpretation through 'interpretants' that is indefinite in principle (although it is always related – through the triadic sign-relation – to 'the real' as its 'transcendental significatum' as any Peircean philosopher would have to insist against Derrida).[17]

Connected with this semiotic transformation of the traditional function of the subject of cognition and truth claims are two other basic features of a Peircean consensus theory of truth.

Second, Peirce's semiotic logic of inquiry which is part of a 'normative science' is distinguished from Morris's and Carnap's conception of empirical and formal pragmatics[18] by the fact that it provides not only a basis for a description of the use of language but a set of regulative principles for the procedures of inference and sign-interpretation that have to be postulated in order to reach in the long run a consensus about the 'logical interpretants' of signs or the 'ultimate opinion' about 'the real' through the joint enterprise of an indefinite community of investigators.

In particular the pragmatic maxim of 'how to make our ideas clear'[19] is distinguished from other pragmatic theories about the use of signs in the practical contexts of life (e.g. from Wittgenstein's suggestions) by the fact that the pragmatic maxim is part of a normative and methodologically relevant theory which relies on 'counterfactuals'. It does not tell the scientist who asks for the real meaning of a concept that she should look for the usage, that is for the usual behaviour and experiences associated with the use of signs. This would be of little help to her in cases of difficult concepts. Instead, the pragmatic maxim provides a normative guideline for thought experiments according to which *if . . . then . . .* connections between possible actions or operations and possible experiences can be discovered. Thus even the unconscious 'background' of our ordinary use of signs ('background' as meant by John Searle in his book on intentionality)[20] may be progressively brought to light, and a deeper understanding of the meaning of terms and a novel use of them in the language games of science and philosophy may be brought about. I would exemplify this by Einstein's 'special theory of relativity' which can be seen as an ingenious experiment of thought in order to clarify – in accordance with the prescriptions of the pragmatic maxim – what the phrase 'two events are occurring simultaneously' could mean when we seek how the simultaneity could be measured.

The normative character of Peirce's semiotic logic of inquiry and the fact that it provides postulates and regulative principles as conditions of inter-subjectively valid sign interpretation and thus of truth by consensus – this feature testifies to the fact that it grew out of Kant's 'transcendental logic' and that it even preserves the status of a semiotic transformation of that logic.[21] Therefore it is not a part of empirical science – not even of hypothetical metaphysics in Peirce's sense.[22] Rather, it accounts for the conditions of the possibility of all enterprises of progressive sign interpretation as search for the truth. On this level the postulate of an ultimate consensus of an indefinite community takes the place of Kant's 'synthesis of apperception' as the 'supreme point' of the 'transcendental deduction' of 'principles'. The Peircean 'principles' that are functionally related to the highest point of an ultimate consensus are no longer 'synthetic judgements a priori' but the procedural conditions of the validity of the three kinds of inferences (deduction, induction and abduction) and of sign interpretation.[23]

Third, there is also an internal connection between the normative-transcendental character of Peirce's semiotic logic and the fact that his consensus theory of truth can also function as a semiotic integration of Husserl's phenomenological evidence theory of truth.[24] The crucial feature in this context is constituted by the fact that Peirce's semiotics must not treat the subjective or inter-subjective conditions of sign interpretation merely as intramundane objects of the semantic reference of signs (more precisely: of the semantic reference of the signs of a meta-language of semanticized pragmatics) as is suggested by Morris's and Carnap's conception of pragmatics.[25] Instead, a transcendental semiotic of Peircean provenance preserves the status of the interpreter or the community of interpreters as the transcendental subject of cognition and truth. For only thereby can it preserve the special place of the interpreter in the triadic relation of semiosis, as has been shown.[26]

From this it follows that phenomenological evidence for one's consciousness must not be abstractively excluded from semiotic logic as a merely empirical-pragmatic, that is psychological, fact, say, a certain feeling that may function as a cause of my judgements (e.g. of my 'basis sentences') as Carnap and Popper supposed. Instead, the evidence of the suchness of a phenomenon given to my consciousness can function as a cognitive reason or as a criterion for true perceptual judgements as Husserl supposed in his phenomenology. But Husserl equates the phenomenological evidence of a given suchness with the truth of a perceptual judgement, overlooking the fact that the latter rests on a linguistic interpretation of the phenomenon as well, whereas Peirce considers the pure evidence of suchness, that is the 'firstness' of a given phenomenon, as only a necessary ingredient of the unconscious abductive inference which as a whole is constitutive for the meaning and possible truth of a perceptual judgement.

Hence for Peirce the immediate intuitive awareness of pure 'phenomenological' or 'phaneroscopic' evidence does not yet amount to the truth of cognition. As it is immediately given to my consciousness, a phenomenon of firstness (of being so-and-so) and of secondness (i.e. a relation of I and non-I) is not yet interpreted as being something, that is mediated by the general meaning of a conceptual sign (thirdness). This interpretation, which constitutes a perceptual judgement that may eventually be inter-subjectively valid, that is true, requires three further cognitive procedures.

First, the grasping of pure suchness or being so-and-so (i.e. of qualities and their phenomenal relations) must somehow provide a premise for an abductive inference.

Second, the abductive inference, in order to subsume the given phenomenon of suchness under a general concept, must for that purpose introduce a linguistic interpretation through a symbol.

Third, as a predicate, this symbol makes possible the predicative proposition that turns out to be the conclusion of the abductive inference that constitutes the perceptual judgement. That conclusion may then engender further processes of sign interpretation that are subjected to the regulative principle of searching – according to the pragmatic maxim – for the correct 'logical interpretant'. This entire interpretation process is part of the research process through which the truth qua consensus of the reserach community about specific truth claims may be attained in the long run. But the truth about the real *in toto* can be defined only by the regulative idea of the ultimate consensus of an infinite reseach community, that is in terms of a total belief that principally could not be called into question by any further objection.

It seems clear that this ultimate ideal consensus the notion of which defines the idea of truth can never be reached, that is realized in the course of time, since a regulative idea cannot be equated with any empirical fact according to both Peirce and Kant. But the regulative idea of an ultimate consensus is nevertheless criteriologically relevant (in contradistinction to the ontological notion of correspondence) in virtue of the following normative (procedural) implications.

First, it suggests looking for all possible truth criteria and weighing them against each other in order to reach factual but fallible and hence provisory consensus through the argumentative discourse of a real community of investigators.

Second, equally, the regulative idea of an ultimate consensus suggests that we should look for any counter-arguments in order to question every factual consensus of an existent finite research community, thereby keeping open the way of research toward the ultimate consensus of an indefinite community. Only this final consensus, which could no longer be questioned by argument, can and must be be equated with the truth that we can strive for – if striving for the truth is to make sense at all for us in terms of procedural *praxis*.

Thus it turns out, in my view, that the Peircean consensus theory of truth can itself be considered as an application of the pragmatic maxim of meaning clarification on the very idea of truth. It provides the procedures through which the search for truth can be pursued and it yields a conception of the results we can reasonably expect in this way. It does not reduce the pragmatic meaning of truth to the satisfactory or useful effects which the belief in certain opinions could have for the life of some person or some group of human beings. This way of applying the pragmatic maxim on the concept of truth Peirce left to those who borrowed the idea of pragmatism but only to attribute to it different connotations.[27] (The last of them in our day is Richard Rorty who, following in the steps of William James, defines the predicate 'true' by 'what is good for us to believe'.)

For Peirce the context for the application of the pragmatic maxim to the concept of truth is not to be constituted by the finite horizon and subjective perspective of a human life and its vital needs and interests.[28] It is constituted by the potentially infinite horizon of argumentative discourse within an infinite community of researchers. As a moral precondition of their *praxis*, the members of this community must even commit themselves to 'surrendering' all their private or group interests in favour of the long-term interest of the indefinite community in its search for the final consensus by arguments.[29]

Notes

First published in M.A. Bonfantini and E. Martone (eds), *Peirce in Italia* (Naples: Liguori, 1993), 191–208.

1 K.-O. Apel, *Der Denkweg von Charles Sanders Peirce: eine Einführung in den amerikanischen Pragmatismus* (Frankfurt a. M.: Suhrkamp, 1975), English translation: *Charles S. Peirce: From Pragmatism to Pragmaticism* (Amherst: University of Massachusetts Press, 1981); and Apel, 'C.S. Peirce and the Post-Tarskian Problem of an Adequate Explication of the Meaning of Truth: Towards a Transcendental-pragmatic Theory of Truth', in E. Freeman (ed.), *The Relevance of Charles Peirce* (La Salle, Ill.: Hegeler Institute, 1983), 189–223.

2 Aristotle, *Metaphysics*, 1011b 26 f.

3 Aquinas, *Summa Theologiae*, I, 16, 2; *De Veritate*, I, 1.

4 I. Kant, *Logik*, ed. G.B. Jasche (Königsberg: Nicolovius, 1800), 50.

5 E. Husserl, *Formale und Transzendentale Logik* (Halle: Niemeyer, 1929), 140 ff., and *Cartesianische Meditationen und Pariser Vorträge*, Husserliana 1 (The Hague: Nijhoff, second edition, 1963), 55 ff., 92 f., 143.

6 T.S. Kuhn, *The Structure of Scientific Revolutions* (Chicago: University of Chicago Press, 1962).

7 A. Tarski, 'Der Wahrheitsbegriff in den formalisierten Sprachen', in K. Berka and L. Kreiser (eds), *Logik-Texte* (Berlin: De Gruyter, 1971), 447–550, and 'Die semantische Konzeption der Wahrheit und die Grundlagen der Semantik', in J. Sinnreich (ed.), *Zur Philosophie der idealen Sprache* (Munich: DTV, 1972), 5–100.

8 W. Stegmüller, *Das Wahrheitsproblem und die Idee der Semantik* (Vienna and New York, 1968), 47 ff. It has often been objected against Tarski that truth is not a predicate of sentences but of propositions. This is surely correct if by 'sentences' Tarski meant the sign vehicles. This interpretation is suggested by Tarski's sharing the physicalism of Carnap. It seems to me however that Tarski's relativization of truth to the sentences of a semantic system may be understood in a different sense which constitutes the point of semanticism as a first stage of the linguistic turn in philosophy. According to this turn the very meanings of propositions are relative to their being the meanings of certain sentences of a semantic system. This point was brought out by Wittgenstein's statement that 'the thought is the significant sentence' ('Der Gedanke ist der sinnvolle Satz') (*Tractatus*), and even more clearly in the following remark: 'The limit of language shows itself in the impossibility of describing the fact which corresponds to a sentence . . . without repeating the sentence' (*Vermischte Bemerkungen* (Frankfurt a. M.: Suhrkamp, 1977), 27). This remark, I suggest, illuminates the very point of Tarski's 'convention T', e.g. of the equivalence: 'The sentence "p" is true if, and only if, *p*.' It shows that Tarski's semantic theory of truth marks the very counterposition to Husserl's transcendental-phenomenological theory of pre-linguistic evidence.

9 A. Tarski, 'Der Wahrheitsbegriff', 452 ff.; 'Die semantische Konzeption', 60 f.

10 A. Tarski, 'Die semantische Konzeption', 87.

11 The distinction between *designata* as supposed referents of an abstract seman-

tic system and real *denotata* as referents of a cognitive-pragmatic use of language with the aid of 'identifiers' (e.g. 'indexical signs') was introduced by Charles W. Morris in his *Signs, Language and Behavior* (New York: Braziller, 1946).

12 G.W.F. Hegel, *Die Phänomenologie des Geistes* (Leipzig: Meiner, 1949), 79 ff. Cf. M. Kettner, *Hegels 'Sinnliche Gewissheit': diskursanalytischer Kommentar* (Frankfurt and New York: Campus, 1990).

13 L. Feuerbach, 'Zur Kritik der Hegelschen Philosophie', in *Werke in 6 Banden*, vol. 3 (Frankfurt a. M.: Suhrkamp, 1975).

14 Apel, 'Linguistic Meaning and Intentionality: the Compatibility of the "Linguistic Turn" and the "Pragmatic Turn" of Meaning-theory within the Framework of a Transcendental Semiotics', in H.J. Silverman and D. Welton (eds), *Critical and Dialectical Phenomenology* (Albany: State University of New York Press, 1987), 2–53.

15 This fact of a mutual interdependence of coherence and empirical evidence, it seems to me, is presupposed as a matter of course and thus veiled in favour of the suggestion of the sole criteriological relevance of coherence by Leibniz and N. Rescher who seems to follow Leibniz in his books *Leibniz* (Oxford: Blackwell, 1979) and *The Coherence Theory of Truth* (Oxford: Clarendon Press, 1973).

16 C.W. Morris, *Foundations of the Theory of Signs* (Chicago, Ill.: University of Chicago Press, 1938).

17 Apel, 'Transcendental Semiotics and Hypothetical Metaphysics of Evolution', in Apel, *Towards a Transcendental Semiotics* (Atlantic Highlands, N.J.: Humanities Press, 1994); and 'Linguistic Meaning', in K.L. Ketner (ed.), *Peirce and Contemporary Thought* (New York: Fordham University Press, 1995), 366–97.

18 C.W. Morris, *Foundations*; and R. Carnap, 'On some Concepts of Pragmatics', *Philosophical Studies*, 6, 85–91.

19 Charles S. Peirce, *Collected Papers*, ed. C. Hartshorne and P. Weiss (Cambridge, Mass.: Harvard University Press, 1931–35), vol. 5, 388–407.

20 J.R. Searle, *Intentionality* (Cambridge: Cambridge University Press, 1983), chapter 5.

21 Apel, *Der Denkweg*, chapter 3, and 'From Kant to Peirce: the Semiotical Transformation of Transcendental Logic', in Apel, *Towards a Transformation of Philosophy* (London: Routledge & Kegan Paul, 1980).

22 Apel, 'Transcendental Semiotics and Hypothetical Metaphysics of Evolution'.

23 C.S. Peirce, 'Grounds of the Validity of the Laws of Logic', *Collected Papers*, vol. 5, 318–55. Cf. also Apel, *Der Denkweg*, chapter 3, c, e.

24 Apel, 'Das Problem der phänomenologischen Evidenz im Lichte einer transzendentalen Semiotik', in M. Benedikt and R. Burger (eds), *Die Krise der Phänomenologie und die Pragmatik des Wissenschaftsfortschritts* (Vienna: Österreichische Staatsdruckerei, 1986), 78–99.

25 See note 18 and for the direction of a semanticized pragmatics also R. Martin, *Towards a Systematic Pragmatics* (Amsterdam: North-Holland, 1959), and R. Montague, 'Pragmatics', in R. Klibansky (ed.), *La philosophie contemporaine* (Florence, 1968), 102–22.

26 Also Apel, 'Pragmatische Sprachphilosophie in transzendentalsemiotischer

Begründung', in H. Stachowiak (ed.), *Pragmatik*, vol. 4, part 1 (Hamburg: Meiner, 1991); English Eranslation: 'Pragmatic Philosophy of Language Based on Transcendental Semiotics', in Apel, *Selected Essays*, vol. I: *Towards a Transcendental Semiotics* (New Jersey: Humanities Press, 1994), 231–54.

27 C.S. Peirce, *Collected Papers*, vol. 5, 414 and 432.

28 *Ibid.*, 589: 'Detached Ideas on Vitally Important Topics', and vol. 1, 636.

29 *Ibid.*, 354 ff.

4

Can an ultimate foundation of knowledge be non-metaphysical?

translated by BENJAMIN GREGG

If we abandon traditional metaphysics, must we also abandon the notion of an ultimate philosophical foundation, in theoretical as well as in practical philosophy? Most advocates of a post-metaphysical philosophy take this position, as do the more radical advocates of a theory so post-metaphysical that it can only be post-philosophical. Such advocates include the postmodernists in France (inspired by Nietzsche and Heidegger),[1] and the neo-pragmatists in America,[2] as well as Jürgen Habermas. (In fact Habermas seems more concerned to avoid the term *ultimate foundation* than to avoid what the term actually refers to. After all, he seeks a 'normative foundation' for ethics and a critical theory of the social sciences. In other words, he seeks a foundation that would have no alternatives.)[3]

Can we advocate, at one and the same time, a post-metaphysical philosophy *and* the possibility of (or even necessity for) an ultimate foundation? To push this apparent paradox to its limit, I would suggest the following thesis. A post-metaphysical philosophy is needed today for the very sake of an ultimate foundation of knowledge. The greatest single weakness of metaphysics (and of mythical thinking) is that metaphysics can only intimate, but never really prove, an ultimate foundation. Examples of this kind of dogmatic thinking include the doctrine of God qua *causa sui*, as well as the Indian myth that the world rests on an elephant's back, that the elephant in turn rests on a turtle's back – at which point the story breaks off.

Together with Karl Popper's followers (Hans Albert in particular), I believe that rationalistic metaphysics – the type usually associated with the notion of an ultimate foundation – is inescapably entangled in the 'Baron von Münchhausen trilemma', which confronts any project for an ultimate foundation. According to this trilemma, an ultimate foundation leads either to an endless regress (in myths about the world's origin, for example), or to a logical circularity in which what was to be proved (namely, a foundation) is actually assumed by the proof. Or alternatively, an ultimate foundation must break out of the regression by simply declaring, dogmatically, that the notion of an ultimate ground of all things is, quite simply, intuitively obvious – for example, God as *causa sui sive ens a se*.[4]

I direct my criticism at a weakness in the logical structure by which metaphysics attempts to ground itself. I do not dispute the potential profundity of the foundations that might be developed in any particular case, especially those foundations that attempt to put to rest questions concerning foundations. The quality of metaphysical theories of foundations varies widely. We see this, for example, in the great explanatory power of scientific theories, whose basic hypotheses are demonstrably inspired by metaphysics. Yet no one today expects the hypotheses of empirical science to have an ultimate foundation. Rather, we do expect these hypotheses always to be subject to the principle of fallibilism, that is, to an open-ended process of rigorous scrutiny and possible falsification.

Hence the notion of metaphysics as an irreplaceable basis for the universal hypotheses of science does not contradict the critique of traditional metaphysics as a science of ultimate foundations. On the contrary, Charles Peirce's notion (shared by Popper) of a fallibilistic metaphysics, qua science of universal hypotheses, is usually thought to imply that the goal of providing an ultimate foundation must be abandoned – along with the corresponding concept of metaphysics. It should be abandoned because the structure underlying a rational metaphysics does not admit of an ultimate foundation – no more than any science of experience (any science heuristically inspired by metaphysical hypotheses) does. Most logically oriented critics of traditional metaphysics share this view (in later pages I turn to postmodernist critiques inspired by Nietzsche and Heidegger).

I, too, am a critic of the traditional notion of ontological metaphysics. I am persuaded by Peirce's notion of metaphysics (shared by the later Popper) as a speculative discipline of universal hypotheses.[5] I am especially persuaded by the insight that traditional ontological metaphysics, as well as modern hypothetical science, presupposes the same structure of explanation, hence that neither can provide an ultimate foundation for knowledge. But, unlike Popper's followers,

I do not conclude that we must therefore abandon all notions of an ultimate foundation. On the contrary I believe that a post-metaphysical philosophy capable of providing an ultimate foundation is nothing less than necessary. By such a philosophy I mean a philosophy that presupposes a notion of foundation distinct from the notion presupposed by both empirical science and traditional onto-logical metaphysics – hence a philosophy that can provide an ultimate foundation that is specifically philosophical.

The necessity, possibility and functional relevance of a non-metaphysical, yet specifically philosophical, ultimate foundation

Having sketched out my basic position, I now want to develop and ground it. In doing so, I will address myself to three questions.

First, neither empirical science nor hypothetical metaphysics requires an ultimate foundation: why, then, should philosophy? Why would anyone insist on a foundation that (as I concede) is beyond the competence of the logic of science? Does not such insist-ence simply reveal a psychological need for security, a need that could be satisfied only dogmatically, beyond all rational critique? Do I not simply reveal a need for what we nowadays call 'fundamentalism'?

Most people will immediately associate my concept of 'ultimate foundation' (which I offer as an alternative to Albert's notion of ultimate foundation)[6] with a notion of religious-metaphysical 'fun-damentalism'. Indeed some people might expect someone who be-lieves in the possibility of an ultimate philosophical foundation to claim personal infallibility for himself or herself. Given that many people may view me in just these terms – a prospect I find distinctly discomfiting – why would I nevertheless insist that an ultimate philosophical foundation is necessary?

The answer to this first question can hardly be separated from a second one, a question concerning the very possibility of an ultimate foundation not subject to what Hans Albert has called the 'Baron von Münchhausen trilemma'. As I have already indicated, the answer to this question assumes that a specifically philosophical notion of an ultimate foundation is wholly distinct from the notion presupposed by traditional ontological metaphysics as well as by the logic of the sciences.

Third, what can my proposal accomplish both theoretically and practically? Should it – as we might suspect, assuming the standpoint of traditional conceptions of metaphysics – domineer, like some 'Queen of the Sciences', over all sciences, and over moral discourse in both political and legal questions, by claiming a privileged access to truth? Or can we conceive of a completely different relationship between an ultimate philosophical foundation, on the one hand, and the open-ended discourse in science and in the lifeworld, on the other?

Why is a transcendental reflexive, ultimate foundation necessary for a post-metaphysical critical-fallibilistic philosophy?

First, I will attempt to answer the question concerning the necessity of – indeed, need for – an ultimate philosophical foundation. For lack of space, I can only allude to the fact that this question is best answered in the field of ethics. Imagine a young person in the midst of an adolescent crisis who, like Nietzsche, has come to question all traditional moral conventions – who asks: 'Why should I act morally?' What possible comfort could such a person derive from an answer that provides no ultimate foundation, but that immediately relativizes itself as being limited or wholly revisable? I will return to this point later when I examine the very possibility of an ultimate foundation.

Less evident is the need for an ultimate foundation in theoretical philosophy, for example, in epistemology or in the philosophy of science. Why shouldn't we be satisfied in these fields – as we are in empirical science – with continually developing new hypotheses that we then expose to a searching and open-ended critique, as envisaged by an unrestricted principle of fallibilism? As Popper would say, in this way we would replicate, at the level of theory construction, the evolution of life through mutation and selection. In place of ourselves we would expose our epistemological hypotheses to the struggle for existence, a struggle in which solely the best-adapted hypotheses survive.[7] Is this Popperian vision inadequate to explain theoretical knowledge and its possible progress? Cannot the question of an ultimate foundation be regarded as obsolete, indeed, as a source of interference, as a search for security that, in fact, hinders the imaginative construction of hypotheses and precludes the capacity of critique to be thoroughgoing?

To answer this question I would certainly accept Popper's vision of the progress of knowledge; indeed, I take this vision as my point of departure. Nevertheless, I should point out – still in agreement with Popper – that comparing evolutionary theory to the practice of scholarly research involves several additional, specifically human – indeed spiritual – presuppositions. If, in place of ourselves, we are to expose hypotheses or theories to the struggle for existence, such that their falsification may be compared with the extinction of ill-adapted forms of life, then, as humans, we must appreciate what it means to falsify a hypothesis or theory. Unlike the extinction of a species, the falsification of a theory does not simply occur with brute facticity: it must first be accepted by us, on the basis of arguments and justifications. Even a theory of the practice of scholarly research, which regards the falsification of hypotheses as the continuation of evolution by other means, cannot be a merely descriptive or explanatory theory; it must also be normative. Charles Peirce, who anticipated Popper's evolutionary concept, was quite clear on this point.[8]

In this context I need not discuss the barely understood problem of adequate criteria of falsification (in the sense of a falsification sophisticated, not naive).[9] I think it enough to advocate the following general thesis. If we do not want to describe advances in scientific knowledge in terms of a natural process (in which theories simply expire one day, along with their human advocates, as Thomas Kuhn suggests);[10] if, more radically, we do not wish to declare, together with Paul Feyerabend, that 'anything goes' (which implies our inability to distinguish between scientific theories and fairy tales);[11] in short, if, together with Popper (and the later Kuhn),[12] we want to understand science and its advances as a rational enterprise, then we must understand that what it means to advocate a hypothesis or theory is quite different from mere fiction or fairy tales, to put a hypothesis or theory up for discussion, and (where warranted) to falsify a hypothesis or theory through formal or empirical examination.

A question of great importance follows: can everything that we must know and presuppose in order to understand the thematization, examination, critique and (if necessary) falsification of hypotheses be reduced to falsifiable hypotheses, such that we need not presuppose anything as certain *a priori*? So argue the proponents of an unrestricted principle of fallibilism; they consider an ultimate philosophical foundation of epistemological principles not only impossible but also unnecessary. What, then, should we make of the epistemological presuppositions of a fallibilistic logic of science?

In order not to make things too easy for myself, I want to introduce an argument (inspired by the late Wittgenstein[13] and the early Peirce)[14] that only apparently contradicts the unrestricted fallibilism principle. Every concrete doubt which places a scientific theory into question must itself lay claim to paradigmatic certainties, to certainties that are part of a language game and that make that language game possible. Hence my first conclusion is that a universal doubt (or, correspondingly, an unrestricted principle of fallibilism) has no methodologically relevant meaning. It is nothing more than what Peirce called a 'paper doubt'.

The radical fallibilist may counter this argument as follows. Certainly we cannot doubt, or otherwise place into question, at a stroke everything we consider to be certain. We can (indeed, must) concede that every concrete doubt (together with the corresponding language game) presupposes paradigmatic certainties (in Wittgenstein's sense). Yet precisely this circumstance gives rise to a methodologically relevant, virtually universal doubt concerning any language game and its paradigmatic certainties. None of these language games – hence no paradigmatic certainty – is immune from doubts and revisions for all time, or even in the long run. Repeated paradigm changes throughout the history of science show this to be the case. Unlike some Wittgensteinians, I do not think that the renewal of a virtually universal fallibilism principle (at the level of formal methodology or of a theory of science) is completely meaningless. On the contrary, in such a renewal lies the necessary addendum to the 'paper doubt' doctrine, as Peirce himself realized when he introduced the fallibilism principle.[15] Scientific-theoretical enlightenment, which seeks to save itself from dogmatism and 'paper doubt', must recognize both the fact that every substantive doubt about the paradigmatic presuppositions of certainty is itself dependent on a presupposition of certainty and the fact that all factual certainties – including those of language games – can be doubted universally (at the level of methodological reflection).

Does this mean that, at the level of reflection, the unrestricted principle of fallibilism demonstrates the impossibility and non-necessity of every attempt to provide, in *a priori* fashion, an ultimate foundation for *a priori* certainties?[16] What, then, should we make of the presuppositions of certainty that the principle of fallibilism itself must presuppose in order to be understandable within the context of a language game? If we follow Wittgenstein's approach (in *On Certainty*) to its logical conclusion,[17] we will conclude that paradigmatic certainties must also exist for the language game of the theory of fallibilism, in order to make its concepts and statements understandable in the first place. Nor is it difficult to identify the presuppositions concerning existence, and the presuppositions concerning rules, which must themselves be presupposed as paradigmatically certain in the very language game that establishes the fallibilism principle in the first place. Here I would list the following as just a few of these presuppositions.

We must presuppose that there are true statements in distinction to false statements. Further, we must presuppose that there are statements – hypotheses – that can be thematized in an argumentative discourse in which truth claims, although not claims to certainty, are made. We must presuppose that these statements admit of examination, and that they can be proved (by means of criteria) to be inter-subjectively valid (capable of achieving consensus) or to be false. This further implies that there is a community (in principle, an unlimited community) of discourse or argumentation that has at its disposal a sufficiently shared and clear language in which it can formulate not only its problems but also possible solutions to these problems. This further presupposes that certain rules of argumentation are to be followed as normative conditions for the very possibility of discussion, that is of the consensual redemption or critique of truth claims. For example: all discussion participants are in principle equal in the sense that no arguments may be excluded, and solely the better argument (rather than hidden or open force, such as threats or suggestive influences) guides the discussion of truth claims.

I regard these suggestions (incomplete as they are) as sufficient to demonstrate that the fallibilism principle, in order to be understandable, must itself presuppose a discourse principle as the condition of its own possibility. Clearly the latter principle (and the presuppositions about existence and rules implicit in the latter principle) must be presupposed as certain *a priori*, if the fallibilism principle is a meaningful argument and if its methodological application is to be possible.

Therein lies the indispensable ultimate philosophical foundation of the fallibility principle. This ultimate foundation reveals itself as necessary because argumentative discourse, precisely in its anti-dogmatic openness and its freedom from force, must be guaranteed as the normative condition for the very possibility of the critique and possible falsification of hypotheses. Hence the necessity for an ultimate philosophical foundation in no way follows from some need for dogmatic security. Rather, it follows from our interest in guaranteeing the greatest possible scope for the fallibilism postulate of modern science.

As is well known, the 'pan-critical rationalism' of some Popperians in no way concedes this point. The argument here is that the discourse principle's presuppositions concerning existence and rules must themselves be revisable, hence must themselves be subject to the (unrestricted) fallibilism principle. Indeed, the argument goes so far as to suggest that even the fallibilism principle, together with its presuppositions, must itself be regarded as fallible.

I would reply to these arguments as follows. It is true that the presuppositions of the discourse principle – without which the fallibilism principle is incoherent – is itself always in need of explication, and that all such explications are revisable. But what does this mean? Can it mean that we can no longer know *a priori* that the existence of truth and falsehood, and the possibility of investigating it discursively, must be implied by arguments if the fallibilism principle is itself to be meaningful? Clearly this possibility is excluded even when we subject the presuppositions of the fallibilism principle themselves again and again, *ad infinitum*, to the fallibilism principle, in order to do justice to the fact that the presuppositions of the fallibilism principle must themselves always be open to explication. The fallibilism principle is coherent at all conceivable levels of application only if its presuppositions are coherent in their *a priori* certainty.

This argument can be developed and strengthened by the following consideration. Every imaginable revision (revisions that make for greater completeness, for example) in the explication of the meaning of the fallibilism principle's presuppositions must always presuppose *a priori* knowledge of the very presuppositions to be explicated. A possible revision in the explication of the fallibilism principle's presuppositions must be able to appeal to those very presuppositions as a standard.

Thus it is, at most, only self-correction (i.e. through self-reference) that is possible in the explications of the relevant presuppositions' meanings. Under these circumstances possible revisions in the explication of the meaning of *a priori* philosophical knowledge differ from the falsifications of (even very powerful) empirical theories or hypotheses, for the latter presuppose contingent data of experience as the criteria of possible verification or revision. Of course they also presuppose the presuppositions of the fallibilism principle. Yet they presuppose the latter presuppositions, not as criteria of verification but as presuppositions of the concept of investigation or falsification.

If we wanted to contest this difference in principle between the investigation of empirical theories and hypotheses, on the one hand, and the possible revision in explications of meaning of *a priori* knowledge, on the other, we would have to argue that the presuppositions of the meaning of the concepts 'investigation' and 'falsification' admit of empirical examination. This, however, would lead to a paradox: we would have to be able to falsify the presuppositions in question and, at the same time, thereby presuppose these same presuppositions as valid.

This paradox reaches its outer limits in the notion of a fallibilism principle that applies to itself. According to this notion we would have to be able to simultaneously both refute *and* confirm as valid the unrestricted fallibilism principle. This notion not only engenders a logical contradiction but even immunizes itself against possible criticism, which Popper rightly stigmatizes as a mortal sin against the holy spirit of critical philosophy.

We observe here – as in Feyerabend, and as in postmodernism – a dialectic of reason's radicalized self-criticism.[18] In this case reason's self-critique, despite itself, leads to a non-criticizable, hence apparently infallible, position. By contrast, the claim that an ultimate philosophical foundation is needed and is possible does not amount to a claim to personal infallibility. For this equation rests on a psychologistic fallacy. The concession of subjective fallibility, that is that mistakes are possible at any time – in philosophy as in empirical science, indeed, even in mathematics – is consistent with the possibility that, if we made the idealized assumption that a person makes no mistakes whatsoever, certain presuppositions of argumentation (hence critical scholarship as well) reveal themselves to be absolutely necessary. Now, are we entitled to make this idealized assumption, for we simply could not argue that we might be continually duped by some malign god if we could not exclude this possibility through idealization?[19] Similarly, Albert then could not offer the 'Baron von Münchhausen' trilemma as a fatal flaw in the logic of an ultimate metaphysical foundation.

The possibility of a post-metaphysical, ultimate foundation depends on a transcendental reflexive concept of foundation

My effort to understand correctly the necessity of an ultimate philosophical foundation is inseparable from arguments for the possibility of such a foundation. But for all that, I have yet to answer the question of how a non-metaphysical method for attaining an ultimate foundation is possible – a method different from that which Albert criticizes by applying the 'Baron von Münchhausen' trilemma.

Of course, in having discussed irrefutable conditions of possibility and meaning, or the presuppositions of coherence, for fundamental concepts of critical science (hence of the fallibilism principle as well), I have already intimated the kind of question we must ask if we are to establish a non-metaphysical ultimate foundation. Here it is a question of something that we must always presuppose as valid if the examination or critique of possible conditions is itself to be coherent, and therefore possibly valid. Hence my argument implies a combination of two aspects that (as I shall show) distinguish it from the foundationalism criticized by Hans Albert.

The first aspect concerns the necessary conditions of validity. The second aspect involves the fact that this quest also applies to the preconditions of the relevant argumentation of the person who would criticize foundational arguments; and it applies by means of strict reflection.[20]

With regard to the first aspect, we ask, for example, about the conditions requisite for the validity of the fallibilism principle. In answering this question we run up against the precondition of the discourse principle, as a condition for the coherence of our own use of the concept 'fallibilism'. We thereby founder upon the irrefutability of presuppositions of existence, and of presuppositions of rules, for argumentative discourse in general. The criterion for the irrefutability of the presuppositions of argumentation (and thereby of their ultimate foundation) lies in the pragmatic or performative self-contradiction that would occur were the argument ever contested. This would happen if, for example, a person claimed the following:

'on the basis of arguments, I contest the notion that I argue and that I therefore must recognize as irrefutable the presuppositions about the very existence of, and rules for, valid argumentation'.

The principle of performative self-contradiction also contains the criterion for a test by which we can distinguish the method of an ultimate philosophical foundation (concerned with the conditions for the validity of valid argumentation) from any empirical examination of fallible hypotheses of science (and of a metaphysics qua science of universal hypotheses).

The specifically philosophical method of achieving an ultimate foundation cannot be subsumed under the concept of 'foundation' presupposed in traditional ontological metaphysics, or in the modern logic of science, or in Albert's 'Baron von Münchhausen' trilemma.[21] In all these cases 'foundation' may be broadly defined as the derivation of something from something else. In the narrow sense of a compelling proof, this definition refers to logical and mathematical deduction. In broader terms it also refers to the empirical examination of hypotheses through induction, and to the syllogistic form of abduction discovered by Peirce. According to Peirce, these three methods of foundation, in their interdependence (and together with the constant flow of the interpretation of signs), form the normative presuppositions of science (including speculative-hypothetical metaphysics).[22]

To what extent is this conception different from the specifically philosophical method of ultimate foundation that I developed in previous pages? First, it is easy to see why the three syllogistic forms – deduction, induction and abduction – must end in the 'Baron von Münchhausen' trilemma whenever these forms are used to construct an ultimate foundation. As the deduction of something from something else, they must always give rise to further questions if they are to avoid generating a logical circularity and dogmatism. This is quite different from the specifically philosophical concept or procedure of foundation that I propose. As the reflective recourse to the conditions of the validity of argumentation, my method never finds itself in the situation of deducing something from something else, hence it never develops into an endless regress. My method ascertains only what it itself relies on as a method of foundation; it ascertains only those kinds of presuppositions that it itself cannot dispute if it is to avoid performative self-contradiction. It can provide no ontological cosmological explanation of the whole world; rather, it provides solely for the self-ascertainment of argumentative reason. But to the extent that it leads to indisputable statements, does it lead to trivial or insignificant statements?

The practical, everyday relevance of an ultimate, post-metaphysical foundation

With this question I come to the penultimate part of my chapter. This part is concerned with the relevance of a non-metaphysical ultimate foundation. Consider the following example: according to Popper, the most radical question a philosopher can pose himself or herself is 'Why should I be rational?', that is, 'Why should I recognize the normative conditions of a critical-argumentative discourse and not some obscurantist, wishful type of thinking that will submit to no critique whatsoever?' Obviously this question is relevant not only to the philosophy of science but to ethics as well. If we sought to answer this question in the manner of deducing something from something else, we would have to presuppose what we wanted to show – the commitment to reason. We would then be trapped in a logical circularity. In that case, Popper concludes, no foundation is possible whatsoever; rather, solely a pre-rational or irrational (but neverthe-less moral) decision could replace an ultimate foundation.[23]

This answer is coherent and, if we assume the usual non-reflective concept of foundation, unavoidable. But the reflective method of foundation I have developed indicates – contrary to this answer – that the decisionistic situation imputed by Popper never obtains. Whoever poses Popper's question in a serious manner, in other words, whoever thematizes it (at least in lonely conversation with himself or herself), can assure himself or herself that he or she has already entered the territory of argumentative reason, that is of discourse, and that he or she thereby has already recognized the normative conditions for such a discourse. Indeed, he or she can now grasp that this is precisely why we cannot provide a foundation for our being rational, without becoming mired in circularity, if we presuppose the usual, non-reflective concept of foundation.

The fact that Popper, like many others, overlooks the possibility of a reflective ultimate foundation, and instead resorts ultimately to decisionism, may have another reason, indeed one quite under-standable. In a reflective ultimate foundation we realize that we cannot argue (hence that we cannot think in a way that involves validity claims) without recognizing the normative conditions of argumentative discourse. Yet this in no way guarantees that in a concrete situation – where there is a conflict of interest, for example – we will actually pursue the form of reason we recognize to be superior, that we will not in fact reject this form of reason when it is to our selfish advantage to do so. This decisional problem – the problem of a good or evil will – cannot be solved through the reflective ultimate foundation of what *should* be. Consequently many philosophers conclude that the problem of an ultimate foundation must be replaced by the problem of an ultimate decision. I regard this conclusion as mistaken. First, it rests on a confusion between the problem of foundation and the problem of efficient motivation; second, it overlooks the fact that we cannot assume that the insight of a reflective ultimate foundation, which does not determine how any particular human will should decide, therefore is without power to motivate a person. Let us ask anew: wherein lies the possible practical meaning of a reflective ultimate foundation, that is, the possible practical meaning of the proof that we have always already recognized the normative conditions of reason in the manner of argumentative discourse?

I can now formulate an answer (one in keeping with Popper's radical perspective) to the question of relevance. To affirm the discursive principle of reason is to recognize the norms of argumentative discourse presupposed in critical science as well as in a discourse ethics of practical reason. This means that we can always assure ourselves through strict reflection not only that – as in the case of Descartes – it is not possible to gain a level somehow beyond or below or behind our own solitary thought. Through the same reflection we can also assure ourselves of the fact that we are arguing and hence are committed to the rational form of argumentative discourse, which is to be sharply distinguished from the rational form of instrumental and strategic thought.[24] For the theoretical reason of human knowledge and science, this means that we have always already recognized that such reason presupposes an unrestricted critical discourse, in which every participant, from the very start, forgoes the use of strategic – rhetorical or otherwise manipulative – methods for getting others to accept his or her own opinion – or for dogmatically immunizing his or her own thought from all possible criticism. For practical (ethical or political) reason, it means that we know that all binding norms of ethics and law can be legitimized only in the capacity of all concerned persons to find consensus in a discourse free of all force. At the level of an ethic of responsibility capable of finding ideal consensus, we can, of course, also see that the conditions for the application of an ideal discourse ethics do not obtain anywhere in reality. This *conditio humana* requires, in the broadest sense of political *praxis*, mediation (itself capable of finding an ethical consensus) between discursive-ethical rationality and strategic rationality. (I cannot further address this question here.)[25]

A non-metaphysical, ultimate foundation as the task of a post-metaphysical paradigm of *prima philosophia*

In conclusion I want to return to the question of why I call the ultimate philosophical foundation 'non-metaphysical' or 'post-metaphysical'. You may have wondered if my proposed method has any precursors in the philosophical tradition.[26] It most certainly does. The method I propose has its historical roots in the so-called 'indirect proof' (*elenchos*) found in Plato and Aristotle, found in antique refutations in the sceptics (in Augustine, in particular), found in the modern era in Descartes, and found above all in what, since Kant, has come to be known as 'transcendental philosophy' (to which belong the 'transcendental arguments' of the ordinary language philosophy of Peter Strawson and others).[27]

I would not, however, ascribe all of these historical precursors – especially the transcendental approach in philosophy – to the paradigm of metaphysics, but rather to the rejection of metaphysics by reflection on the conditions for the possibility of inter-subjective validity. In the modern era this critical reflection first brought forth the paradigm of the transcendental philosophy of consciousness, or the philosophy of the subject (from Descartes to Kant to Husserl). Finally, in the twentieth century, this paradigm has served as a basis for a language-pragmatic transformation of philosophy qua reflection on the conditions of the inter-subjective validity of argumentation.

Here I cannot adequately explicate my notion of a succession of the three paradigms of *prima philosophia*: ontological metaphysics, the transcendental philosophy of consciousness and a transcendental semiotics or language pragmatics.[28] Moreover, I cannot comment here on the fact that, unlike Thomas Kuhn,[29] I am thinking not of a succession of incommensurable paradigms but rather of a sequence in the Hegelian sense of the 'sublimation' of the directly preceding paradigms by increasingly radical critical reflection. I do, however, want to touch on one major point.

Why do I associate the paradigm of ontological metaphysics with the non-reflective concept of foundation in modern empirical science? Because, unlike transcendental philosophy, both ontological metaphysics and empirical science consider their proper object domain to be a domain of contingent phenomena. Both maintain that we can make a contingent phenomenon into an object of possible knowledge, and that we can place contingent phenomena into question – and that we can do so from a standpoint we need not thematize. The empirical sciences thus ask the 'why? question' of anything in the world that admits of thematization. These sciences do not (and need not) thereby reflect on the conditions for the possibility of such a question. Ontological metaphysics, by contrast, asks the 'why? question' of the world as a whole, including the human being as a subject of knowledge. And, as we have known ever since Kant, metaphysics thereby fails to reflect on the conditions for the possibility of such a question. Of course, at the dawn of the modern era, one regarded as a self-evident truth (indeed, as theologically and metaphysically self-evident) the idea that the fundamental metaphysical question – 'Why does something exist rather than nothing?' (Leibniz) – can be posed by the human being because the human being (as the *imago dei et quasi alter deus* (Cusanus)) can pose the question from the standpoint of God the Creator, and from the standpoint of God's *creatio mundi ex nihilo*. Even for the language philosophy of the early Wittgenstein (*Tractatus*) – a philosophy that is quasi-transcendental, yet one free of transcendental reflection – 'to view the world *sub specie aeterni* is to view it as a whole – a limited whole'. Richard Rorty rightly identifies this as an example of a metaphysical standpoint.[30]

But how can a critical philosophy overcome the reflective deficit of this metaphysical standpoint? Can it do so perhaps (as Rorty argues) by restricting itself, in its questions and reflections, to the empirical sciences, and by declaring *everything* to be contingent (without having to reflect on the conditions for the possibility of thinking about contingency?)[31]

Transcendental philosophy – which, of course, in Descartes and even in Kant is still connected with (ontological) metaphysics in a manner not well understood – was the first to ask (adequately) about the (rational) conditions of valid knowledge from which we cannot distance ourselves (as we can distance ourselves from something contingent) because any thematization of contingency must itself presuppose those conditions of valid knowledge. From Descartes to Husserl, philosophers believed that only self-consciousness could or should be thematized, and thematized in the sense of 'transcendental solipsism', through transcendental reflection, as a residuum of bracketing everything else in the world. But since Peirce and Wittgenstein, we know that a solitary, autarkic subject of inter-subjectively valid interpretations of the world is unthinkable. Such a subject is unthinkable because all inter-subjectively valued conception of 'something as being something' (Heidegger) depends on language. (This in no way implies that the great achievements of modern subject-philosophy – in theoretical philosophy: the insistence on evidence for me; in practical philosophy: the notion of the autonomy of the conscience – are somehow *passé* and should be abandoned. The point of the third paradigm is rather that, with the evidence of 'categorical intuition' (Husserl), I can realize that even irreplaceable pieces of experiential evidence – evidence for sense perception, and even more so: categorical evidence in the sense of *ego cogito, ergo sum* – are always linguistically interpreted pieces of evidence, and that truth qua inter-subjective validity is not guaranteed until the last possible synthesis of interpretations capable of consensus, and not merely by the synthesis of my apperceptions.[32] Likewise, an insight of conscience tells me that I must not arbitrarily break off the discourse on claims to moral correctness by appealing to my subjective conscience as a court of final appeal.)[33]

Contemporary philosophy, seeking to draw the proper consequences from the 'linguistic turn' in philosophy, stands before the following two alternatives. The first alternative would be to abandon the approach of universalistic transcendental philosophy, because of the contingency of all thinking on language games and on sociocultural life forms. We would simply classify the conditions for subjective and inter-subjective knowledge, as well as for argumentation, as the contingent, innerworldly objects of science or of everyday knowledge. Most postmodernists – especially the American neopragmatists – see in this kind of 'detranscendentalization'[34] the definite overcoming of metaphysics. It seems to me, however, that ignoring the transcendental (hence non-contingent) presuppositions of the valid discussion of contingency merely leads us back to the naive attitude of pre-Kantian metaphysics. Of course the neo-pragmatists want to avoid any kind of metaphysics. But I think 'detranscendentalization' leads to a situation where we must either completely abandon discursive philosophy and its claim to truth – say, in favour of its becoming *belles lettres*, as Rorty recently proposed – or fall victim to a reductionistic metaphysics in the manner of an absolutized empirical science.

We can contrast the latter option for contemporary philosophy with the following alternative. While recognizing the dependence of our thought and understanding on contingent, 'background' pre-suppositions of the lifeworld, on its language games and life forms,[35] further, in reflecting on the universal validity claims that belong to argumentation, we must also recognize the conditions of valid knowledge about contingent phenomena, namely, conditions beyond or below or behind which we cannot go, hence noncontingent conditions. These transcendental-pragmatic conditions of thought – as conditions of language-based communication about anything admitting of thematization – are distinguished from the contingency of the finite conditions of human reason solely by counterfactual postulates. One example would be the postulate of (and counterfactual anticipation of) an infinite, ideal community of communication, as the transcendental subject of a definitive consensus about truth and normative correctness.[36]

Here the determination of the transcendental conditions of validity is displaced to what Kant called the 'regulative ideas' of 'reflective judgement' – and, correspondingly, to the process of inference and argumentation that, in the long run, guarantees the exhaustion of all criteria of investigation.[37] This displacement enables the transcendental-semiotic or transcendental-pragmatic paradigm of transcendental philosophy to expose even what Kant called the 'constitutive' conditions of objectively valid knowledge (the 'forms of intuition' and the 'categorical schemes') to a fallibilistic relativization – by restricting their validity to that of a protophysics having to do only with the *mesocosmos* of possible human experience. (Rorty's demand for a 'detranscendentalization' finds itself a transcendental-philosophical justification in this *a priori* relativization of Kant's *constitutive* principles.)

But a relativization of the knowledge-constitutive apriorism of transcendental philosophy's Kantian paradigm – a relativization undertaken according to the theory of the regulative ideas and the process of inference and argumentation – cannot mean that we thereby forgo an ultimate transcendental foundation for the conditions of the validity of argumentation and thereby of cognition, and that everything must be seen to be contingent. To postulate any regulative ideas (and conditions) of procedure whatsoever (so as not to have to say 'anything goes'), we must assume that we are already, so to speak, 'in truth'. For example, we must assume that (contrary to Derrida's suggestion)[38] we can share sufficiently identical meanings of signs in a sufficiently adequate language. Earlier I pointed out that the most basic understanding of the meaning of fallibility (hence also the understanding of the meaning of what some people today appeal to as an 'other of reason', by means of which our own reason could be refuted) already presupposes the paradigmatic certainty of the principle of discourse and hence a transcendental-pragmatic explication of (communicative) reason.

Every attempt to dispute the implications of the *a priori* conditions of argumentation unavoidably leads to a performative self-contradiction. This indicates that the implications of the argumentation principle are more fundamental in a transcendental-philosophical sense than what Kant thematized as the categorical *a priori* conditions of possible knowledge of a world of objects. These implications refer not to a structure (considered to be necessary *a priori*) of the propositional contents of knowing but rather to the presuppositions (presupposed even in the relativization of these structures through arguments) of the performative aspect of acts of argumentation and to the corresponding validity claims.[39] Hence a performative self-contradiction, with its own validity claim, must at the same time sublate the possibility of criticizable argumentation. If the possibility of an overcoming or 'getting over' metaphysics depends on enduring the performative self-contradiction (as many post-Nietzscheans or postmodernists today claim), then I for my part would still prefer to be called a metaphysical philosopher.

However, it seems to me that the attempt to see everything – even our claim to reason – as contingent, and in this fashion to imitate the reflective innocence of the empirical sciences, merely leads back not only to a performative self-contradiction but beyond that to the perspective of dogmatic metaphysics. Namely, in so far as the philosopher, in apparently critical fashion, reduces everything – including his or her claim to reason – to contingent grounds (or else to what Heidegger calls *Seinsgeschick*) as the basis for all contingency, he or she once again assumes a quasi-divine standpoint from which they believe that they can think the world in its contingency, as a 'limited totality' – without ever having examined the conditions of the validity of such thought.

Notes

First published in *Journal of Speculative Philosophy*, 7, 3 (1993), 171–90.

1 J. Habermas, *The Philosophical Discourse of Modernity* (Cambridge, Mass.: MIT Press, 1987); Apel, 'Die Herausforderung der totalen Vernunftkritik und das Programm einer philosophischen Theorie der Rationalitätstypen', *Concordia*, 11 (1987), 2–23; K. Baynes, J. Bohman and T. McCarthy (eds), *After Philosophy: End or Transformation?* (Cambridge, Mass.: MIT Press, 1987).

2 R. Rorty, *Philosophy and the Mirror of Nature* (Princeton: Princeton University Press, 1979); Rorty, *Consequences of Pragmatism* (Minneapolis: University of Minnesota Press, 1982); Rorty, *Contingency, Irony, and Solidarity* (Cambridge: Cambridge University Press, 1989). See also K. Baynes *et al.* (eds), *After Philosophy.*

3 Apel, 'Normatively Grounding "Critical Theory" through Recourse to the Lifeworld? A Transcendental-Pragmatic Attempt to Think with Habermas against Habermas', in A. Honneth, T.A. McCarthy, C. Offe and A. Wellmer (eds), *Philosophical Interventions I: The Unfinished Project of Enlightenment* (Cambridge, Mass.: MIT Press, 1992), 125–70.

4 H. Albert, *Treatise on Critical Reason*, trans. M.V. Rorty (Princeton: Princeton University Press, 1984).

5 Apel, 'Transcendental Semiotics and Hypothetical Metaphysics of Evolution: a Peircean and Quasi-Peircean Answer to a Recurrent Problem of Post-Kantian Philosophy', in K.L. Ketner (ed.), *Peirce and Contemporary Thought: Transactions of the Sesquicentennial International Congress* (Texas: Texas Technical University Press, forthcoming).

6 Apel, 'The Problem of Philosophical Fundamental Grounding in Light of a Transcendental Pragmatic of Language', *Man and World*, 8 (1975), 239–75, repr. in K. Baynes *et al.* (eds), *After Philosophy*, 250–90.

7 K. Popper, 'The Death of Theories and of Ideologies', in Ecole Libre de Philosophie 'Plethon' (ed.), *La reflexion sur la mort* (Athens: Ecole Libre de Philosophie 'Plethon', 1977), 296–329; Popper, *Objective Knowledge: An Evolutionary Approach* (Oxford: Clarendon Press, 1972), 248.

8 See note 5.

9 I. Lakatos, 'Falsification and the Methodology of Scientific Research Programmes', in I. Lakatos and A. Musgrave (eds), *Criticism and the Growth of Knowledge* (Cambridge: Cambridge University Press, 1970), 91–196.

10 T.S. Kuhn, *The Structure of Scientific Revolutions* (Chicago: University of Chicago Press, 1962).

11 P. Feyerabend, *Against Method* (New York: Verso, 1988).

12 T. Kuhn, 'Anmerkungen zu Lakatos', in W. Diederich (ed.), *Theorien der Wissenschaftsgeschichte* (Frankfurt a. M.: Suhrkamp, 1974), 120–36.

13 L. Wittgenstein, *Über Gewissheit/On Certainty*, ed. G.E.M. Anscombe and G.H. von Wright (Oxford: Basil Blackwell, 1969).

14 C. Peirce, 'The Fixation of Belief', in *Collected Papers*, ed. C. Hartshorne and P. Weiss (Cambridge, Mass.: Harvard University Press, 1931–35), vol. 5, 358–83.

15 C. Peirce, *Collected Papers*, vol. 1, 141–75.

16 So maintains H. Albert in *Transzendentale Träumereien* (Hamburg: Hoffmann und Campe, 1975), 118 ff.

17 See the text I mention in note 6, as well as Apel, 'Fallibilismus, Konsenstheorie der Wahrheit und Letzbegründung', in Forum für Philosophie Bad Homburg (ed.), *Philosophie und Begründung* (Frankfurt a. M.: Suhrkamp, 1987), 116–211.

18 C. Radnitzky, 'In Defense of Self-applicable Critical Rationalism', in International Cultural Foundation (ed.), *Absolute Values and the Creation of the New World* (New York: International Cultural Foundation Press, 1983), vol. 3, 1025–69.

19 This transcendental argument (and critique of meaning) is inspired by the principle that we must avoid performative self-contradiction. The argument renders superfluous all of Descartes's efforts (by means of a proof of the existence of God) to preclude the possibility of a *deus malignus* who continually deceives us. By analogy we can also refute Descartes's dream argument: if everything we take to be real were in fact simply a dream, then the argument (that everything we take to be real is simply a dream) itself can only be part of that dream.

20 W. Kuhlmann, 'Reflexive Letztbegründung: Zur These von der Unhintergehbarkeit der Argumentationssituation', *Zeitschrift für Philosophische Forschung*, 35 (1981), 3–26; Kuhlmann, *Reflexive Letztbegründung: Untersuchungen zur Transzendentalpragmatik* (Freiburg and Munich: Alber, 1985).

21 In this context see Apel, 'Begründung', in H. Seiffert and G. Radnitzky (eds), *Handlexikon zur Wissenschaftstheorie* (Munich: Ehrenwirth, 1989).

22 Apel, *Charles S. Peirce: From Pragmatism to Pragmaticism* (Amherst: University of Massachusetts Press, 1981).

23 K. Popper, *Conjectures and Refutations*, fourth edn (London: Routledge & Kegan Paul, 1972), 357 ff.; Popper, *The Open Society and its Enemies* (London: Routledge & Kegan Paul, 1966).

24 Apel, 'Die Herausforderung de totalen Vernunftkritik'; Apel, 'Types of Rationality Today: the Continuum of Reason between Science and Ethics', in T. Geraets (ed.), *Rationality Today* (Ottawa: Ottawa University Press, 1979), 307–40; Apel, 'Lässt sich ethische Vernunft von strategischer Zweckrationalität unterscheiden?', in W. van Reijen and Apel (eds), *Rationales Handeln und Gesellschaftstheorie* (Bochum: Germinal Verlag, 1984), 23–80.

25 Apel, *Diskurs und Verantwortung* (Frankfurt a. M.: Suhrkamp, 1988) (English translation forthcoming).

26 W. Kuhlmann, *Reflexive Letztbegründung*, chapter 5.

27 In this context see the comprehensive study by M. Niquet, *Transzendentale Argumente: Kant, Strawson und die Aporetik der Detranszendentalisierung* (Frankfurt a. M.: Suhrkamp, 1991).

28 Apel, 'The Transcendental Conception of Language Communication and the Idea of First Philosophy', in Herman Parret (ed.), *History of Linguistic Thought and Contemporary Linguistics* (Berlin and New York: W. de Gruyter, 1976), 32–61.

29 T. Kuhn, *The Structure of Scientific Revolutions*.

30 L. Wittgenstein, *Tractatus*, trans. D.F. Pears and B.R. McGuiness (London: Routledge & Kegan Paul, 1961). See R. Rorty, 'Wittgenstein, Heidegger, and the Hypostatization of Language', in J. Habermas (ed.), *Der Löwe spricht . . . und wir können ihn nicht verstehen* (Frankfurt a. M.: Suhrkamp, 1991).

31 J. Habermas (ed.), *Der Löwe spricht.*

32 Apel, 'Fallibilismus, Konsenstheorie der Wahrheit und Letztbegründung'; Apel, 'Linguistic Meaning and Intentionality: the Compatibility of the "Linguistic Turn" and the "Pragmatic Turn" of Meaning-theory within the Framework of a Transcendental Semiotics', in H.J. Silverman and D. Welton (eds), *Critical and Dialectical Phenomenology* (Albany: State University of New York Press, 1987), 2–53; Apel, 'Das Problem der phänomenologischen Evidenz im Lichte einer transcendentalen Semiotik', in M. Benedikt and R. Burger (eds), *Die Krise der Phänomenologie und die Pragmatik des Wissenschaftsfortschritts* (Vienna: Österreichische Staatsdruckerei, 1986), 78–99.

33 In the preface to *The Phenomenology of Mind* Hegel writes: 'Since the man of commonsense appeals to his feeling, to an oracle within his breast, he is done with anyone who does not agree. He has just to explain that he has no more to say to anyone who does not find and feel the same as himself. In other words, he tramples the roots of humanity underfoot. For the nature of humanity is to impel men to agree with one another, and its very existence lies simply in the explicit realization of a community of conscious life' (G.W.F. Hegel, *The Phenomenology of Mind*, trans. J.B. Baillie (New York: Macmillan, 1931), 127). In § 139 of his *Philosophy of Right* Hegel concludes, correspondingly, that 'once self-consciousness has reduced . . . itself to the sheer inwardness of the will, . . . it has become potentially evil' (*Hegel's Philosophy of Right*, trans. T.M. Knox (Oxford: Clarendon Press, 1942), 92). In this context see D. Bohler, 'Das Verhältnis von Gewissen und Argumentationsgemeinschaft', in Apel, D. Bohler and K. Rebel (eds), *Funkkolleg: Praktische Philosophie/Ethik*, Studientexte, vol. 2 (Weinheim and Basle: Beltz-Verlag, 1984), 347.

34 See especially R. Rorty, 'Epistemological Behaviorism and the De-transcendentalization of Analytic Philosophy', *Neue Hefte für Philosophie*, 14 (1978), 115–42; and Rorty, 'Transcendental Arguments, Self-reference, and Pragmatism', in *TAS*, 77–103.

35 See especially J.R. Searle, *Intentionality* (Cambridge: Cambridge University Press, 1983), chapter 5 ('The Background'); and J. Habermas, *The Theory of Communicative Action*, trans. T. McCarthy (Boston: Beacon Press, 1984–87).

36 Apel, *Towards a Transformation of Philosophy*, trans. G. Adey and D. Frishy (Boston: Routledge & Kegan Paul, 1980).

37 *Ibid.*; Apel, 'Fallibilismus'.

38 J. Derrida, *Of Grammatology*, trans. G.C. Spivak (Baltimore: Johns Hopkins University Press, 1976); J. Derrida, *Writing and Difference*, trans. A. Bass (Chicago: University of Chicago Press, 1978).

5

Meaning constitution and justification of validity: has Heidegger overcome transcendental philosophy by history of being?

The problem as a consequence of the present impact of Heidegger's philosophy

Let me start out with a question: what explains the fascination of Heidegger's philosophy in the present era? Certainly, this fascination no longer emanates from the so-called philosophy of 'existence', which was, no doubt, formulated in *Being and Time* in an expressive and appealing way. Nor is it, I suppose, the concern of a 'fundamental ontology', that is the response to the question as to the 'meaning of being', which Heidegger himself opposed to what he called the 'existentialist misunderstanding' of his main work. The source of fascination in our day is rather, it seems to me, his venture of a 'destruction' of occidental metaphysics which was postulated already in *Being and Time* but later, after the so-called 'turn' (*Kehre*), was directed against the conception of fundamental ontology as well. In other words: at present, the following programme of Heidegger's seems to stand in the foreground of interest: his attempt at thinking back – by critical reconstruction and destruction of all current conceptual schemes, metaphysics and science – beyond the beginnings of classical Greek philosophy, in order possibly to regain the 'free space' (*Spielraum*) of an 'initial thinking' that might have existed in the time of myth or even of the pre-Socratic philosophers. This free space, on Heidegger's account, might eventually open up the preconditions for a post-metaphysical and post-technological thought to the extent that such a possibility may be actualized by the 'happening of being', that is through a 'clearance' of the meaning of being.

It is especially the last suggestion of a post-metaphysical, nay even post-philosophical and post-rational (although not – according to Heidegger – 'irrational'),[1] thinking that within the last decade has aroused the greatest fascination – for example in the sphere of

French and Italian postmodernism,[2] but even beyond this in a special version of American neo-pragmatism which thinks it possible – although with certain political reservations – to bring into line the thought of Dewey, Wittgenstein and Heidegger.[3]

However, beyond this vague outline of the history of Heidegger's impact, let us ask more closely: which forms or schemes of Heidegger's thought lend support to these aspects of its reception history in the present era? I will try to sum up the answer to this question in a thesis that allows me to introduce the topic that I indicated in the title of this chapter.

The fascination of the later Heidegger and the far-reaching implications of the reception of his thought by the postmodernists and the post-Wittgensteinian neo-pragmatists derive primarily from the fact that in Heidegger's late philosophy (of the history of being) the initially transcendental-phenomenological problem of the constitution of meaning is subject to a detranscendentalization and historicization. In Heidegger's philosophy this is a consequence of his conception of truth as *aletheia*, a conception that was already implied in *Being and Time* in the existential-hermeneutical analysis of the 'pre-structure' of all world-understanding, conceived as 'disclosedness' of being-in-the-world and later terminated in the conception of the *clearing* (*Lichtung*) of (the meaning) of being. The latter, as a happening of disclosure and simultaneously concealment, precedes the possibility of true and false judgements. Within the context of French post-structuralism – for example in the work of Derrida – the structure of the 'ontic-ontological difference', which in Heidegger's philosophy was connected with the 'happening' of 'clearance' as a condition of the possibility of linguistic meaning constitution, came to be fused with Saussure's notion of a semiotical constitution of difference and Derrida's conception of *différance* as the happening of simultaneously opening up and shifting of meaning.

But why or in what respect may one say that by Heidegger's analysis of 'disclosedness' in *Being and Time* a transcendental or quasi-transcendental problem is raised and at the same time is tendentially subject to a detranscendentalization?

To address this question I will first distinguish and elucidate two pertinent dimensions of Heidegger's so called 'pre-structure' of existential world-understanding and self-understanding. For this pre-structure of what is 'always already pre-understood' has a quasi-transcendental function in *Being and Time*.

The 'pre-structure' of the 'disclosedness' of being-in-the-world as an answer to the transcendental question as to the conditions of the possibility of the world's meaning constitution

Heidegger's analysis shows that the subject–object relation of scientific knowledge is always already embedded in the contextual structure of being-in-the-world as understanding the coherent significance of the world. The beings encountered within the world are not primarily understood as existing or present (*vorhandene*) objects of theoretical observation and predicative determination but (rather) as equipment to hand (*zuhandenes Zeug*), looked upon from the viewpoint of care, and pre-understood from this point of view 'as something' (i.e. as significant). Therefore, the world itself is not primarily an aggregate of present objects or – as for Kant and natural science – the 'existence of things in as far as they make up a coherence according to laws'; but, for Heidegger, the world is 'the situational context of understanding according to reference-marks as a (teleological) horizon of possible encounterings of beings that have a specific significance'. (In German: 'Das Worin des sich-verweisenden Verstehens als Woraufhin des Begegnenlassens von Seiendem in der Seinsart der Bewandtnis.')[4]

On the presupposition of this Heideggerian concept of the world, those critical-epistemological (*erkenntniskritische*) questions that are suggested by the traditional reflection upon the pure objectivity of beings prove to be pseudo-problems: for instance, the question whether perhaps all objects (and that means: even all human subjects of action and knowledge qua objects) might be only within human consciousness. This must be a pseudo-problem, since those modes of being-in-the-world that are supposed in the critical question – namely 'being with' mere representations or sense data or being solitary in principle – can be understood by us only as 'deficient modes' of being-in-the-world as 'being with the beings themselves' and 'being-together-with' other people.[5]

This Heideggerian analysis, which is phenomenological and existential-hermeneutical, is almost exactly confirmed by a

Wittgensteinian analysis of language games – namely of the interwovenness of language games, world interpretations and activities as parts of life forms. For this analysis reveals that the idealistic and solipsistic paradigms of the philosophy of consciousness are parasitic upon non-idealist and non-solipist everyday language games, that is on language games that even Descartes (and Husserl) must make use of in order to articulate their problems linguistically. Thus with regard to the Cartesian dream argument, one may prove that the meaning of the phrase 'all that is considered to be real, might possibly be merely my dream' is parasitic upon a language game, according to which there must be a difference in principle between a real world outside my consciousness and that which might be 'merely my dream'. Thereby one may justify also Heidegger's objection to Kant that the 'scandal of philosophy' does not lie in the lack of a proof for the existence of an outer world but rather in demanding such a proof.[6] To put it briefly: the hermeneutic-phenomenological reflection on the 'being-always-already-in-the-world' proves its priority with regard to the post-Cartesian reflection on the 'object-consciousness' in the same sense as the pragmatically oriented analysis of language games can prove that those language games of ordinary language that are interwoven with the *praxis* of life are presupposed by the philosophical language games – and also by the constructive languages of the logic of science.

Thus far we have already shed light on the point of Heidegger's interpretation of what the late Husserl called *Lebenswelt* and of the fundamental relation of this lifeworld to the abstractive and idealizing world-thematization of the sciences. And the point of Heidegger's analysis of the lifeworld appears to me to be more radical and more illuminating than that which can be found in the remaining part of Husserl's last writings on the *Krisis*.[7] This holds especially with regard to the quasi-transcendental function of our pre-understanding of the lifeworld as a precondition of the subject–object relation of scientific knowledge. For, on Heidegger's account, it becomes clear that a pure transcendental consciousness of objects does not suffice as a basis for the constitution of a world of significance – and this for at least two reasons. On the one hand, there is a lack of the horizon of practical engagement and hence of cognitive interests that could guide our searching and asking for something 'as something'. On the other hand, there is also a lack with regard to the medium of language by which the interpretation of something as something must be mediated in order to be inter-subjectively valid.

However, given the features of the lifeworld that we have eluci-dated thus far, we have not yet revealed the whole significance of what Heidegger always characterizes as the 'pre-structure' of 'being-in-the-world' by using the phrase 'always already' (*immer schon* or *je schon*). Our explanation of this by pointing to the lifeworld as a presupposed embedding of the object-consciousness could still be understood in the abstract sense of claiming only necessary precon-ditions of knowledge as Kant does in his transcendental logic. And already on the ground of this understanding, one could speak of a heightening of the transcendental problematic of the conditions of meaning constitution beyond the special problematic of the constitu-tion of 'objectivity' in the Kantian sense. But in this case the dimen-sion of existential temporality, which is also indicated by Heidegger's using the terms 'always already', would not yet be taken into consid-eration. In fact the world- and self-understanding of human *Dasein* according to Heidegger is dependent on its 'pre-structure' not only in an abstractive transcendental-logical sense but also in the temporal sense of being 'always already ahead of itself' (*sich vorweg*). The *Dasein* cannot pull up, so to speak, its 'thrownness' into a historically conditioned situation-world (and its having always already become addicted to this world in a specific way).

Now, if one carries through the analysis of the temporality structure of being-always-already-in-the-world, then the inescap-able insight into the 'historicity' of the finite *Dasein* and its possible understanding of meaning must be the result. It is in this respect, I suggest, that the most radical effects of Heidegger's philosophy on the rest of contemporary philosophy have been exerted: those effects that, as being quasi-transcendental conditions of the world-meaning constitution, have contributed most effectively to the detranscendentalization of contemporary philosophy – in Rorty's sense, for example.

Thus the following Heideggerian insight, which was further elaborated by Gadamer, has presumably found a world-wide accept-ance: there is a temporally and historically determined (conditioned) pre-understanding of the world that belongs to the pre-structure of all cognition – that of every day as well as that of the sciences. This pre-understanding is always already linguistically articulated in the sense of the 'public interpretation' of the lifeworld. This is what Heidegger elucidated in *Being and Time* as follows:

> The *Dasein* is never able to escape this everyday world-interpretation to which it has been familiarized from the beginning. Within, from, and against it, all genuine understanding, interpreting and communicating, all appropriation afresh is performed. It is not the case that a *Dasein* should ever be posed before or confronted with the open space of a world in itself, i.e., untouched by the pre-interpretation, just to gaze upon what is presented to it.[8]

Here is an elucidation of that dimension of the pre-structure of being-in-the-world by which Heidegger's hermeneutical phenomenology is definitely distinguished from Husserl's optical and pre-linguistic type of 'evidence-phenomenology'. And it is this dimension that made possible the convergence of the hermeneutic phenomenology with the post-Wittgensteinian development of linguistic philosophy.

But, in what respect may those insights into the temporality and historicity still be considered as dimensions of a possible reconstruction and transformation of transcendental philosophy? Does this question really expose the problematic and intriguing aspect of our topic?

First it has to be pointed out that it is Heidegger himself who, in his early work, established an internal relationship between his analysis of the pre-structure of the disclosedness of being-in-the-world and the problematic of transcendental philosophy.

Heidegger's attempt at understanding his 'fundamental ontology' as a radicalization of Kant's project of a transcendental philosophy

In *Being and Time* Heidegger emphasized that his programme of a 'fundamental ontology', which placed the question as to the 'meaning of being' before the question of traditional ontology and tried to answer this question by recourse to that 'understanding of being' that belongs to human *Dasein*, may by no means take its orientation toward a pre-Kantian understanding of cognition as an innerwordly relation between a subject and an object. Thus far Heidegger dissociated himself from Max Scheler's and furthermore from Nicolai Hartmann's conception of 'ontology' or of cognition as an ontological relationship between beings. He wrote: 'Scheler as well as Hartmann, notwithstanding their different phenomenological point of departure, overlook the fact that ontology in its traditional basic orientation fails with regard to (human) *Dasein* and that precisely that "relationship of being" that is implied in cognition enforces a revision and not only a critical repair of ontology.'[9] The 'relation of being' that is at stake here cannot, on Heidegger's account, be regarded as a relation between two beings in the world but has to be thought of as 'transcendental' in so far as, along with *Dasein*'s understanding of being, the horizon of a world, which transcends every possible object as well as every possible subject, is projected and, so to speak, extended in a primordial way.

Thus far in *Being and Time* Heidegger can still maintain (in connection to Husserl's ideas): 'compared with realism, idealism, however opposed and untenable it is in effect, has a priority in principle, if it does not misunderstand itself as "psychological" idealism'.[10] And he explains: 'if the term "idealism" means as much as understanding that being [*Sein*] can never be explained by beings, since it is always already the transcendental with regard to each being, then idealism implies the only and right possibility of a philosophical problematic'. But he adds: 'if idealism means reducing all being to a subject or consciousness that is distinguished only by the fact that it remains undetermined in its being and at best is negatively characterized as "non-substantial" (*undinglich*), then idealism is no less naive than the crudest realism'.[11] Here Heidegger seems to make explicit the need for a fundamental-ontological transformation of Kant's transcendental philosophy.

But Heidegger clarified the relationship between his programme of fundamental ontology and transcendental philosophy much more precisely and thoroughly in his first book on Kant, *Kant and the Problem of Metaphysics*.[12] There he also had to pose the most difficult question with regard to the relation of his own approach to classical transcendental philosophy: the question regarding the relation of 'pure reason' to human *Dasein*, which precisely in (or on the ground of) its temporality and historicity is presupposed as condition of the possibility of the understanding of being. A transcendental philosopher might ask immediately: how is it possible to compare the pre-structure of the temporal-historical being-in-the-world – characterized by Heidegger as that of a 'thrown project' (*geworfener*

Entwurf) – with the transcendental basic structure of pure reason, which is presupposed by Kant?

In his first book on Kant Heidegger tried to solve this problem by interpreting Kant's 'pure reason' primarily as 'finite reason'. In this sense he tried to lay open the root of the transcendental synthesis of apperception as that of 'understanding being' in Kant's faculty of imagination (*Einbildungskraft*) and to understand this faculty as 'original temporality' of the transcendental projection of the world. For Heidegger the transcendental faculty of imagination is the capacity of 'pure synthesis' and thereby of projecting by which the finite reason of human beings must display the horizon of all understanding of being in advance of all possible affect by beings. As a projecting of 'pure intuition' in the Kantian sense, the transcendental faculty of imagination must generate (*bilden*) the horizon of time in such a way that it simultaneously engenders the ecstatic dimensions of the present, the past and the future and thereby opens up the conditions of the possibility of the 'pure succession of the nows' as providing a 'schema-image' (*Schemabild*) for the possible givenness of object representations.[13]

Thereby Heidegger reconstructed Kant's transcendental faculty of imagination as a testimony and illustration for what he himself had claimed in *Being and Time* to be the threefold ecstatic temporalizing function of the 'original time'. And Heidegger left no doubt about the fact that the original function of ecstatic temporalization, which corresponds to Kant's 'faculty of imagination' as 'original synthesis', constitutes the essence of understanding – that is of the 'synthesis of apperception' and moreover the essence of theoretical and practical reason.

However, already in Heidegger's first book on Kant there is some evidence for the fact that Heidegger's separation of empirical intratemporality (*Innerzeitlichkeit*), that is of the succession of the nows within the horizon of time, from the original time as ecstatic temporalization or 'pure synthesis' is counter-intuitive and cannot be sustained. It does not seem to be possible for Heidegger simply to draw a parallel between his distinction of original and vulgar time and Kant's transcendental distinction of reason as synthesis and *Innerzeitlichkeit* as empirical succession of moments. For at the end of his first book on Kant, where he summarizes his interpretation of the *Critique of Pure Reason* along the lines of a fundamental ontology, Heidegger is compelled to abandon the analogy between Kant's and his own 'architectonics'. This happens, I think, as a result of his discussion – apparently only in passing – of the occurrence of the finiteness of the understanding in *Dasein* and the 'transcendental subject'. According to Heidegger, this occurrence is to constitute after all 'the transcendental subjectivity' of the subject, the finiteness of reason.

The failure of the Heideggerian quasi-transcendental interpretation of 'original time' and the abandonment of transcendental philosophy after the turn of his philosophy

In what sense may one say that the use of the word 'occurrence' or 'happening' (*Ereignis* or *Geschehen*) amounts to an overthrowing of the Kantian 'architectonics' of transcendental philosophy? I think that the word 'happening', which, as is well known, is characteristic of Heidegger's later philosophy and has also a central significance in Gadamer's *Truth and Method*, points to a difficulty of Heidegger's analysis of time already in *Being and Time*. It is a difficulty that must become visible, if (or, rather, when) one parallels Heidegger's 'ontic-ontological difference' with Kant's 'empirico-transcendental difference', as Heidegger himself in his first book on Kant still endeavours to do.

Heidegger asserts time and again that the 'original time', which constitutes the essence of the transcendental synthesis, is radically different from the vulgar conception of time in the sense of a succession of moments within the horizon of time because the original ecstatic time precedes the 'intratemporality' as a condition that generates the horizon for the succession of moments. This appears quite *transcendental* – even in the Kantian sense. But the question is whether in this case Heidegger is right to talk meaningfully about a 'happening' of 'transcendence', or of the 'transcendental synthesis' generating the horizon? Is it possible to speak in a meaningful way of a 'happening' without already making use of the traditional concept of time as a succession of moments, that is to say, of intratemporality?

One may easily grant Heidegger that the traditional concept of time does not heed the moment of (quasi-transcendental) 'temporalization' (*Zeitigung*), that is of generating the three ecstatic dimensions of the present, the past and the future, and that this ecstatic structure of temporalization (which may be paralleled to the triadic structure of the 'apprehensive', 'reproductive' and 'recognitive' faculty of imagination) is always already presupposed in our talk of 'now' (in contradistinction to 'a minute ago' and 'soon'). At the same time, however, one has nevertheless to insist that, by referring to a 'happening', the factual 'one after another' of a succession of moments and thus far empirical 'intratemporality' in the Kantian sense is presupposed too. If one abstracts completely from 'intratemporality' – as Heidegger seems to suggest in *Being and Time* and still in his first book on Kant – that is if one tries to conceive of an 'original time' only in the sense of the simultaneous originating of the three 'ecstasies', then one can no longer understand the moving of the time. (It is not accidental that most philosophers, for example Kant, James and Husserl, used the metaphor of a stream in talking about the time or the consciousness of time. But a stream – being a continuous happening – is something that in Kant's sense is also 'intratemporal'. It can be experienced within the frame of Kant's temporal form of intuition, and that means: it must be empirically ascertainable, e.g. by the distinction between the simultaneity and the succession of two events.)

Thus far the suspicion arises that Heidegger's reconstruction of Kant's conception of transcendental synthesis in terms of 'original time' may be doomed to failure. And this suspicion, I think, is fully confirmed by the changes in philosophical 'architectonics' that are connected with Heidegger's *Kehre*. The quasi-transcendental understanding of the ('original') time, and thereby also the quasi-Kantian distinction between ecstatic 'temporalization' and 'intratemporality', is now tacitly given up together with the whole philosophy of subjectivity which now has to be overcome.

Heidegger now speaks quite openly of a 'happening' of 'clearing' and simultaneously 'concealing' of being and thus far of a 'history of being'. Still it may not be overlooked that Heidegger, by the 'happening' (*Ereignis*) of the mission (*Schickung*) of being, still means 'temporalization' (and 'spacing' or 'spacialization') as primordial constitution of meaning horizons of a lifeworld rather than 'occurrence' within the world that has been already constituted. The quasi-transcendental notion of 'temporalization' qua meaning constitution by *Dasein*'s project is transformed into the notion of a world- and meaning constitution by the mission (*Schickung*) of being. But it must not be overlooked also that Heidegger now talks of 'epochal' happenings of the 'history of being', that is of happenings that followed each other and may be considered as corresponding to the well-known intratemporal and intra-historical epochs of the history of philosophy, as for instance the foundation of metaphysics by the Greeks, the transformation of this foundation by the Romans and Christianity, and finally the instauration of modern science and technology as the frame (*Gestell*).

It is precisely this intratemporality and intra-historicity of 'happenings' (*Ereignisse*), which at the same time are considered to have opened up and thus originated the meaning of being, that precedes the possibility of true and false judgements. And it is this intertwining of quasi-transcendental temporalization and intratemporality that makes up the challenge of Heidegger's later philosophy to a transcendental philosophy that is oriented toward Kant's conception of a universally valid constitution of the world's objectivity by the synthetical functions of understanding or reason. This challenge culminates in Heidegger's claims that the whole philosophy of the transcendental subject – and, moreover, the whole philosophy in general as an enterprise of the *logos*, or reason (*Vernunft*), as a faculty of demanding and providing reasons – is now to be understood with regard to its validity as a finite result of an originating event of the history of being.

Here a question might arise: how can this Heideggerian thesis itself still be thought or stated with a claim to universal validity? Does it not turn out, after all, that time in the traditional sense, which was already considered by Parmenides and Plato as the most serious endangering of the possibility of thought's validity – that time in this sense in Heidegger's late philosophy holds sway over reason which according to the earlier Heidegger was to be identical with 'orignal time'?[14] (With Gadamer the same problematic reappears – the only difference being here that Gadamer does not take pains to deny the intratemporal character of what he calls *Sinngeschehen* or even *Wahrheitsgeschehen*. He still wishes to respond in a sense to the transcendental question as to the 'conditions of the possibility of understanding',[15] but he no longer sees any difficulty in answering this question exclusively in terms of historical happenings or even processes – finally in terms of ontological or cosmological processes of playing that seem to be conceived in a pre-Kantian sense of ontology.)[16]

Nevertheless, after this reconstruction of Heidegger's 'time' philosophy which finally amounts to a destruction of transcendental philosophy, we must again ask the question whether Heidegger's approach is justified as an answer to the question about the conditions of the possibility of the meaning constitution for the lifeworld. With regard to this question we have suggested that it points to the need for a transformation of transcendental philosophy, since a pure transcendental consciousness cannot explain the constitution of the concrete pre-understanding of the significance of the lifeworld that is presupposed by all cognition. To this extent Heidegger's transformation of Kant's transcendental philosophy seems to be plausible to me.

But our reconstruction of this transformation has also led us to make the following point: Heidegger's presupposition of a meaning-constitutive temporality and historicity of world-understanding, which finally leads to the meaning-constitutive happenings of the history of being, turns out to be incompatible with the possibility of answering Kant's question as to the conditions of the possibility of the universal objectivity and hence inter-subjective validity of our understanding. Which consequence may be drawn from this dilemma? Do we perhaps – following Heidegger – have to consider the possibility that all objective validity of knowledge and thus far the possible truth and falsehood of judgements is dependent, in a unilateral way, on the preceding happenings of a world disclosure that articulates and delivers itself in the historical languages?

The spirit of our time appears to be prepared to accept this principled subordination of the question of the validity of knowledge (and, by the way, also of norms) under the question of historical world disclosure qua meaning constitution. Thus the truth and falsehood of scientific discoveries – according to Thomas Kuhn – may be understood as dependent upon the preceding constitution of the 'paradigms' of 'normal science' which themselves may be compared with the historical 'clearings' or 'concealings' of the 'history of being'. In accordance with this conception also the rightness or wrongness of moral norms seems be dependent on a particular, contingent 'consensus-basis', as Rorty suggests. In brief: the validity of the *logos* (reason) and its modes, which serve universality and identity, seems to be subordinated to a meaning-constitutive happening of temporal-historical generation of differences (what Derrida terms 'la différance').

However, there is a transcendental-reflexive argument that we could oppose to this tendency: the universal validity claim of the detranscendentalization arguments themselves is not compatible with the propositional content of these arguments: arguments that relativize their own validity claim to temporal-historical happenings cannot state at least this relativization itself with a corresponding validity claim. Apart from this central paradox, the question arises whether there is in fact a unilateral relation of dependence between the truth and falsehood of (empirical) judgements and the preceding clearing-concealing world disclosures as suggested by Heidegger's theory of truth. Could it not be that there is rather a relation of reciprocal dependence between both sides – such that also the linguistic disclosure of meaning on its part is dependent on its being tested in those processes of experience and learning that itself has made them possible? In *Being and Time* Heidegger himself had suggested the possibility of such a relation of mutual correction by introducing his notion of the 'hermeneutic circle'.

However, even if one defends the latter strategy, as I would, one is blatantly supposing – in contradistinction to classical transcendental philosophy – that the question as to the conditions of the possibility of meaning constitution is not the same as the question as to the conditions of the possibility of justifying the validity of knowledge (or of norms). This distinction, which, on its part, makes possible a new relating of both dimensions of the transcendental problem, appears to me to turn out as an interim result of our reconstruction of Heidegger's transformation of transcendental philosophy.

In my opinion this interim result may serve as a vantage point for another strategy which is an alternative to the fashionable strategy of detranscendentalization: this alternative should do justice, on the one hand, to the historicity of the world's meaning constitution and its being the precondition for true and false judgements, but also to the conditions of the universal and timeless validity of these judgements, on the other. (This holds not only for the empirical judgements that have been made possible by the meaning constitution but also for the philosophical judgements about the relationship between meaning constitution and the validity of judgments.)

To corroborate this thesis I must discuss in a detour the internal relation and the difference between the problematic of meaning constitution and of the justification of validity within the history of transcendental philosophy.

The relationship of meaning constitution and justification of validity in the frame of a transcendental pragmatics of language

The relation between the question of meaning constitution and the question of validity within the history of transcendental philosophy

Let me first state that for Kant the question as to the conditions of the possibility of the objective validity of scientific knowledge coincides with the question as to the transcendental conditions of the constitution of the *a priori* meaning of objectivity (i.e. *Gegenständlichkeit*). More specifically, Kant does answer the first question by reducing it to the second. This constitutes the point of the 'Copernican turn' which is inspired by the basic *topos* of modern philosophy, according to which we can understand *a priori* only what we ourselves have made or in a certain sense can make.[17] But Kant could make plausible this solution of the transcendental problem only by confining his entire problematic to the question of the constitution of the *a priori* valid form of objective experience and hence of the objectivity of the world to be experienced.

This situation was changed however in a fundamental way by Husserl's expanding of the Kantian problematic of 'transcendental constitution', that is by Husserl's transcending Kant's question in order to account for the constitution of the concrete manifoldness of the meaning contents of experience of the lifeworld – such as it expresses itself in language. Such an expansion implied as its immediate consequence, I believe, that the Kantian identification of the formal *a priori* conditions of meaning constitution with the conditions of the justification of the validity of knowledge could no longer be redeemed. For the presuppositions of meaning constitution in the sense of the concrete manifoldness of world disclosure refer indeed to those temporal-historical conditions that were assumed by Heidegger.

Be that as it may, the peculiarity and the deficiency of Husserl's transformation of transcendental philosophy are due to the fact that he preserved the solution strategy of Kant's philosophy of the transcendental subject even with regard to his expanded problematic of meaning constitution. For although he had extended the question in the way I pointed out, he nevertheless wished to give the answer – in a certain analogy to Kant – by reducing the meaning constitutions of the lifeworld to the intentional achievements of a transcendental consciousness, without taking into account the language mediation of the vast variety of the meaning contents of the lifeworld. Thus he was able, as it appeared, to escape Heidegger's problematic of a temporal-historical world-meaning constitution and thereby adapt his newly detected problematics of the pre-scientific meaning constitution of the lifeworld to that of a Kantian transcendental philosophy. But this restoration of the programme of classical transcendental philosophy was evidently doomed to failure because Husserl totally overlooked the role of linguistic mediation and thus of the dependence on history of concrete meaning constitution.

Does this rejection of Husserl's project of transcendental philosophy allows for an alternative to Heidegger's transformation and destruction of transcendental philosophy? Must the alternative to Husserl's strategy of reducing the justification of the validity of experience to meaning constitution by the transcendental subject be – necessarily – the reduction of all validity to the meaning constitution by the history of being, as suggested by Heidegger?

A transcendental-pragmatic renegotiation of the analysis of the 'pre-structure' of understanding in *Being and Time*

In my opinion there is an alternative to the Heideggerian suggestion. It is opened by the same reflection that – as a first step – enforced the assumption of a temporal-historical meaning constitution: namely by the reflection on the language mediation of our understanding of the lifeworld. For this reflection points not only to the undeniable historicity of meaning constitution but also to the fact that, already on the level of communicative understanding of the meaning of our utterances, a claim to universal validity of meaning is presupposed: a claim to the validity of meaning which can be definitively redeemed – if at all – only by the possible consensus of an indefinite, ideal community of communication and interpretation (as understood by Peirce and Royce).[18] In a semiotically transformed transcendental philosophy this 'regulative idea' has to take the place (so to speak) of the transcendental subject of meaning constitution (which on Husserl's account was to warrant the universal inter-subjective validity of meaning by its solitary intentional achievements).

If the definite consensus of the ideal community of interpretation may be presupposed – which of course can never be supposed empirically – then the universally valid redemption of all justifiable

meaning claims would be identical with the historical meaning constitution (i.e. everybody would at least understand anybody else).[19]
And therefore, under this ideal presupposition and the additional
supposition of an exhaustion of all truth criteria that are available to
an indefinite community of researchers – for example of all possible
criteria of evidence and coherence – the redemption of all discursively justifiable truth claims would also be possible.[20]

I argue that this counterfactual supposition of the ideal of a
consensual justification of validity claims (which was first envisaged
by Peirce) represents the alternative, or, so to speak, 'counter-
instance' of reason, to Heidegger's conception of the history of being,
and to the transcendental subject of classical transcendental philosophy. Being a counterfactual supposition and a regulative idea of
what consensual justification of validity would be, it obviously does
not contradict the factual dependence of our understanding, for
example of our capability of asking questions and hence also of the
truth or falsehood of possible answers, on the temporal-historical
meaning constitution of the lifeworld, as it is articulated in the
language as medium of understanding. Nevertheless, we have to
insist that from this dependence – which was explored by Heidegger
– it does not follow that the possible justification of validity – of
meaning and truth – is conditioned in a unilateral way by the
preceding historical meaning constitution.

In light of the variety and diversity of languages or language
games, the postulate of consensual justification of validity firstly
functions as a regulative idea of translatability and hence for a
progressive translation and hermeneutic interpretation of meaning;
furthermore it functions as a regulative idea for the progressive
research qua searching for the truth under the restrictive conditions
of abstractive meaning constitutions. Even these restrictive conditions however do not constitute themselves merely in dependence
on the background conditions of the lifeworld as they are always
already opened up by the history of being. For they are also always
already constituted in dependence on learning processes in the sense
of 'trial and error', and this means, in the age of science, on methodi-
cally controlled processes of discursive redemption or refutation on
the basis of criteria.

It has to be conceded that we shall always remain under the
sway of the historical and socio-cultural 'background' assumptions of
the lifeworld. Up to this point, a view that, along with Heidegger and

Wittgenstein, focuses only on the factual conditions of understanding may appear as if it finally considers only the historical happening of meaning and truth. However, such a position would be blind to the actual, performative validity claims that are brought forward in the situation of communication, and it is finally the validity claims of the philosophers themselves who argue for the historicist position that have to be put under scrutiny.

As I see it, Heidegger himself, who discovered the idea of the temporality of being (which is not to be confused with the abstract beingness of traditional ontology), could never bring to bear, as against the generative power of time, a counter-instance of reason, for example such a thing as Kant's 'regulative ideas'. This fundamental deficiency seems to be caused, in the last resort, by the fact that Heidegger, already in *Being and Time*, in his analysis of the pre-structure of being-in-the-world or of understanding being, did not account – by strict transcendental reflection – for the claim to universal validity and the presuppositions of his own analysis of the (existential-ontological) structures of being-in-the-world. Instead, his analysis, so to speak, fell upon the contingent, historically conditioned structures of 'facticity' (*geworfener-Entwurf*). Hereby he indeed discovered for the first time those structures that today are called 'background' presuppositions of the lifeworld. Thus in *Being and Time* the later turn of his philosophy in the sense of deriving the 'thrown project' from the 'happening' of the 'mission of being' had already been grounded – at least in the sense that there was no *logos* of the philosophical thought itself that could be counterposed to the history of being. The way to 'detranscendentalization' which today seems so plausible for many people was paved then.

But this whole surrender of the *logos* to the superiority of time – at least in Heidegger – rests on the fact that one part of the pre-structure of world understanding was overleapt, so to speak: namely that part which contains the specific validity claims and presuppositions of the philosophical analysis of being-in-the-world. In short: a deficiency of reflection came about that – by contrasting it with Heidegger's talk of 'oblivion of being' (*Seinsvergessenheit*) – we may call it 'oblivion of the *logos*' (*Logosvergessenheit*). And it should be noted that by '*logos*' I would not understand the *logos* of the *Gestell*, that is of making available by objectifying or making present in Heidegger's and Derrida's sense, but a much wider *logos*, which is presupposed by a communicative understanding and – finally in a form that cannot be reflectively denied without self-contradiction – by the philosophical discourse itself.[21]

At this point the task of a reiteration of Heidegger's analysis of the pre-structure of world-understanding arises, if we desire a transformation of transcendental philosophy that would be oriented toward a pragmatics of language communication. Such a transformation should avoid Heidegger's reflection deficit of the *Logosvergessenheit* without losing sight of his discovery of the temporal-historical background presuppositions of the lifeworld – especially of the clearing–concealing structure of the meaning constitution by the linguistic world disclosure. It seems clear that this task cannot be carried through to the end by a return to a transcendental philosophy of the transcendental subject or consciousness, that is neither by a restriction of the problematic of meaning constitution to the constitution of objectivity in Kant's sense nor by recourse to a meaning constitution that – along Husserlian lines – could be conceived as an intentional achievement of a self-sufficient subject in the wake of 'transcendental solipsism'. Instead I suggest that, at the beginning of the philosophical venture, we reflect on those transcendental-pragmatic presuppositions of arguing, that is of the argumentative discourse, that must be acknowledged – in order to avoid a performative self-contradiction – by each interlocutor, in other words, even by each subject of empirically solitary thinking. And I do insist on this suggestion, even if, at present, this appears to be very unfashionable with regard to the opening move of the philosophical language game.

Notes

First published in E. Agazzi (ed.), *Entretiens sur philosophie et histoire*, Actes du Congrès de Santa Margherita Ligure et Genes 1989 (Genoa: Academia Ligure di Science e Lettere, 1990), 127–46.

1 M. Heidegger, 'Das Ende der Philosophie und die Aufgabe des Denkens', in *Zur Sache des Denkens* (Tübingen: Mohr, 1969), 79.
2 K.O. Apel, 'Le défit de la critique totale de la raison et le programme d'une théorie philosophique des types de rationalité', *Le Débat*, 49 (1988), 141–63.
3 R. Rorty, *Consequences of Pragmatism* (Minneapolis: Univerity of Minnesota Press, 1987), and 'Pragmatism and Philosophy', in K. Baynes, J. Bohman and T.A. McCarthy (eds), *After Philosophy: End or Transformation?* (Cambridge, Mass.: MIT Press, 1987), 26–66.
4 M. Heidegger, *Sein und Zeit* (Halle: Niemeyer, 1941), 86.
5 *Ibid.*, 89 ff.

6 *Ibid.*, 205.

7 E. Husserl, *Die Krisis der europäischen Wissenschaften und die transzendentale Phänomenologie* (The Hague: Nijhoff, 1962).

8 M. Heidegger, *Sein und Zeit*, § 35.

9 *Ibid.*, 208.

10 *Ibid.*, 207 ff.

11 *Ibid.*, 208.

12 M. Heidegger, *Kant und das Problem der Metaphysik* (Frankfurt a. M: Kostermann, 1951).

13 *Ibid.*, 159 ff.

14 In his first book on Kant, Heidegger claimed 'that the I, the pure reason, in its essence is temporal' (*ibid.*, 174); after the *Kehre*, 'reason', as it is understood by occidental philosophy, is conceived as an epochal and hence restrictively valid result of the 'history of being'.

15 Gadamer, *Wahrheit und Methode*, preface to the second edition (Tübingen: Mohr & Siebeck, 1965), xv ff.

16 *Ibid.*, part 3.

17 For the history of this *topos* cf. Apel, *Die Idee der Sprache in der Tradition des Humanismus von Dante bis Vico* (Bonn: Bouvier, 1963, 1980), 321 ff., and 'Das "Verstehen" (eine Begriffsgeschichte als Problemgeschichte)', *Archiv für Begriffsgeschichte*, 1 (Bonn: Bouvier, 1955), 142–99.

18 Apel, 'Szientismus oder transzendentale Hermeneutik?', in *Transformation der Philosophie* (Frankfurt a. M.: Suhrkamp, 1973), vol. 2, 178–219; English translation: *Towards a Transformation of Philosophy* (London: Routledge & Kegan Paul, 1980); cf. Apel, *Der Denkweg von Charles Sanders Peirce* (Frankfurt a. M.: Suhrkamp, 1975).

19 Apel, 'Linguistic Meaning and Intentionality: the Compatibility of the "Linguistic Turn" and the "Pragmatic Turn" of Meaning-theory within the Framework of a Transcendental Semiotics', in H.J. Silverman and D. Welton (eds), *Critical and Dialectical Phenomenology* (Albany: State University of New York Press, 1987), 2–53.

20 Apel, 'Fallibilismus, Konsenstheorie der Wahrheit und Letztbegründung', in Forum für Philosophie Bad Homburg (ed.), *Philosophie und Begründung* (Frankfurt a. M.: Suhrkamp, 1987), 116–211.

21 Apel, 'Die Logosauszeichnung der menschlichen Sprache: die philosophische Relevanz der Sprechakttheorie', in H.-G. Bosshardt (ed.), *Perspektiven auf Sprache* (Berlin and New York: De Gruyter, 1986), 45–87.

6

Wittgenstein and Heidegger: language games and life forms

translated by CHRISTOPHER MACANN

Thirty years on: a retrospective overview

I would like to take up once again and develop still further the comparison between Wittgenstein and Heidegger which I undertook at the beginning of the 1960s in a series of papers.[1] In what follows I shall therefore be concerned with such questions as: what new insights have been opened up since the beginning of the 1960s with regard to the evaluation of Wittgenstein and Heidegger? And what follows therefrom for the critical development of the comparison I made at that time between the two thinkers?

First, it seems to me that my positive evaluation of the epochal significance of both thinkers and of their – at that time still surprising – affinity has been confirmed both by the worldwide influence and by the now apparent convergence of their thinking. We no longer – as in my student days in the decade after 1945 – have to contend with the hermetically sealed and starkly opposed fields of (Anglo-Saxon and Scandinavian) analytical philosophy and (continental European) phenomenological philosophy. Rather, a convergence along the lines of a linguistic-pragmatic, or even a hermeneutical, turn has taken place – right up to (post-Kuhnian) philosophy of science – and this situation is due largely to the historical impact of the convergence between Wittgenstein and Heidegger – whereby American pragmatism functions as the sounding-board and amplifier.

On the other hand, it seems to me that my critique of Heidegger and Wittgenstein – or, more exactly, of both thinkers' inadequately conducted reflection upon the *logos* (i.e. of discursive language games and their unquestionable presuppositions)[2] – which was intended only as provisional at the beginning of the 1960s, has, in the meantime, acquired an increased relevance. Briefly, the reduction of philosophy to self-therapy, a reduction which Wittgenstein's critique of language and meaning linked with the pseudo-problems of traditional metaphysics, was paradoxical from the very beginning; for it represented a negation of critical philosophy's own claims to meaning and truth. Precisely this tendency created its own disciples. Moreover, in Heidegger's ever more radical 'destruction' of Western metaphysics (and more completely in Derrida's 'deconstruction' and in Lyotard's 'postmodernism', which refer back to Heidegger and Wittgenstein) this tendency is strengthened to the point of attesting to something like the self-destruction of philosophical reason.[3] The opportunity opened up by Wittgenstein and Heidegger of effecting a post-metaphysical transformation and reconstruction of philosophy – from the standpoint of discursive language games containing the conditions of the possibility and validity of a critical hermeneutics and a philosophical critique of language and meaning – seems to have gone to ground in a self-destruction of philosophical discourse through an all too uncritical pursuit of the more problematic suggestions of two of the most prominent thinkers of the century.

The theme of this chapter is already indicated in advance with this ambivalent retrospective view of the historical impact of Wittgenstein and Heidegger.

In this first part of the chapter, I would like once again to set out the main points of convergence of the positive achievements of Wittgenstein and Heidegger in the form of a summary and a supplementation of my previous comparison. Admittedly, and owing to the lack of space, this cannot be done with reference to the Wittgenstein and Heidegger editions which have appeared in the meantime. Instead we shall concentrate upon a selection and a description of what is essential in the historical impact of the two thinkers from the distancing perspective of the present.

In the second, critical part of the chapter, which will carry the most weight, I would like to enter more closely into an argument with Heidegger and Wittgenstein. Finally I would like to show that neither thinker was fully cognizant of (and so both failed to measure up to) the primary requirement of philosophical *logos* or language game, namely a rigorous reflection, in the medium of public language, upon what is undertaken, believed in and presupposed when philosophical questions are raised and theses developed – or even only suggested. These latter, no matter how self-critical they may turn out to be, must after all claim to consist of statements capable of eliciting assent about how things are in general, that is, about the status of philosophy and its relation to the world.

First of all then, let us proceed with our comparison between the positive achievements of Wittgenstein and Heidegger.

The linguistic and hermeneutical turn in philosophy

As already indicated, what the achievements of Wittgenstein and Heidegger have in common is the rendering possible of a philosophical critique of language and meaning, on the one hand, and a pragmatic hermeneutic, on the other. What is meant by this? Let us first try to point out the paradigmatic function of the critique of language and meaning with reference to a problematic which plays an exemplary role in modern philosophy.

Wittgenstein's and Heidegger's critique of the mentalism of modern philosophy

The way in which the problem is posed in modern philosophizing might be expressed in the following train of thought.

In reality – and this is the basic assumption – only that is certain which is evident to me in inner experience, therefore not the existence of things and persons in the external world but only that I believe I am perceiving something here and now. Thus my sensational experience or at best my representation of the external world is the only genuine object of my consciousness whilst the things and persons which occupy the external world, including thereunder the common world, are at best a result of justified conclusions drawn on the basis of the data of immanental consciousness. Indeed, even the fact that such conclusions are justified in principle must, in principle, remain doubtful for epistemological philosophy. In the end, everything I take to be real could be something which only appears in my consciousness, for example, could only be my dream. Or, the being of things might consist only in their being perceived, and so on.

With this sketch of a problem, which could always be extended and spun out further, I wanted to point to the paradigmatic presuppositions of modern philosophy, which already figured with Augustine and with the Ockhamism of the late Middle Ages, and which have at least served to determine the problem of consciousness in modern philosophy from Descartes to Husserl. Even today philosophers can be found who take the questions mentioned above to be meaningful and pressing. But one may then be sure that they are thinking in accordance with a pre-Wittgensteinian and a pre-Heideggerian paradigm. The 'intellectual revolution' implied in the critique of meaning which has taken place here can be most effectively illustrated with reference to the 'language games' of late Wittgenstein: more precisely, with reference to the famous thesis that a 'private language' is impossible, in other words, that 'a solitary individual' cannot follow a rule.[4]

From this standpoint, precisely what, after Ockham, and even more so after Descartes, featured as the only certainty of human knowledge – the evidence of my inner experience – became irrelevant in the framework of an inter-subjectively valid world and self-understanding.

With this however the subjective certainty of inner experience, for example the certainty that I have pains or the Cartesian certainty that I think or that I have specific representations, is not called in question. What is denied is only that this purely subjective certainty can be distinguished epistemologically and that an (epistemological) primacy can be accorded to it over any inter-subjectively valid knowledge of the external world.

The reason why the epistemological primacy of inner experience cannot be legitimately sustained is that our knowledge claims are bound up with the assumption of a shared language (not only with regard to their possible truth but also with regard to their intelligible meaningfulness) and to this extent are, in the course of the language game, bound up with a publicly controllable rule-following procedure. In this linguistically founded assumption of the inter-subjectively valid understanding of something lies the new paradigm for philosophy. For it follows therefrom that the never certain but still publicly intelligible (and with regard to criteria controllable and correctable) experience of the external world must assume a primacy over the subjectively private certainty of inner experience.

Should the epistemological primacy of inner experience be upheld, it would have to be possible for the epistemological subject to validate the certainties of inner experience (for example, the certainties of pain sensations or of a reflection about thinking or about representations immanent to consciousness), in a private language, that is, in a language which no one else could understand because it would be characterized only by 'private ideas' in John Locke's sense.

Such a language is however unthinkable, because its rules – both syntactical and semantical – cannot be learned and taught with reference to rule-following criteria.

If the certainty of inner experience were to furnish the basis for the introduction and application of semantic rules, there would then, according to Wittgenstein, have to be something like a 'dictionary' which would exist only in my mind; that is, its word meanings would have to be established by means of definitions relating to private sensations or representations. And in order to re-identify these sensations and representations one would have to refer the table of meanings in the dictionary to the representations in question. In other words, with a view to justifying the correctness of my application of the semantic rules I would never be able to appeal to anything independent of my consciousness. Rather, I would have to rely upon memory. According to Wittgenstein, this would be as if I could decide about the question of 'whether I had correctly noted the departure time of a train' only by remembering an image of the page of the timetable and not by testing this memory image with reference to a publicly accessible timetable.[5] This means however that it is impossible to establish the distinction between right and wrong. For without recourse to an instance independent of my consciousness there could be no distinction between 'following the rule' and 'thinking one is following the rule'.[6]

In fact the indubitable certainty of inner experience in the post-Cartesian philosophy of modern times exists precisely because the distinction in question between doing and thinking one is doing, that is between being and appearing, would be suspended. And this positive paradigm serves to account for the direction of the modern critique of knowledge, namely scepticism. For Descartes's 'problematic Idealism' which was taken so seriously by British empiricism and which Kant accepted as meaningful even if refutable, this doubt fundamental to the modern critique of knowledge rests on the supposition: whatever is not certain in the sense of inner experience, that is those judgements which are at times true and at times false because they relate to an external world independent of me, these judgements could always be false because there might be no external world, because it might be the case that everything which is taken to be real simply exists as my dream.

At this point the critique of meaning implicit in the consideration of language games underlying all world and self-understanding

will become still clearer than with the destruction of the paradigmatic illusion of the epistemological primacy of 'inner experience'.
For it is enough to check the language game with reference to the
phrase *'simply* my dream' (i.e. *'simply* in consciousness') in order
to recognize the meaninglessness of the statement 'everything . . .
could simply be my dream' (i.e. could *simply* be in consciousness).
For the language game which makes the dramatic meaning of the
phrase *'simply* my dream' possible clearly presupposes as a paradigmatic certainty that not everything is my dream but that a real world
exists. For this language game would have to be suspended as a
possible language game if everything were simply my dream. But
then, in practice, nothing has changed. One has only introduced a
new language game of such a kind that what was previously understood by *'simply* my dream' now has to be introduced with the
description 'dream'.

In his last book (unpublished in his lifetime), *On Certainty* (*Über
Gewissheit*),[7] Wittgenstein brought out even more pointedly the suspension of the language game in question through the Cartesian
dream argument. He says there: 'the argument, perhaps I am dreaming, is simply devoid of meaning because in that case I would have
had to dream the expression of it, indeed, that these very words are
themselves meaningful' (383). The self-suspension of this language
game is, in the final analysis, traced back here to the performative
contradiction inherent in the argument – a point to which I will
return.

The arguments brought forward so far might suffice to elucidate
the point of the revolution brought about by Wittgenstein's critique
of language and meaning. It should also be noted however that
Kant's transcendental epistemology is in no way immune to what is
in question in this critique of meaning. To be sure, Kant tried to
refute the primacy accorded to 'inner experience' and, accordingly,
to 'subjective Idealism'. And Peter Strawson has undertaken a critical
reconstruction of this argument in *The Bounds of Sense*.[8] But at the
same time he also pointed out that the presupposition underlying a
'transcendental Idealism of consciousness', that, namely, of a transcendental realism, of unknowable things in themselves, itself rests
upon a metaphysical claim which is undermined by a critique of
language and meaning.

It is for example simply not possible to distinguish, along
Kantian lines, the concept of 'appearances' or of the 'world of

appearances', on the one hand, from that of 'mere semblance' – in the sense of the 'empirical reality' of objects of experience – while, on the other hand, distinguishing the former from the concept of 'unknowable' but still 'thinkable' things in themselves in the sense of pure appearances.[9] A language game containing these distinctions – or so Wittgenstein would have said – cannot function because it cannot be learnt. The sense in which the concept of 'pure appearances' can be learnt presupposes the concept 'knowable reality' just as much as it does that of 'mere semblance'. Thus, the reality which we can know cannot be distinguished over again as 'pure appearance' from a 'noumenal' reality. (In fact Kant took note of the problem of the consistency of this conceptual usage in his *Critique of Judgement*, where he found himself obliged to introduce a 'symbolic use of language' with an 'analogical schematism' to accommodate the epistemological talk about 'things in themselves'.)[10]

It is now time to consider the correspondences and convergences between the 'intellectual revolution' implied by this critique of meaning and the philosophy of Heidegger.

Significantly, a correspondence can be most easily established between Wittgenstein and Heidegger on the basis of the latter's early major work *Being and Time*, even though in this work Heidegger has not yet introduced language as the 'house of being' and as the 'habitation of mankind' as he will later in *The Letter on Humanism*. But even here the pre-linguistic, so to speak, visual-eidetic suppositions of Husserlian phenomenology have already been transcended in favour of the hermeneutic of a being-in-the-world which has always already been linguistically interpreted, as for example in the following paradigmatic statement:

> This everyday way in which things have been interpreted is one into which Dasein has grown up in the first instance, with never a possibility of extrication. In it, out of it, and against it, all genuine understanding, interpreting, and communicating, all rediscovering and appropriating anew, are performed. In no case is a Dasein, untouched and unseduced by this way in which things have been interpreted, set before the open country of a 'world in itself' so that it just beholds what it encounters.[11]

It is evident that this passage cannot be fitted into the context of a Wittgensteinian critique of language and meaning without further ado. Rather, it contains the key to a hermeneutic of language and refers to the so-called 'pre-structure of understanding being-in-the-world' and, as such, of an 'already' linguistically disclosed and so prefigured pre-comprehension of the lifeworld. In *Being and Time* a dimension of temporality or historicality is therewith already in question, a dimension which, with Wittgenstein, is not articulated in this form. For Wittgenstein concedes that language games are historically engendered and transformed. But he hardly ever investigates the historical dependence of our thinking upon the tradition of Western philosophy, a tradition which preoccupied Heidegger throughout his life. Wittgenstein prefers to construct functional models of as many simple language games as possible – 'objects of possible comparison', as he likes to call them – which are supposed to facilitate the description of everyday language usage. To this extent Wittgenstein remains throughout his life a trained aircraft engineer who does not have much feeling for the humanities, while Heidegger continually embodied the *modus vivendi* of a philosophically and historically oriented scholar.

For all that, this distinction, which is certainly relevant, does not prevent the two kinds of analysis, the analysis of the 'everydayness' of understanding being-in-the-world, an analysis drawn from *Being and Time*, and the analysis of 'everyday' language games, bound up as they are with activities, concrete expression and world interpretation and representing as they do 'cross-sections of life forms', from throwing light upon each other, substantiating and completing each other, at least in part.

In relation to the key points of the hermeneutical stance, cited by us, an even more direct relation between Heidegger and Wittgenstein can be set up. It is for example clear that Wittgenstein emphatically substantiates Heidegger's construction in the sense of an entanglement in the linguistic world interpretation and in the sense of having always already been seduced by it. He would admittedly have placed less emphasis upon the aspect of a 'concealing–revealing' world disclosure made possible by the foregoing and more upon the aspect of everyday speech patterns and, to this extent, upon the emergence of the vacuous language games of philosophy, games which are no longer connected to a meaningful life *praxis*.

But it is possible to establish direct correspondences with Heidegger even on the plane of just such a critique of meaning. Such a correspondence is for example to be found in *Being and Time* in the hermeneutical indication that we are able to understand immanental objectives made up of sense data or pure presentations only on the assumption that our ordinary understanding of the world assumes the form of being-in-the-world and, to this extent, uncovers the real being itself 'as something' in a 'relationship' or 'meaning context' – the 'roaring car', the 'motor bike' and the 'tapping woodpecker', not the corresponding noises in consciousness.[12] If we wanted to try to grasp our being-in-the-world as 'being-alongside' the immanental sounds in consciousness, qua sense data, such a 'being-alongside' could be understood only as a 'deficient modus' of being with things themselves – originally disclosed and comprehended as something. (Analytical philosophers would talk here of a parasitic relationship.)

Moreover, Heidegger established not only the Cartesian position with regard to immanental consciousness as a deficient mode of being-in-the-world, but – as an extension of this critique – also that represented by Husserl under the auspices of 'methodological solipsism', that is, the primordial 'solitariness' of the transcendental ego, which now figures as a deficient mode of being-in-the-world under the auspices of being-with-others.[13]

On the basis of this analysis of being-in-the-world and the world understanding which belongs to it, Heidegger was able to formulate a hermeneutical equivalent to the epistemological critique of Descartes's dream argument in his own critique of Kant's demand for a proof of the 'existence of things outside me'.[14] He shows that Kant set out from the Cartesian assumption of an 'isolated subject present at hand' and from the primacy of the inner experience of this subject and does not get beyond this assumption even in the proof of a necessary coincidence of the changing and the persisting through time. For this very reason Kant has to concede that 'problematic Idealism' is both 'reasonable and in accordance with a thorough and philosophical mode of thought', and so 'allows for no decisive judgement until sufficient proof has been found'.[15] Against this position Heidegger contends that both the distinction and the connection of 'inner' and 'outer' in relation to my consciousness can be rendered intelligible only if the primacy of being-in-the-world as being alongside external entities has already been presupposed. (The corresponding analysis of the way in which language games are learnt arrives at precisely the same result.) In this way Heidegger arrives at his conclusion that the 'scandal of philosophy' against which Kant rails consists not in this, that the proof of the existence of an external world has not yet been provided, but in this, 'that such proofs are expected and attempted again and again'.[16]

It is understandable that Heidegger's analysis of being-in-the-world as being-with should also lead to a similar conclusion relative to the traditional problematic of the existence of 'Other Minds'. Heidegger explicitly rejected the theory (represented by middle-period Dilthey and by Husserl) of the constitution of the other subject on the basis of 'empathy', for example through an analogical inference, because such a conception wrongly presupposes the reflective self-understanding of an isolated first-person subject.[17] In opposition to such a stance Heidegger shows that 'empathy' does not constitute being-with in the first instance but 'is itself first possible on this basis' and 'gets its motivation from the deficiency of the dominant modes of being-with'.[18] Even this phenomenological reference can be strengthened and deepened through a language-game analysis which starts out from possible ways of learning the meaning of personal pronouns, and in such a way that statements of Hegel, Humboldt, G.H. Mead and Rosenstock-Huessy on the equi-primordiality and the reciprocity of communication roles thereby become applicable.

The deconstruction of world understanding and of the idea of truth in Western metaphysics in general

Up to now the point of departure for my comparison of the positive results of the thinking of Wittgenstein and Heidegger has been the heuristic standpoint of the critique of mentalism and the methodological solipsism which goes along with it. My aim has been to bring out the hermeneutical-phenomenological equivalences in Heidegger. A still broader horizon opens up for the comparison when one sets out from Heidegger's 'destruction' of the ontology of pure 'presence-at-hand' or, in other words, from the standpoint of a hermeneutical-pragmatic analysis of the 'relational' world – more precisely, in Heidegger's sense: from the world as the 'wherein of self-referring understanding', that is the 'upon which' of a letting be encountered of entities in the kind of being that belongs to involvements.[19] On one occasion Heidegger formulates this conception of the pre-theoretical constitution of the life world in terms of the possible structural pre-stages of any theoretical use of language.

Between the kind of interpretation which is still wholly wrapped up in concernful understanding and the extreme opposite case of a theoretical assertion about something present-at-hand, there are many intermediate gradations: assertions about the happenings in the environment, accounts of the ready-to-hand, reports on the situation, the recording and fixing of the facts of the matter, the description of a state of affairs, the narration of something that has befallen. We cannot trace back these sentences to theoretical statements themselves; they have their 'source' in circumspective interpretation.[20]

It is clear that these passages can be read in the Wittgensteinian sense of a reference to the multiplicity of non-theoretical language games. Even with regard to the Heideggerian point – the founding of 'theoretical statements' about what is present in a pre-theoretical ('circumspective') 'interpretation' of the 'relational-world' – it is possible to find a fairly close equivalence in Wittgenstein, namely – as has yet to be shown – in his pragmatically oriented critique of the traditional absolutizing of that nominative or descriptive function of language in which the latter is referred to objects.[21] The basis of comparison which is in question here goes further than the Cartesian critique of meaning in the sense that, with Heidegger as also with Wittgenstein, it reaches back to the beginnings of Western ontology and philosophy of language in Plato and Aristotle. Let us first consider Heidegger's 'destruction' of the ontological (or objectively theoretical) world understanding.

First of all we need to show that, on the assumption of a purely theoretical distancing from beings as simply 'present-at-hand', something like a *de-worlding* has to make its appearance.[22] This means: the connection of the 'significative-references' inherent in the lifeworld, in the sense of relatedness or meaningfulness of entities, is dissolved. In so far as there is now only a 'staring' at the present-at-hand, nothing like a 'hermeneutical synthesis' of 'letting something be as something' is conceivable, and this implies that the basis for a predicative synthesis of the apophatical *logos* also falls away. Putting this together one might conclude: the fact that something is confronted as something standing over against presupposes that beings were encountered previously as something in a pragmatically relational-totality. And, according to Heidegger, this in turn presupposes that human *Dasein* as being-in-the-world is able to disclose the 'significance' of the world out of the horizon of being-ahead-of-oneself in the mode of 'care', and of 'concernful having to do with'. A purely theoretical consciousness of objects of the kind Husserl assumes is given originally is quite incapable of conferring 'significance' upon the world.[23] (This circumstance was not properly thought through by Husserl even with his introduction of the concept of the 'lifeworld' in *Crisis*, which seeks to respond to Heidegger's *Being and Time*.)

I would however like to note here that this pragmatic conception of the lifeworld has to be applied even to the constitutive conditions of scientific theorizing and its connection with experimental *praxis*, if one wants to think with Heidegger beyond the Heidegger of *Being and Time*. For the latter cannot be rendered intelligible in terms of Heidegger's purely theoretical limiting case of being-in-the-world, which implies simply staring at the present-at-hand. For example, the meaning constitution of the categories of proto-geometry and proto-physics can be reconstructed only under the assumption of a human measuring practice, as Hugo Dingler and Paul Lorenzen and Peter Janich have shown.[24] Something similar is to be found with the category of the causal necessity of the succession of two events, for example the expectation that, when iron is heated, it expands. This understanding of causal necessity, which differs from mere (Humean) regularity (as is seen in the proposition 'when iron is heated, the earth rotates'), can be constituted – as G.H. von Wright has shown[25] – only on the pragmatic assumption that the experimental *praxis* of physics (and before that of human labour) is, through our intervention in the course of nature, able to bring about something which, without that intervention, would not have happened.

If one's point of departure is that these pragmatic conditions of the possibility have to be rooted in a world constitution already presupposed by science, Heidegger's concept of 'de-worlding' can then be supported with a famous example from the history of philosophy, namely David Hume's conclusion that nothing like a necessary relation between the occurrence of one natural event and a preceding or succeeding event can be discovered. In my view Hume arrived at this conclusion simply because he conducted his analysis from the standpoint of a purely theoretical remoteness from the world, because he had abstracted altogether from the worldly involvement of experimental *praxis*. His discovery therefore depended upon a de-worlding. (I am, like Paul Lorenzen, convinced that even the most abstract relations (those, for instance, of logic and mathematics) would fall to the ground if, through a total abstraction from the life *praxis*, we effected a de-worlding in Heidegger's sense.)

However, if the above-mentioned conclusions concerning lifeworldly constitutional foundations apply equally to science, an important reservation must be voiced against the Heideggerian thesis about the ontological primacy of the relational world of concernful dealings (i.e. everyday being-in-the-world) over any world conception in the sense of objectivity, an objectivity founded by Descartes and Kant but already laid down in that understanding of being implicit in Greek ontology (e.g. nature as the being-there of things in so far as they belong together in a law-governed connection). A state of affairs makes itself known which is never taken into consideration in *Being and Time*. Between the existential relational-world, a relational-world which is itself related to a being-in-the-world founded in mineness or ourness and which is, to this extent, subjectively perspectival and historically pre-structured, and the limiting case of de-worlding which arises as the correlate of a simple staring at things (therefore of a complete disengagement from my life *praxis*), between these two poles which were thematically articulated by Heidegger, a world understanding which takes on a destinal significance for the West emerges, that of an objective (and this means at least in principle inter-subjectively valid) science. This world understanding does indeed abstract, and in principle, from any 'purely subjective' (and so also from any collectively subjective) presuppositions but it does not abstract – as does the purely theoretical world understanding outlined in *Being and Time* – from any practical involvement that, as an epistemological interest, might open up the worldly significance of a referential totality of signs. Rather, it does itself rest upon the quite unique 'discovery' of an objectivity which constitutes itself for every 'consciousness as such' and as that which can be measured and causally explained. That 'existential fore-structure' of the historically determined world understanding which first made possible the concrete theoretical constructions of science has not prevented scientific theories and experiments from being inter-subjectively reproducible, and, to this extent, universally valid.

What I have just pointed out was recognized by later Heidegger to the extent that, in his concept of the *Gestell*, scientific world understanding (an understanding whose roots can be traced back to classical ontology) is explicitly related to a *praxis* which furnishes the *a priori* conditions for the latter – that of technology.[26] But he fails to connect this discovery with any appreciation of the phenomenon of

strictly inter-subjective validity, which requires that scientific statements (as also those of philosophy) should be validated through a
procedure of argumentative discourse. Still less did he appreciate the
circumstance that that objectivity which makes the world available
to science does not have to lead to a scientizing conception of
the world as absolute – a 'making available' in the sense of an
'enframing' – quite simply because the making available of the world
in the sense of the subject–object relation 'always already' presupposes that complementary communicative understanding of one's
co-subjects which proceeds from the existence of a discursive community. That through this complementarity a definitive success, that
is, an absolutization of methodologically reductive scientism, is excluded a priori is even today hardly recognized.

Instead, late Heidegger will conceive of the objectivity of science
(and the claim of philosophy itself to the inter-subjective validity of
its statements) as a merely contingent pre-condition of world understanding, a pre-condition which is grounded in the 'thrown projection' of being-in-the-world – and, after the Kehre, this means in a
world-establishing, epochal event in the history of being. I will come
back later to this question of the threat represented by the above to
the validation of philosophical statements, as also to Heidegger's
statements about the historical conditions of the possibility (and
validity) of Western science and philosophy. But first I would like
to maintain that a peculiar reflective deficiency with regard to the
constitution of objectivity (and connected therewith to the inter-
subjective criteria of validity for a scientific experience – as Kant had
shown) attaches to the genial analysis of the pre-theoretical
relational-world in Being and Time. Already in Being and Time
Heidegger had only the following to say about the meaning of the
Kantian idealization of the epistemological subject in the sense of a
'pure ego' or a 'consciousness in general':

> Is not such a subject a *fanciful idealization*? With such a conception
> have we not missed precisely the *a priori* character of that merely
> 'factual' subject Dasein? Is it not an attribute of the *a priori* character
> of the factical subject (that is, an attribute of Dasein's facticity) that
> it is in the truth and in untruth equi-primordially?[27]

After the turn introduced by Heidegger's 'hermeneutical revolution' no philosopher is going to deny that the world understanding
which comes before the truth of science and which makes it possible

has the character of 'revealing–concealing'. But surely the possibility of the simple inter-subjective validity – and of absolute truth in this sense – of the findings of science must therewith also become a questionable issue. Heidegger's answer to this question in *Being and Time* can be found in the following passage:

> There is truth only in so far as Dasein is and as long as Dasein is. Entities are uncovered only when Dasein is: and only as long as Dasein is, are they disclosed . . . To say that before Newton his laws were neither true nor false, cannot signify that before him there were no such entities as have been uncovered and pointed out by those laws. Through Newton the laws became true; and with them, entities became accessible in themselves to Dasein . . . That there are 'eternal truths' will not be adequately proved until someone has succeeded in demonstrating that Dasein has been and will be for all eternity . . . Even the 'universal validity' of truth is rooted solely in the fact that Dasein can uncover entities in themselves and free them . . . Why must we presuppose that there is truth? What is 'presupposing'? What do we have in mind with the 'must' and the 'we'? . . . 'We' presuppose truth because 'we', being in the kind of being which Dasein possesses, are 'in the truth'.[28]

But even this answer to the question posed by us with regard to the possibility of a strictly inter-subjective validity remains ambiguous. That the truth of 'propositions' can no longer – as Thomas Aquinas and even Bolzano held – be regarded as independent of human knowledge on the ground of the creative knowledge of an *intellectus divinus* can be accepted as following from Heidegger's 'methodological atheism'. But that the validity of true statements for any 'epistemological subject in general' has to be regarded as relative to the temporal duration of a world disclosure which belongs to human *Dasein* is already problematic. In his first Kant book Heidegger tried to align his thesis with regard to the dependence of truth in general upon the world understanding of human *Dasein* with Kant's transcendental philosophy, more specifically with the first edition of the *Critique of Pure Reason* and not with the second.[29] But after the historico-ontological 'turn' of his interpretation of human *Dasein* and its 'disclosiveness' as that of 'thrown-projection', Heidegger radicalized the thesis about the relativity of the truth as the unhiddenness of the world with regard to the temporal-historical *Dasein* of human being in this sense, that even this relativity can be understood as relative to a specific epoch in ontological history, for example as the relativity of the concept of the universal validity of scientific and philosophical truth with regard to the epoch of metaphysics which began in Greece and which is coming to an end today. At this point a difficulty inherent in Heidegger's philosophy can, I suggest, be noted, a difficulty to which we shall have to come back, namely, the pragmatic contradiction between the relativity thesis and its own claim to universal validity. For the historico-ontological relativization of the universal validity of truth will itself have to be true, that is universally valid, as an insight into the necessity of this very relativization, and this in a sense which cannot itself be relativized – and that means for any possible epistemological subject in the context of an ideal dialogical community of human beings as potentially rational beings.

Here we see that even the much vaunted pragmatism of the *Dasein*'s analyses undertaken in *Being and Time* is ambiguous. It may well be that it displays – as Richard Rorty has suggested[30] – an affinity to William James's and John Dewey's reduction of scientific and philosophical truth to practically serviceable aims in the sense of the needs of (individual or collectively individual) human beings who happen to exist in a given world. But it has nothing to do with Peirce's pragmatism, for instance, with what Peirce, in opposition to James and Dewey, later called 'pragmaticism'. To be sure, the latter also interpreted the meaning of any possible true or false statement in terms of a possible life *praxis*. But he also distinguished the inter-subjective validity of experimental procedures and the dialogical *praxis* of an 'unlimited community of scientists' as the only possible regulative context for the pursuit of truth in practice. In distinction from Heidegger, he did not attempt to found the ultimate validity of truth upon the 'factical apriori' of being-in-the-world, but upon the ability of the truth to establish a consensus for all rational human beings, a consensus which is counterfactually anticipated in advance.[31]

So much for Heidegger's 'destruction' of world understanding and for that idea of truth to which Western philosophy and science subscribe. With regard to what has already been said, where are we to locate the correspondence between Wittgenstein's critique of language and meaning and Heidegggger's ambition to undertake a comprehensive philosophical destruction?

In the first place, a positive correspondence between language-game analysis and the pragmatically oriented existential-hermeneutical analysis of the relational-world, together with the transition from world understanding to the deficient mode of de-worlding (simply staring at what is present-at-hand), can very easily be found. It is to be sought in this, that the privileging of the denominative language game (taken for granted since the founding of ontological philosophy in Greece), a strategy pushed to the limit by Wittgenstein himself in the *Tractatus* through his characterization of objects and states of affairs, is radically called in question in his later language-game analysis. But it is not so much a matter of Wittgenstein completely giving up his earlier conception of name-giving and ostensive definition later on. Rather, he made it clear that a quite special language game operated here, one which always presupposed other language games which for their part were intimately bound up with the practice of a given life form. The following passages from *Philosophical Investigations* will suffice to bring out these presuppositions.

> The ostensive definition explains the use – the meaning – of the word when the overall role of the word in language is clear . . . One has already to know (or to be able to do) something in order to be capable of asking a thing's name. (1, § 30)

And:

> When one shows someone the king in chess and says: 'This is the king', this does not tell him the use of this piece – unless he already knows the rules of the game up to this last point . . . Only someone who already knows how to do something with it can significantly ask a name. (1, § 31)

A remark by Wittgenstein should also be seen in this connection, a remark which, so to speak, marks the semiotic equivalence with Heidegger's theory of 'de-worlding'. It shows how a self-sufficient theory of meaning constitution through name-giving, taken out of the pragmatic context of language games bound up with life forms, exactly corresponds to the transition described by Heidegger from contextual world understanding to the deficient mode of simply staring at the present-at-hand. Wittgenstein formulates this as follows:

> Naming appears as a queer connection of a word with an object – And you really get such a *queer* connection when the philosopher tries to bring out *the* relation between name and thing by staring

at an object in front of him and repeating a name or even the word 'this' innumerable times. For philosophical problems arise when language *goes on holiday*. And here we may indeed fancy naming to be some remarkable act of mind, as it were a baptism of an object. (1, § 38)

To the Heideggerian limiting case of 'de-worlding' (in which what is present-at-hand is simply stared at and so can have no more 'meaning' for us) there corresponds, with Wittgenstein, the limiting case in which language 'goes on holiday', that is, is no longer bound up with its use in a given life *praxis*. In this limiting case it is indeed only possible to substitute a name for the 'this-there', a name which no longer carries with it any intelligible meaning. And this naturally implies that under these conditions the constitution of the meaning of linguistic predicates cannot be rendered intelligible.

It is therefore quite impossible to find a universally valid theory of linguistic meaning by the co-ordination of pure 'sensations' with 'logically proper names' as the elements out of which a given world can be constructed, as Russell, for example, sought to do. Rather, the naming language game – or even the question concerning the correct way of naming some given entity – already presupposes those very language games in and through which the context of a life *praxis* determines the possible role of words in the language game and so also, to this extent, their meaning.

We are now in a position to pull together the philosophical achievements of Wittgenstein and Heidegger. I would like to appeal here to the concept of the 'lifeworld' employed by late Husserl and advance the thesis that Wittgenstein and Heidegger each discovered the lifeworld in his own way and, moreover, that they were able to work out this concept (in opposition to the world conception of the philosophical tradition) in a much more radical way than Husserl was able to do in *Crisis*.[32] To be sure, Husserl had seen that the abstract idealizing objectification of European science presupposed the emergence of meaning out of the lifeworld (and so had to be understood philosophically out of the latter). But, as the last classical representative of the post-Cartesian philosophy of consciousness, he assumed that even the meaning constitution of the lifeworld and its inter-subjective validity could be traced back to the intentional op-erations of a solipsistically transcendental consciousness, an 'I think', and, in the last analysis, had to be so understood. That the meaning constitution of the lifeworld, as publicly valid, was always dependent upon language and that, to this extent, it was always dependent upon a historical and socio-culturally determined life form, was something he did not appreciate.

While with Husserl the pre-linguistic intentional operation of an Ego consciousness is supposed to found the meaning constitution of the lifeworld, it is this very lifeworld which, with Heidegger and Wittgenstein, assumes the role of the ultimate bedrock: with Heidegger, in the form of a historically determined 'thrown projection' of 'being-in-the-world' and, with Wittgenstein, in the guise of the 'life forms' which make up the background of those very 'language games' which have already been taken account of. In fact, bound up with the latter we find insights into the quasi-transcendental conditioning of our world and self-understanding, beyond which, at the present time, philosophy cannot go back. Belonging thereto we find, on the one hand, the insights I have mentioned concerning a critique of the meanings involved in metaphysical pseudo-problems, meanings which result from the non-reflection upon the linguistic *a priori* of language games and, on the other hand, the corresponding existential-hermeneutical insights into the dependence of our positive understanding of worldly significance upon human being-in-the world and, in connection therewith, upon the worldly disclosiveness of historical language(s).

With reference to this linguistically and historically conditioned pre-understanding of the lifeworld, we are no longer able to go back to a null-point of presuppositionless thinking about whatever is present, for example, to the self-givenness of phenomena. This can today be regarded as generally accepted by a philosophizing which has gone through the linguistically pragmatic and hermeneutically oriented turn introduced by Wittgenstein and Heidegger. That things are like this can be shown also through a complementary turn in the philosophy of science which, since Thomas Kuhn's analysis in *The Structure of Scientific Revolutions*, has also brought out the dependence of scientific thinking and its possible development upon a historically conditioned agreement between a community of scientists.[33]

This reference to Kuhn's philosophy of science, in which Wittgensteinian motifs join together with motifs drawn from the hermeneutical philosophy inspired by Heidegger (and Gadamer), is intended to point to the questionable suggestions inherent in Wittgenstein's and Heidegger's thinking: the absolutization of the contingently *a priori*, the historically conditioned lifeworld, which does not lend itself to the forming of a consensus because it calls in question the conditions of the possibility of a universal philosophical consensus. I am here deliberately harping upon the pragmatic requirement of philosophical consistency, that is, upon the requirement of avoiding any performative contradiction in argumentation. And I am drawing attention to the fact that, in his *reductio ad absurdum* of the Cartesian dream argument in *On Certainty*, Wittgenstein himself offered an example of the very self-suspension of a philosophical language game which has to be avoided.

With reference to Heidegger I have already had occasion to point to the danger which results from the inconsistency inherent in his destruction of that idea of truth which underlies Western metaphysics. Let us now take a closer look with reference to Wittgenstein. Consider Wittgenstein's radical critique of the vacuity or the 'disease' of language games. As is well known, in his *Philosophical Investigations* Wittgenstein did not really take back the dictum of 'non-sensicality' expressed in the *Tractatus*, a dictum directed against the propositions of philosophy in general – including those of the *Tractatus* itself – at least, not in the form indicated there. For he did not answer the question of how that critical language game of philosophy, the language game in which one talks about language games in general (their function and dys-function) and so is able to 'show the fly the way out of the fly-bottle', is itself possible and valid. To these questions he seems only to have given critically therapeutic answers which apply equally to the language game needed to cure the disease and which, at the very least, seem not to recognize that the legitimacy of his characterization of philosophical problems in general as a linguistic disease itself rests upon a specifically philosophical insight which lays claim to universal validity.[34]

If, as has been shown, the proof of the self-suspension of the philosophical language game through the performative self-contradiction involved turns out to be the most radical form of the critique of language and meaning, it then becomes possible to think with Wittgenstein against Wittgenstein and to conclude that the recommended programme of a total self-therapy of philosophy as a disease proves to be defective. It then becomes possible to counter the exaggerated emphasis laid upon the contingently *a priori* character of the many life forms, for instance, that of the historically determined own lifeworld, with one argument which, in the final analysis, so far from reclaiming a metaphysical standpoint beyond language and the world, simply recognizes the impossibility of getting behind that language game which is philosophy as the legitimate form of reflection with regard to all thinkable language games and life forms and, to this extent, of any historically conditioned lifeworld.

And so I come to the second part of my comparison between Wittgenstein and Heidegger.

Philosophy: self-criticism or self-suspension?

Thomas Kuhn's theory of the 'paradigms' of the history of science can with good reason be taken up as a particularly instructive example for the convergence of the historical efficiency of the thinking of Wittgenstein and Heidegger. For the concept of a paradigm, a concept which is introduced by Kuhn in the double role of the positive condition of the possibility and of the historical relativization of scientific progress,[35] this central and multi-faceted concept can be elucidated both out of the perspective of Wittgenstein's language games and their paradigms of 'certainty' and out of the perspective of the epochal revealing–concealing establishment of the world in Heidegger's history of being.

Seen from a Wittgensteinian perspective, Kuhn's 'incommensurable' paradigms of science and their possible development appear as illustrations of the idea that language games, as part of 'life forms', are 'bound up' with 'activities' and grammatically conditioned *a priori* valid forms of world interpretation. To this extent they function as 'norms' for language usage, experimental *praxis* and for any acceptable research findings which can be expected to yield true or false conclusions and which for this reason cannot be called in question by empirical science since they have to be known *a priori* as conditions of the possibility of the functioning of the scientific language game and the *praxis* which belongs to it. The provocative point of the Kuhnian paradigm concept (both for the traditional linear representation of progress and for the unitary rationality of science) is to be sought along the lines of Wittgenstein's suggestion that one cannot go behind the multiplicity and the variety of language games and the life forms which support them, that the multiplicity of life forms, functioning as they do as the background for the different language games, can even make comprehension through the medium of language impossible. Lions, for example, could not be understood by us humans even if they could talk;[36] more pertinently, a similar limitation of our understanding must perhaps be assumed for the understanding of foreign human life forms, that is, so-called primitive cultures.[37]

To this primarily synchronous relativism of the Wittgensteinian perspective there now largely corresponds the primarily diachronic relativism of epochal world clearing which (as has been shown above) with Heidegger emerges out of the historical transformation of a *Dasein*-related concept of truth as 'disclosure'. Above all it is the following intellectual configuration which seems to correspond to the function of Kuhn's concept of a paradigm. In a later statement in *The Task of Thinking*[38] Heidegger conceded on the one hand that it would be 'inappropriate' to interpret his concept of world clearing (for example, revealing–concealing or *aletheia*) as the 'original concept of truth'. For the element of correctness, in the sense of a correspondence with something pre-given, is lacking. On the other hand, he emphasized once again that, with the concept of 'lighting', a dimension had been opened up which systematically preceded the traditional concept of truth. For in this instance it was a question of the condition of the possibility of true or false judgements, that is statements about beings.

The connection of this intellectual configuration with the function of the Kuhnian paradigm is clearly to be found in this consideration: that in both cases where the possibility of an advance in knowledge is in question – including the process of verification and falsification – the latter is, in a one-sided manner, made to appear dependent upon a preceding condition. To Kuhn's normative paradigm there corresponds Heidegger's clearing, a clearing which, as linguistically world-disclosive, first opens up the meaning horizon for possible scientific questions. And true or false judgements must, as Gadamer has shown, be understood as answers to actual, or at least to possible, questions.[39] To this extent it would be true to conclude that the findings of Western science in general are dependent upon paradigmatic meaning or interrogative horizons, horizons which could not be opened up at all in cultures with different linguistic modes of world disclosure – for example the Hopi people of New Mexico.[40] At this point the convergence between Heidegger's hermeneutical understanding of language and Wittgenstein's analytical understanding of language games becomes even clearer.

One difference between Heidegger and Kuhn or Wittgenstein

seems to consist in this, that the uncovering–covering, meaning-clearing inherent in Heidegger's understanding of Western world history is as a whole quite explicitly characterized by the 'event' of the founding of philosophy as metaphysics by the Greeks. To this extent the different scientific paradigms which follow therefrom can obviously not be regarded by Heidegger as 'incommensurable' in every respect since they have to be understood as consequences of the founding of metaphysics. The point of Heidegger's supposition is to be found in the thesis that already in the metaphysical uncovering of the meaning of being with Plato – that is, in the so-called 'theory of Ideas' – the mode of uncovering of the world assumes the form of the subject–object relation and therewith also of an 'enframing' of scientific technology, that is of the technological science of modern Europe.

By comparison with this Heideggerian vision (which corresponds to his lifelong attempt at a reconstruction and destruction of Western metaphysics) the Wittgensteinian representation of infinitely many language games and life forms is, on the one hand, and as we have already noted, marked by an a historical intellectual model – especially in the transitional period between the *Tractatus* and the *Philosophical Investigations*. On the other hand, it is illustrated in late Wittgenstein along the lines of ethnological examples and, globally, with reference to the idea of a 'natural history'.

These differences do not however make it impossible for us – as the example of Kuhn has already shown – to establish a convergence of the Heideggerian and the Wittgensteinian perspectives, in the sense, too, of a relativistic and historicalistic orientation of Western philosophy in general. Frequently these very characteristics are rejected as a misunderstanding – as the consequence of a way of thinking which is itself metaphysical and which has not learned how to assimilate the new standpoint 'beyond relativism and objectivism'. At the end of the chapter I would like to resist precisely this suggestion.

To this end, I would like first to set out what, in my opinion, constitute the most important philosophical results of the historically effective convergence of the intellectual claims of Wittgenstein and Heidegger. With Heidegger the most important claim consists in this, that meaning-clearing and the truth which, in the final analysis, is dependent upon it, must be thought as a meaning (or truth) event, that is, in its most radical accentuation. Even the insight – opened up with the philosophical truth claim – that our ability to pose questions is genetically dependent upon the clearing event of the history of being is clearly, according to Heidegger, itself dependent upon the temporal occurrence of the history of being for its validity. The *logos* of our thinking (for instance, our argumentative procedures) which was above all taken to be independent of time by the Greek of philosophy now has to be regarded as dependent upon the 'other of reason' – the temporality of being. Nevertheless it should be possible to frame this insight in the form of a universally valid philosophical thesis about the history of being. Is this claim, a claim which has been carried over from Heidegger into philosophical postmodernism, tenable from the standpoint of a critique of meaning? Or does it not rather lead to a self-suspension of the language game of philosophy?

With a view to answering these questions we shall have recourse to Wittgenstein's critique of language and meaning. However, it must be said that Wittgenstein and the Wittgensteinians do not offer much in the way of helpful objections but rather tend to complete and to strengthen the Heideggerian claims. To be sure, Wittgenstein tirelessly traced the disease of seemingly unsolvable philosophical problems back to a misunderstanding of the function of language. And in this sense he did indeed – as shown above – take into consideration the phenomenon of the self-suspension of the philosophical language game. But he never applied these kinds of analyses in a strictly reflective manner to his own, suggestive statements about philosophy as a disease resulting from a misuse of language. Above all (and particularly after the paradoxical self-suspension of the philosophical language game in the *Tractatus*) he never again posed the reflective question concerning the linguistic conditions of the possibility of one's own language game, that is, the question concerning the presuppositions not of the pseudo-language-games of metaphysics which were to be critically resolved by him, but about the language game involved in his own critically therapeutic philosophy which, clearly, could only 'show the fly the way out of the fly-bottle' and cure the sickness through linguistically formulated insights, and not through the dispensing of medicaments.

At this point we have to take account of the following circumstance. The well-known statements by Wittgenstein in the *Philosophical Investigations* on the method of philosophy such as, for example, 'we may not advance any kind of theory . . . We might do away with all explanation, and description alone must take its place' (1, § 109) or 'Philosophy simply puts everything before us and neither explains nor deduces anything. Since everything lies open to view there is nothing to explain. For what is hidden, for example, is of no interest to us' (1, § 126). Statements of this kind certainly attest to the originality of his method. But they do not make it clear to what extent they make it possible for Wittgenstein to communicate, through the summoning-up of examples, those insights into the 'workings of our language' (1, § 109) which should help us to get things 'straight' and which are so complete 'that philosophical problems should completely disappear' (1, § 133). It is just not enough to simply set out, or to describe, the everyday language games on the one hand and, on the other, the empty language games of philosophy. Rather, it is necessary at least to point out the reasons – that is the universally valid insights of philosophy – which make it possible to play off the one language game against the other. These reasons are at least suggested by Wittgenstein in his ever-renewed intimations towards philosophical theory-building at the level of a specific philosophical language game in which he, as much as any other philosopher, was obliged to participate.

Here we run up against a reflective deficiency which is bound up with his – in many instances helpful – predisposition for the 'pure describing' of examples. Certainly it is possible – as Wittgenstein's work demonstrates – to correct the *a priori* assumptions and over-hasty generalizations of systematic philosophy with the analysis of examples. But one cannot hope to render intelligible in this way the specific claims to validity of all philosophical statements – even those statements which bear the brunt of the critique of language and meaning. To put it otherwise: one cannot render intelligible the actual function of philosophical language games through language-game analysis in this way; by presenting this language game as just one language game among these or alongside others, which means embedded in a particular form of life with particular 'conventions', 'uses' or 'customary practices'. For the claim that is raised by the philosophical language games practised by Wittgenstein in the descriptive presentation of particular 'conventions' has to rise above the embedding of all language games in particular life forms and, to this extent, above the facticity and contingency of all language games and life forms and so express something that is universally valid. This unavoidable claim to universality can be rendered intelligible only in the following way, one that seeks to analyse the function of the philosophical language game in strict reflection[41] upon what one does and presupposes as a philosopher, with the description of particular language games and life forms. Such a methodological claim would however, at least for the post-*Tractatus* Wittgenstein, be taboo – as though, for the pragmatic language-game analysis, the view oriented towards the semantics of the statement were still true, the view, namely, that any actual reflection upon language has to lead to semantic antinomies.[42]

A radically pragmatic questioning of the semantic paradigm, of the kind introduced by Wittgenstein in his language-game theory, leads however to the conclusion that the pragmatic function of language games must also be analysed, which means suspending the semantically oriented prohibition against the self-reference of the speech act. Only in this way does one find oneself in a position to recognize the denial of the specifically philosophical claim to universality as a performative contradiction and, to this extent, as self-suspension of the philosophical language game.[43]

As things stand today, Wittgenstein's one-sided and unsatisfactory thematization of the philosophical language game – just as Heidegger's one-sided (forgetfulness of the *logos*) analysis of the facticity of being-in-the-world (as a historically 'thrown projection') – has tended to promote a very general confusion concerning the self-understanding of philosophy and to provoke an era of pragmatically inconsistent philosophical statements. I would like to support this with reference to two famous Wittgensteinian theses: the argument against the possibility of a 'private language' and the argument against the possibility of universal doubt in *On Certainty*.

In both cases I am deeply indebted to Wittgenstein's theses. And I would here like to interpret these theses in a transcendentally pragmatic fashion – as I have attempted to do elsewhere.[44] What does this mean?

In the case of the argument against the possibility of a private language, the emphasis should be placed on two points. First, it is not possible to talk meaningfully about a person S following a rule – for example, speaking a language – if it is not in principle possible for other subjects – for a community – to control the following of the rule on the basis of public criteria which make it possible for them too to follow the rule, for instance, to enter into communicative relations with the person S. Second, in addition, the following must also be emphasized. The person S – for example the speaker S – must link up with an already existing procedure for rule-following – for example an actual language usage. To this extent, one might say, S is in fact subjected to a factical *a priori* and to historicality.

These two requirements can be grounded in a pragmatically transcendental manner. Their rejection through arguments which must be capable of eliciting acceptance must lead to a performative contradiction in the argumentative procedure. The latter could not of itself avoid the objection of having, in the course of his or her argumentative procedure, followed a rule which is in principle private. For in that case he or she would have suspended the language game of arguing – rather like the one who says (or thinks): 'Perhaps I am always dreaming.'

So far, so good. But the difficulties with Wittgenstein's argumentative procedures begin when one asks with him the question who – on the basis of what criterion – decides whether a rule – for example addition in arithmetic – has been followed correctly. Two possible answers for Wittgenstein can be distinguished here, even though both will have to be rejected in the end.

First, the possibility of recurring to the remembered rule-following intentions of individual subjects as the actual states of a possible inner experience. Here Wittgenstein can quite appropriately object that in inner experience no distinction can be established between following the rule correctly and thinking that one has followed the rule correctly. The last of these alternatives can only be subjective, as I pointed out earlier.

Second, for Wittgenstein the possibility is also excluded of positing the criterion of validity for following rules with Plato or Frege – or with Karl Popper – as the ideal content of a third world (beyond the material outer world and the subjective world of inner experience). Wittgenstein is always able to object to such a rule-determining Platonism[45] that it is by no means clear how the individual subjects of the rule-following procedure are going to relate or be referred to this ideal criterion without once again recurring to the purely subjective evidence of their inner experience. They cannot have recourse to the ideal rule-following criterion in the same way that one has recourse to a public timetable.

If things are like this, however, then what remains of the possible criterion for correct rule-following? Painfully tedious passages in the *Philosophical Investigations* and in the *Remarks on the Foundations of*

Mathematics are devoted to thought experiments which show, over and over again, that a rule – for example addition – could be followed quite differently from the way that is normally supposed and that these discrepant rule-following procedures cannot be excluded on the grounds that we would be referred to a mental fact pertaining to the intention to follow a rule. How then is it going to be possible to distinguish between 'right' and 'wrong'?

Wolfgang Stegmüller has characterized the calling into question of 'rule Platonism' by Wittgenstein as follows: Wittgenstein rejects even that objectivity which is recognized by mathematical intuitionism. In Wittgenstein's sense one could say:

> that, in so far as we have explained the meaning of a logical expression by means of a convention, we should think that such and such must now be recognized as a logical truth or as a logical inference – *this is* once again simply a new form of the Platonic myth . . . It is the belief in a logical 'must', in a logical necessity which forces us even if only in the form of the binding consequences of specific assertions.[46]

If however we are serious about letting go of these presuppositions, what possible meaning can it then have to raise questions about the problem of 'rule Platonism' on the plane of philosophical discourse? Surely, at least on this plane, are we not assuming the 'unconstrained constraint' (Habermas) of arguments as an ineradicable element?

As a matter of fact it seems to me that Wittgenstein's point does not consist in saying that I can decide *ad hoc* that 'this sentence or that relation has to be regarded as irrefutable, so that nothing could count as an objection' (Stegmüller), even though it must be conceded that the non-necessity of the criteria of rule-following can be rendered intelligible in the light of 'rule Platonism' in the sense of decisionism. But then in what, according to Wittgenstein, is the non-arbitrary basis of the 'criterion' of rule-following – for example linguistic usage – supposed to consist?

It seems to me that no other answer can be found in Wittgenstein's work than a reference to actual rule-following customs in actual situations in an actual rule-following community – in the same way as his theory of meaning relies, in the final analysis, upon actual linguistic usages under pragmatically determined circumstances. This is, or so it seems, the sense in which such typically obstinate expressions of later Wittgenstein in the *Philosophical Inves-tigations* are to be understood: 'this language game is played' (1, § 654); 'this is simply what I do', or more explicitly: 'If I have ex-hausted the justifications I have reached the bedrock, and my spade is turned. Then I am inclined to say: "this is simply what I do"' (1, § 217). And finally: 'What has to be accepted, the given is – so one could say – forms of life' (2, § 226).

If one takes these communications as ultimate answers, a whole series of difficult questions immediately arises. What happens with innovations in the rule-following procedure – in the context of scientific progress, for instance, or in an ethical or political context? Is it its correspondence with the actually existing usages of a commu-nity which provides the criterion for establishing a consensus over the right way to follow a rule or even over which rule or norm should be followed? Charles Peirce called this the 'method of author-ity', a method which is superseded by philosophy and science.[47] Or should the answer to our question even lie in Wittgenstein's talk about learning through a 'training' (or drill) by way of a 'blind' following of rules? It seems to me that this affirmation of Wittgenstein's can mean only that the learning of rules by children cannot begin with an interpretation (and the equivocation which belongs thereto) since the field for possible rule interpretations is in principle unlimited and therefore does not lend itself to 'usages' which could be adopted along these lines. In my opinion, on the Wittgensteinian assumption of a learning through 'training' it is simply not explicable how human children, as distinct from animals, are able to develop a capacity for interpreting and reflecting upon rules which manifests itself in a communicative competence that is not tied down to the linguistic competence of using one's mother language, but consists, for example, in an ability to translate out of one language into another.

The following question, a question which moves beyond the conception of the learning of rule-following, in the sense of the following of an already existing usage, seems to me to be decisive: is it possible for Wittgenstein to argue that an individual (for example, a scientist or a philosopher or a reformer of customary practices) might be right against everyone else and might be capable of con-vincing them that his or her own conception of rule-following is the right one in cases where a dispute arises concerning the right way of following a rule or even concerning the right rule? Unless one is going to observe and describe language games behaviouristically from the outside rather than as intelligible components of a cultural reality in which the describer must be capable of participating, the latter must be possible. And then it is going to be necessary to allow for a relation of reciprocity between a rule-following community and an innovator of new rule-following procedures or between the former and the philosopher who describes language games and life forms. In which case the same problem arises anew: on the basis of what criterion can one or should one arrive at a consensus over the right rule-following procedure?

Faced with this situation I have, with Charles Peirce, J. Royce and G.H. Mead, fallen back upon the normative conception of an ideal consensus to be established within an ideal and unlimited communicative community, that is, upon the conception of a regulative Idea regarding the building-up of a consensus concerning rule-following. In this connection the latter also leads to a regulative Idea regarding the normatively correct meaning of concepts (as for example over the simultaneity of two events or over justice or truth) which, in accordance with the 'pragmatic maxim' of Peirce, has to be tried out first in thought experiments and therefore does not have to be reducible to actually existing linguistic usage even though it has to stand in relation to the latter. So it has to be emphasized that there would also have to be publicly accessible criteria for the establishment of a consensus in any post-conventional situation in which a consensus had to be established (experimental evidence, logical coherence and incoherence or even requirements or interests which could be transformed into morally valid claims), and this whether we are talking about scientific language rulings or extensions of knowledge or a matter of the practical founding or application of norms. Such criteria would never be sufficient in themselves to build up a consensus. However, in the context of an experience which could be brought under the regulative principle of an ideal consensus, they could furnish the basis for a preliminary consensus, as also for a calling in question of any actual consensus with a view to arriving at a better solution to relevant problems.[48]

But this transcendentally pragmatic way out seems in the end not to be reconcilable with Wittgenstein's suggestions. In any case this is the impression one gets when one tries to understand the convergence between the historical efficacy of Wittgenstein's thinking and the American neo-pragmatism of our time. Richard Rorty has done us the service of openly drawing all those radically re-lativistic and historically bound consequences of the thinking of Wittgenstein and Heidegger, which consequences are ordinarily only drawn in a marginal way. I mean such consequences as the denial of all universal (and if possible also transcendentally founded) criteria of philosophical discourse and also the ethically relevant thesis with regard to the necessity of falling back upon the only available basis for a consensus, namely, that of a contingent life form, for example the political and cultural tradition of America.[49] Fortunately, it is a matter here of a tradition which, in distinction from the politico-cultural tradition of the Nazis in Germany, itself goes back to an institutional foundation which has not betrayed its philosophical legitimation with reference to universally valid principles, those of human rights. In this way Rorty is able to avoid the philosophical call to universal criteria of rectitude with reference to a political alle-giance to rights already institutionalized in the American constitu-tion: with the result that only the pragmatic inconsistency of the philosophical thesis – itself obviously claiming universal validity – that in a philosophical discussion one can only fall back upon a contingent basis for establishing a consensus remains indicative of the paradox inherent in this understanding of Wittgenstein.

The paradox of an understanding of Wittgenstein which relies upon an actual 'usage', for example a 'life form', which is even more crass than that of Rorty is to be found in the Norwegian philosopher Viggo Rossvaer. For the latter has advanced the thesis that one can see – in so far as one has been taught to see by Wittgenstein – that in a certain sense even the SS in Auschwitz could have been observing the 'categorical imperative'.[50] This argument is supported by the claim that Wittgenstein has shown that the concept of a rule be-comes meaningful only in conjunction with the appropriate app-lication within the context of an actual life form; to elaborate: the meaning of a rule is not given in a counterfactual anticipation of a possible practice which can be represented as the correct application of the rule in Peirce's sense.

It is perfectly obvious that the understanding of Wittgenstein illustrated above actually operates a suspension of the good sense of anything that might be called a rule – and especially any meaningful moral norm. For the latter are clearly only there – at least upon the plane of a post-conventional human culture – to provide a point of orientation for the practice, and that means calling forth in advance and legitimizing a comportment in conformity with the rule through an application appropriate to the situation. One often has the impression with Wittgenstein that the post-conventional function of rules and norms has to be traced back to just such conventions and usages which always already preclude any possible explication and justification of the normative meaning of rules. And this fits in well with the conservative and populist tendency (inherent in the idea of a therapeutic philosophy) to suppose that in the lifeworld prior to philosophical clarification and its artificially constructed and so irresolvable pseudo-problems everything is already in order, both with respect to language usages which are intricately bound up with a life *praxis* as also with respect to what Hegel would have called 'naively substantialized moral conventions'.[51]

It is admittedly – perhaps – possible to interpret the ultimacy Wittgenstein attributes to language games (or the practice of a life form which upholds them) in another sense. And this second interpretation can, in particular, be supported by the last writings *On Certainty* where statements can be found such as the following:

> Any proof, any validation or invalidation of a claim already takes place within a system. This system is not a more or less arbitrary and dubious starting point for all our reasonings. Rather it belongs to the very essence of what we call an argument. The system is not so much the point of departure as rather the vital element of the argument. (aphorism 105)

Here it is once again pertinent to think about a transcendental-pragmatic interpretation of the impossibility of going beyond or behind the language games constitutive of philosophical argumentation, and in particular the paradigmatic certainty of those presuppositions whose denial inevitably leads to the suspension of the philosophical language game. As a matter of fact, interpretations are to be found which do adhere to such a conception.[52] However, it seems to me today that they cannot be presented as Wittgensteinian interpretations, for the simple reason that Wittgenstein never reflected upon (and indeed never noticed) the difference in principle between those life forms which are always presented in the plural and so as already contingently relativized and the discursive language game of philosophy itself in which a relativization of the many contingent life forms, together with that paradigmatic certainty which belongs to them, can be carried through. It is therefore more plausible to conclude with Peter Strawson that Wittgenstein's argumentative procedure in *On Certainty* is to be understood as 'soft naturalism' and, to this extent, as the detranscendentalized substitute for the foundational claims of transcendental argumentation.[53] The point would then be the following: that in place of the foundational claims of transcendental philosophy it would become apparent that it is simply unavoidable that certain presuppositions of the argumentative procedure (together with the life *praxis* that goes along with them) should be presented as certain.

Many people today would be pleased with this. They would like to see an alternative to a transcendentally pragmatic foundation for philosophy – even for ethics. However it does seem to me that, with Strawson (who has given his assent to this view), the decisive objection against such a substitution thesis has been voiced. For any philosophy which adopts a practical standpoint the task remains of distinguishing between the universally valid presuppositions of its critically reflective language game – the argumentative discourse – and the purely contingent, historically conditioned presuppositions which make up the background of the lifeworld, that is of the many and various life forms.

But for those who in a certain sense belong to a given life form (e.g. a given language game) the latter would also furnish an ultimate bedrock. To be sure it is only in a historically factual sense (in Collingwood's sense) that they are ultimate. On the other hand, since the philosophical enlightenment in Greece and again in modern times, they are already relativized by philosophical discourse as non-ultimate. Only those presuppositions – presuppositions of the entire argumentative procedure – are in a strict and methodologically relevant sense ultimate which function in the self-reflective language game of philosophy as conditions of the possibility of the relativization of all specific life forms and which, in so far as they must still be presupposed, cannot be challenged along with the condemnation of the performative contradiction involved in philosophical argumentation; as, for example, the presupposition that in any argumentative discourse a whole series of claims to validity are always going to make themselves known, and amongst these are the universal claims to validity and consensual legitimacy of certain basic moral norms.[54]

It is easy to see today that it is no longer possible to found a concrete life form (e.g. some form of customary morality in Hegel's sense or even any recommendation for the individual realization of the good life) on the basis of such universally valid presuppositions of philosophical discourse alone. The only ultimately founded and universally valid discursive principles are those which are formal and procedural, which, as such, moreover establish limiting conditions for the complementary task of realizing the good life with respect to concrete, historically evolved life forms. On the basis of this complementarity thesis, a tendency inspired by Wittgenstein and/or Heidegger, a tendency shared by so many contemporary philosophers such as Winch, the later Rawls, Rorty, Williams and MacIntyre, a tendency which consists in understanding moral norms simply as the reflective convictions of a historically contingent life form, this tendency not merely becomes intelligible but begins to betray its limitations.

What seems to me to be decisive here is the assumption of the unavoidable complementarity of the ultimate presuppositions of philosophical discourse, on the one hand, and the contingent presuppositions which lie at the root of concrete life forms, on the other. From the standpoint of the philosophical presuppositions of Wittgenstein and Heidegger such an assumption does not seem to me to be possible. In both cases it is obstructed by a certain forgetfulness of the *logos*, that is, a reflective deficiency with regard to their own intellectual and argumentative presuppositions. With Wittgenstein this leads quite obviously to a tendency to confuse his own philosophical language game with the descriptively objectifiable and, at the same time, contingently relativized language games – together with the concrete life forms which underline them. With Heidegger it leads to a deliberate overstepping of the philosophically universal validation of his own claims in favour of a hermeneutics of the facticity of understanding being-in-the-world; and this means in *Being and Time* the temporality and historicality of 'thrown projection'. In the late work it goes even further in the direction of a total historicism, a reduction of the philosophical *logos* itself to an epochal event in the history of being. As was mentioned earlier, so-called postmodernism latches on at this point to a thinking which starts out from the standpoint of an 'alternative to reason'.

I hardly need to emphasize that I find in this outcome of the historical impact of two outstanding thinkers of this century the signs of a dangerous crisis in philosophy. Instead of moving towards a critique of meaning and a hermeneutical clarification of the presuppositions of philosophical and scientific thinking that would deepen and complete the previous phases of philosophical enlightenment and critical thinking, we seem to be moving towards a paralysis of post-conventional reason. The reflective concern for the rationality of argumentative discourse, a concern which lies at the root of both philosophy and science and which even today still links them together, this concern is (to the extent that there is any awareness of it left at all) understood to be just a reflex reaction left over from a contingent 'usage' or a hangover from a 'metaphysical' epoch in the history of being. 'What people accept as a justification – is shown by how they think and live.'[55] Indeed!

Notes

First published in C. Macann (ed.), *Martin Heidegger: Critical Assessments*, vol. 3 (London: Routledge, 1992), 341–74.

1 K.O. Apel, *Transformation der Philosophie* (Frankfurt a. M.: Suhrkamp, 1973), vol. 2, part 2.
2 *Ibid.*, 247 ff., 269 f., 272 ff.
3 Apel, 'Die Herausforderung der totalen Vernunftkritik und das Programm einer philosophischen Theorie der Rationalitätstypen', *Concordia*, 11 (1987), 2–23.
4 L. Wittgenstein, *Philosophical Investigations* (Oxford: Basil Blackwell, 1958), 1, §§ 138–242, also §§ 243–363.
5 *Ibid.*, § 265.
6 *Ibid.*, § 202.
7 L. Wittgenstein, *Über Gewissheit/On Certainty*, trans. G.E.M. Anscombe and G.H. von Wright (Oxford: Blackwell, 1969).
8 P.F. Strawson, *The Bounds of Sense* (London: Methuen, 1966), 125 ff.
9 *Ibid.*, 247 ff.
10 E.K. Specht, *Der Analogiebegriff bei Kant und Hegel*, Kantstudien, Ergänzungs-Hefte, 55 (1952).
11 M. Heidegger, *Sein und Zeit* (Halle: Niemeyer, 1941), trans. John Macquarrie and Edward Robinson as *Being and Time* (New York: Harper & Row, 1962), 213 (169) (German page numbers in parentheses).
12 *Ibid.*, 207 (163).
13 *Ibid.*, § 26.
14 *Ibid.*, 248 (204 ff.).
15 See I. Kant, *Kritik der reinen Vernunft*, trans. Norman Kemp-Smith as *The Critique of Pure Reason* (London: Macmillan, 1929), B 275, p. 244.
16 M. Heidegger, *Being and Time*, 249 (205).
17 *Ibid.*, 160 (123).
18 *Ibid.*, 162 (125).
19 *Ibid.*, 119 (86).
20 *Ibid.*, 201 (158).
21 L. Wittgenstein, *Philosophical Investigations*, 1, §§ 1–60. Later references are given in parentheses in the text.

22 M. Heidegger, *Being and Time*, 105 (75), 147 (112) 190 (149).
23 Erich Rothacker, *Zur Genealogie des menschlichen Bewusstseins* (Bonn: Bouvier, 1966).
24 G. Böhme (ed.), *Protophysik* (Frankfurt a. M.: Suhrkamp, 1976).
25 G.H. von Wright, *Explanation and Understanding* (Ithaca, N.Y.: Cornell University Press, 1971), chapter 2; also Apel, *Die Erklären/Verstehen-Kontroverse in transzendentalpragmatischer Sicht* (Frankfurt a. M.: Suhrkamp, 1979), trans. G. Warnke as *Understanding and Explanation: A Transcendental-pragmatic Perspective* (Cambridge, Mass.: MIT Press, 1984), 57 ff. and 83 ff.
26 M. Heidegger, 'Die Frage nach der Technik', in *Vorträge und Aufsätze* (Pfullingen, 1954).
27 M. Heidegger, *Being and Time*, 272 (229).
28 *Ibid.*, 269 (226).
29 Apel, 'Sinnkonstitution und Geltungsrechtfertigung: Heidegger und das Problem der "Transzendentalphilosophie"', in Forum für Philosophie Bad Homburg (ed.), *Martin Heidegger: Innen- und Aussenansichten* (Frankfurt a. M.: Suhrkamp, 1989), 131–75; abridged English translation: Chapter 5 above.
30 R. Rorty, *Consequences of Pragmatism* (Brighton: Harvester Press, 1982).
31 Apel, *Der Denkweg von Charles Sanders Peirce: eine Einführung in den amerikanischen Pragmatismus* (Frankfurt a. M.: Suhrkamp, 1975).
32 E. Husserl, *Die Krisis der europäischen Wissenschaften und die transzendentale Phänomenologie*; English translation: *The Crisis of European Sciences and Transcendental Phenomenology*, trans. David Carr (Evanston, Ill.: Northwestern University Press, 1970).
33 T.S. Kuhn, *The Structure of Scientific Revolutions* (Chicago: University of Chicago Press, 1962).
34 Cf. Wittgenstein, *Philosophical Investigations*, 1, §§ 133, 255, 309.
35 M. Masterman, 'The Nature of Paradigm', in I. Lakatos and A. Musgrave (eds), *Criticism and the Growth of Knowledge* (Cambridge: Cambridge University Press, 1970), 59–89.
36 L. Wittgenstein, *Schriften* (Frankfurt a. M.: Suhrkamp, 1960–), vol. 1, 536.
37 This is the sense in which Peter Winch first interpreted Wittgenstein's philosophy. See *The Idea of a Social Science and its Relation to Philosophy* (London: Routledge & Kegan Paul, 1958).
38 M. Heidegger, *Zur Sache des Denkens* (Tübingen: Mohr, 1969), 76 ff.
39 H.-G. Gadamer, *Wahrheit und Methode* (Tübingen: Mohr, 1960), 344 ff.
40 B.L. Whorf, *Sprache, Denken, Wirklichkeit* (Reinbeck: Rowolt, 1963). Also H. Gipper, *Gibt es ein sprachliches Relativitätsprinzip?* (Frankfurt a. M.: Fischer, 1972).
41 W. Kuhlmann, 'Reflexive Leztbegründung: zur These von der Unhintergehbarkeit der Argumentationssituation', *Zeitschrift für Philosophische Forschung*, 35 (1981), 2–26.
42 It should not be overlooked that the penetrating distinction made in the *Tractatus* between what can be said and what can only be shown – the logical form of language and of the world – relies upon a transcendental and mystico-metaphysical transformation of Russell's theory of types. In the paradox of the self-suspension of the *Tractatus* only the pragmatic inconsistency – the performative self-contradiction – of the theory of types is reproduced, an inconsistency which can now be reformulated in a meta-language which could not have been foreseen and which holds for all signs.
43 Apel, 'Fallibilismus, Konsenstheorie der Wahrheit und Letztbegründung', in

Forum für Philosophie Bad Homburg (ed.), *Philosophie und Begründung* (Frankfurt a. M.: Suhrkamp, 1987), 116–211, 130 ff., 174 ff.

44 Apel, 'Das Problem der philosophischen Letztbegründung im Lichte einer transcendentalen Sprachpragmatik', in B. Kanitschneider (ed.), *Sprache und Erkenntnis* (Innsbruck, 1976), 55–82; trans. as 'The Problem of Philosophical Fundamental Grounding in Light of a Transcendental-Pragmatic of Language', *Man and World*, 8, 3 (1975), 239–75, repr. in K. Baynes, J. Bohman and T.A. McCarthy (eds), *After Philosophy: End or Transformation?* (Cambridge, Mass.: MIT Press, 1987), 250–90.

45 W. Stegmüller's reconstruction of Wittgenstein's 'philosophy of logic and mathematics', in *Hauptströmungen der Gegenwartsphilosophie* (Stuttgart: Kroner, 1969), 673 ff.

46 *Ibid.*, 685 ff.

47 C.S. Peirce, *Collected Papers*, ed. C. Hartshorne and R. Weiss (Cambridge, Mass.: Harvard University Press, 1931–5), vol. 5, §§ 58–387.

48 Cf. here my work cited in note 43; also 'Linguistic Meaning and Intentionality: the Compatibility of the "Linguistic Turn" and the "Pragmatic Turn" of Meaning-theory within the Framework of a Transcendental Semiotics', in H.J. Silverman and D. Welton (eds), *Critical and Dialectical Phenomenology* (Albany: State University of New York Press, 1987), 2–53.

49 R. Rorty, 'The Priority of Democracy to Philosophy', in M. Peterson and R. Vaughan (eds), *The Virginia Statute of Religious Freedom* (Cambridge, Mass.: MIT Press, 1987), and Rorty, 'Pragmatism and Philosophy', in Baynes *et al.* (eds), *After Philosophy*, 26–66. Cf. also my argument with Rorty in Apel, *Diskurs und Verantwortung* (Frankfurt a. M.: Surhkamp, 1988), 394 ff.

50 V. Rossvaer, 'Transzendentalpragmatik, transzendentale Hermeneutik und die Möglichkeit, Auschwitz zu verstehen', in D. Bohler, T. Nordenstam and G. Skirbekk (eds), *Die pragmatische Wende* (Frankfurt a. M.: Suhrkamp, 1986), 187–201.

51 In my paper 'Wittgenstein und das Problem des hermeneutischen Verstehens' (1966), repr. in *Towards a Transformation of Philosophy* (London: Routledge & Kegan Paul, 1980), I have already advanced the thesis that late Dilthey's distinction between 'pragmatic' and 'methodological-hermeneutical understanding' opened the way for an important critical re-evaluation of Wittgenstein's contribution to the theory of understanding. Today I would want to give this point even greater emphasis, as follows. Wittgenstein's clarification of understanding seems to reach just as far as Dilthey's concept of 'pragmatic understanding', for which Dilthey, just like Wittgenstein, adopted as his criterion of validation factical agreement in a comportmental *praxis* (e.g. in a 'common sphere' of work). According to Dilthey, however, the conditions of the possibility and the criteria of validity are precisely not made available in this way for a – I would like to say post-conventional, e.g. post-traditionalist – 'methodological understanding' of 'hermeneutics', for instance for the understanding of foreign cultures or documents stemming from one's own culture from which one has become estranged. Here, where the hermeneutical reflection upon Enlightenment culture took its start, it is not possible to adopt the factical agreement in comportmental *praxis* as a sufficient criterion for reciprocal understanding (otherwise it would have to be admitted that the members of a particular community understood each other better in every respect than any re-

searcher could ever possibly do). Worse, it cannot even be assumed that the methodologico-hermeneutical understanding of a foreign life form (at the limit, the quasi-hermeneutical understanding of the behaviour of a pride of lions which does not even assume that the lions are capable of language!) suffices for a clear recognition of any such factical agreement with the comportmental *praxis* of the life form in question (this would exclude a critical understanding from the very outset). In any case, this post-conventional, critically hermeneutical understanding would have to recognize a counterfactual ideal for the communicative understanding of differing forms of *praxis* in an ideal 'interpretative community' (J. Royce). Moreover, in the course of a hermeneutical discussion with the representatives of other life forms, it would also have to be assumed that there existed succinct agreement with regard to the normative conditions for an understanding of the differences implicit in the life form. Cf. here also Apel, 'Szientismus oder transzendentale Hermeneutik?', *Transformation der Philosophie* (Frankfurt a. M.: Suhrkamp, 1973), vol. 2, 178–219.

52 Cf. for example my paper cited in note 44.

53 Cf. P. Strawson, *Scepticism and Naturalism: Some Varieties* (London: Methuen, 1985); also the excellent work of M. Niquet, *Transzendentale Sinnkritik: Untersuchungen zum Problem transzendentaler Argumente* (Frankfurt a. M.: Suhrkamp, 1991).

54 J. Habermas, *Theorie des Kommunikativen Handelns* (Frankfurt a. M.: Suhrkamp, 1981), vols 1–3, and also *Moralbewusstsein und Kommunkatives Handeln* (Frankfurt a. M.: Suhrkamp, 1983). I have to admit I am concerned by the proposal (inspired by Wittgenstein) for a solution to the problem on p. 198 of the last-mentioned work. Cf. here Apel, 'Normative Begründung der "Kritschen Theorie" durch Rekurs auf lebensweltliche Sittlichkeit? Ein transzendental pragmatisch orientierte Versuch, mit Habermas gegen Habermas zu denken', in A. Honneth (ed.), *Zwischenbetrachtungen: Festschrift für J. Habermas* (Frankfurt a. M.: Suhrkamp, 1989), 15–65; English translation: *Cultural-Political Interventions in the Unfinished Project of Enlightenment* and *Philosophical Interventions in the Unfinished Project of Enlightenment* (Cambridge, Mass.: MIT Press, 1992).

55 Wittgenstein, *Philosophical Investigations*, 1, § 325.

7

Regulative ideas or sense events?
An attempt to determine the *logos*
of hermeneutics

translated by DALE SNOW

Introduction

The question of the relation between hermeneutics and practical philosophy is one which presents a challenge for the contemporary philosophical situation. This way of posing the problem provides one of the two stimuli for my attempt to determine the *logos* of hermeneutics. The other resides in the fact that in contemporary philosophy a tendency has persisted for quite some time to define the internal relationship between hermeneutics and practical reason in such a way that one is no longer able to identify (the element of) practical *reason* therein.

The difficulty is already apparent, for example, in view of the following suggestion: on the one hand, the hermeneutic understanding is to be grasped from the pre-scientific connection of communicative agreement in dialogue;[1] on the other hand, as a 'sense event' that is 'transmitted by tradition' through a 'fusion of horizons', which 'plays itself out' – a cosmic event in nature – in such a way that, in the end, there will be no more point to assuming a regulative principle of a deeper or better understanding. Instead one must come to terms with the fact that, especially when the interpreter can use the 'temporal distance' between himself or herself and the *interpretandum* in the sense of a 'historically effective consciousness', one can always achieve only a 'different understanding'.[2] This is supposed to be the case because the existential fore-structure of understanding is determined through a pre-understanding of the world and by 'prejudices' which can never be fully taken into account by the critical consciousness of the interpreter. For in the end, temporal being, which rules the interpreter, is more powerful than his or her critical consciousness. So, as is well known, Hans-Georg

Gadamer argues in his grounding of hermeneutics, inspired by Heidegger, in *Truth and Method*.

Already in view of this surrender of the regulative idea of a possible progress in understanding – and that means also in the judgement of related validity claims in communicative agreement – it is difficult to establish the simultaneously maintained internal connection of hermeneutics to practical philosophy and thus to ethics and to an ethically understood politics. For is it then supposed to be possible to uncouple ethics from the claim, indeed from the responsibility to a binding judgement, for example, of normative claims to validity? And does not the impossibility of this uncoupling imply that progress in understanding a judgement's claim to truth and of normative, finally moral, claims to rightness must be held to be possible in principle?

It should be emphasized that of course it is not necessary to hold that the history of the world or of humanity has a 'necessary path' or must be conceived of or prophesied as a causal or teleologically determined process. This *meta-récit* of modernity (Lyotard) as deployed by Hegel, Comte or Marx may well be declared to be dead.[3] But before this *hubris* on the part of reason arose, Kant had introduced an entirely different concept of progress. He had, as befitting the subject at hand, already established that it is our moral duty to hold a morally relevant progress of humanity to be, at least in principle, possible and, in an attitude resisting, so to speak, frustration, to reconstruct history again and again such that its practical continuation from a moral perspective can appear to be possible.[4] A post-Heideggerian or post-Gadamerian hermeneutic must hold this morally grounded idea of a practical progress, (one) which would be internally related to a progress in understanding, also to be a *meta-récit* of modernity which, in the meantime, has died! What would then still remain?

Gadamer at least does not wish to give up the idea of moral obligation. For him and his German followers there still remains a neo-Aristotelian ethic with neo-pragmatic and Wittgensteinian undertones. In its name one could explain how there still can be an ethic of *phronesis* and of the commonly accepted (Wittgenstein would say: the 'practices' of a 'life form', which determine respectively the language game and to that extent also the fore-structure of our pre-understanding of the world), even if there can be no ethic with a claim to universal validity and thus a claim to ground the progress of

humanity. In this sense Gadamer would continue to hold the obligation of a contemporary valid understanding for us (for whom?) to be
possible, a hermeneutic, so to speak, whose internal connection with
practical reason should be uncoupled from the regulative idea of a
universally valid progress in understanding and judgements of claims
to validity.

It is in this apparently moderate direction of the 'hermeneutic-
pragmatic' turn that something of a liberal-conservative synthesis
seems to be emerging in Germany and the Anglo-Saxon countries
today.[5] For me this synthesis would be, as I have already indicated,
no longer acceptable either as a basis for a hermeneutic or as a
basis for an ethic. The reasons for this disapproval will be laid out
later, but in the present connection I can already hint at them by
referring to the radicalization of the post-Heideggerian hermeneutic
by some postmodernists. What is their situation with respect to
the internal relationship between hermeneutics and practical
philosophy?

The first thing to be noted about those postmodernists who rely
upon Heidegger and Nietzsche is a subversive style which cannot be
rendered compatible with Gadamer's conservatism which ties
hermeneutics to the received tradition – and to that extent also to
Plato and Kant. This becomes clear in the latest discussion between
Gadamer and Derrida in Paris in 1981.[6] Like the later Heidegger,
Derrida wants to give up ties to the received tradition of Western
metaphysics and also the connection to *logos* and therewith, consistently, even ties to the discipline of hermeneutics. Here, apparently,
the concern is no longer with 'interpretation' at all, let alone with a
'holding in validity' (*in Geltung halten* – Gadamer), but rather with
'deconstruction' in an extension of that which Heidegger – still in the
name of an existential hermeneutics – called 'destruction' of traditional ontology.[7]

Heidegger demands that we should 'think' the meaning of Being
that, owing to the ontic-ontological difference, escapes from us in the
'event' of the 'clearing–concealing' (*lichtend–verbergenden*) disclosure
of world meaning – finally thinking this meaning of temporal Being
in its difference from the entity (*Seienden*), and from the abstract
'entity-ness' (*Seiendheit*). But even this demand, like the demand of
a hermeneutic of Being by Derrida's deconstruction, would aspire
only to question meaning as still being a product of the concealed
will to 'logocentric metaphysics' – the will to the presence of the

signifié. This is supposed to be achieved with the help, so to speak, of a post-structuralist semiotic of the infinite 'play' of 'difference', which sets free the symbolic sense, but at the same time 'displaces' it, so that only the infinite play of the 'dissemination' of the signifiers remains for us – the always fruitless attempt, as it were, to discover and root out the 'trace' of the transcendental *significatum* – in search of the 'archi-*écriture*' in the *écriture* that for its part takes the place of the presence of the world.

Where, in this case, could the normative obligation of symbolic sense and its internal connection to practical philosophy lie – if we assume that this question or its formulation were not also to be deconstructed? It would seem that according to Derrida there remains only the leap, the 'rupture', in the attempt to understand the claim of a foreign symbolic sense and – as an equivalent for the inter-subjectively binding character of meaning – the aesthetic suggestion of the 'grand style', which manifests itself in Nietzsche as will to power.[8]

For Heidegger himself there remained the quasi-norm of the 'event', the 'consignment' (*Zuschickung*) of Being in 'the fate of Being' (*Seingeschick*), once he distanced himself from the brutality of the will to power as being itself grounded in the metaphysics of subjectivity. However, we can no more speak here of normative bindingness in the sense of practical reason than we can for Nietzsche's posing of values through the will to power. And through even more careful consideration it can be seen that for the late Heidegger, just as in *Being and Time*, the *logos* of an inter-subjectively valid understanding and claims to validity of normative judgements are replaced by the immediate connection of the 'conscience' to the 'silent voice of Being'. Essential to this thought from the beginning is the questioning of the *logos* of inter-subjective validity through temporal Being. It, and not some kind of principle of reason, is what the human being must 'correspond' to, whether it is in the project (*Entwurf*) of one's own Being or in the grasping of the *kairos* – thus 1933 – or finally in 'devotion' with respect to the 'fate of Being'. The ultimate result of this kind of thinking is the suspicion that the *logos* of philosophy, reason, is to be thought of as itself an epochal event in the history of Being – that is, in the revealing–concealing temporalization (*Zeitigung*) of Being.

How is this challenge to be met? How can one pronounce as valid, or even be able to understand, the claim that reason, as principle of validity, it itself a contingent historical product, a function of time?

It seems that here reason, just as for Nietzsche in the end – from the standpoint of the 'other of reason' – must undergo a critique, not from the standpoint of the will to power but rather from the standpoint, so to speak, of temporal Being. And this paradox of a radical critique of reason, in which reason functions merely as object and no longer as subject of critique, has in the meantime established itself as one of the fundamental characteristics of postmodern thought.

In the light of these obvious paradoxes it can be seen that even Gadamer's apparently moderate hermeneutic has, regardless of its conservative attitude towards the tradition of metaphysics, already crossed the Rubicon of post-rational 'thought' – whatever that may be. For Gadamer too, along with the late Heidegger, wants the condition for the possibility of understanding – and, the Kantian formulation suggests, the condition also for the validity of understanding – to be seen only in the historicity of understanding; that is in the context-dependency of the always 'other (different) understanding'. Precisely in the admission of this dependency on history, not as a hindrance to objectivity but rather simply as a condition of the constitution of sense, does Gadamer want to see the overcoming of historicism, the overcoming of the difficulties in which Dilthey remained entangled because he held fast to the methodological ideal of objectivity.[9]

Gadamer does not deny the difficulties, even the paradoxical nature, of the solution to the historicity problem which he champions. On the contrary, he explicitly discusses this in *Truth and Method*, and this fact distinguishes him from the unconcerned – or rather, from the provocatively stylistically employed – irrationalism of deconstructionists. Gadamer takes on Hegel at a decisive point in his work: Hegel who, as Gadamer admits and even emphasizes, had thoroughly recognized the historicity of our thinking, but still wanted at the same time to 'mediate' it with the claim to the universal validity of thought. The uniqueness of Gadamer's assessment of Hegel consists, on the one hand, in his holding Hegel's 'absolute mediation of history and truth' for the unsurpassable position of reason to which there is no alternative, which from the standpoint of reflection is 'not to be overturned'. Yet, on the other hand, he is convinced that the actual truth is against it, that in the end the demand of the young Hegelians, Kierkegaard, Feuerbach and the young Marx for a self-overcoming of the philosophy which found its completion in Hegel was somehow justified.[10]

This uniquely ambivalent and finally unwarranted assessment of Hegel as the absolute mediator of *logos* and history makes it understandable, and even has as a necessary consequence, that Gadamer no longer holds a paradox-free solution to the historicity problem to be possible or even required on the level of argumentation. Since he sees the 'dialectical superiority of reflective philosophy' in Hegel as unsurpassable and formally irrefutable, he seeks a way out of the dilemma, to a certain extent, by hacking through the Gordian knot. He explains the dialectical superiority of reflective philosophy in general as simply a 'formal (false) appearance'.[11] This means that Gadamer now employs the reproach of 'sophistical' not only against Hegel but rather against all reflective philosophy, and at the same time employs mere hints about the factual success of the refuted opposing positions in history as, so to speak, arguments against the validity of arguments. With respect to the problem of historicity, that reads as follows:

> Heinrich Rickert, who in 1920 thoroughly refuted 'life philosophy' through argument, was unable to come anywhere near the influence of Nietzsche and Dilthey, which was beginning to grow at that time. However clearly one demonstrates the inner contradictions of all relativist views, it is as Heidegger has said: all these victorious arguments have something about them that suggests that they are attempting to bowl one over. However cogent they may seem they still miss the main point. In making use of them one is proved right yet they do not express any superior insight of any value. That the thesis of skepticism or relativism refutes itself to the extent that it claims to be true is an irrefutable argument. But what does it achieve? The reflective argument that proves successful here falls back on the arguer, in that it renders the truthfulness of all reflection suspect. It is not the reality of skepticism or of truth-dissolving relativism, but the claim to truth of all formal arguments that is affected.[12]

This appears to be, I must confess, a very peculiar argument for many reasons, of which I will mention here only the most important.

First, I wish to pose a general question: how could one know or how could one as a philosopher show that 'irrefutable arguments' fail to address the 'real problem'? Perhaps by a reference to the factual success of the refuted position; for example, by reference to the 'reality of skepticism or of truth-dissolving relativism'? But this seems to end in the capitulation of argumentative reason and to open the door to purely rhetorical persuasion and dogmatic assertion. Who at present would contest the victorious 'reality' of scepticism and relativism – if not nihilism? But should that bring to a halt every further discussion and render those assertions uncriticizable?

However, I would like to return from this general position to the concrete bone of contention of philosophical hermeneutics: how does Gadamer know that the refutation of relativism-historicism as a position that one cannot hold without self-contradiction *must* remain unfruitful and without consequences? The following conjecture might be expressed. Gadamer sees himself forced into this questionable verdict because he absolutizes certain historical paradigms of an apparently 'dialectically victorious' philosophy of reflection; for example, on the one hand, the Hegelian paradigm, not at all uncriticizable, of a speculative-dialectical, total or absolute mediation of history and truth, and, on the other, that of the neo-Kantians, a merely formal reflective philosophy which in fact does not take into account the moment of the historicity of knowledge recognized by Hegel.

Is it then the case, especially from the viewpoint of a philosophical hermeneutic, that there can be no alternative to these two versions of a 'reflective philosophy'? Is it settled that for us today only three alternatives are conceivable? There are three possibilities.

First, the attempt, with Hegel, to 'suspend' the historical relativity of knowledge by calling upon 'absolute knowledge', the divine standpoint, so to speak (or, as the case may be, the standpoint of the end of history).

Second, the attempt, with Kant, through purely formal reflection to maintain the claim to validity of knowledge, without taking the historical conditioning of the content of the 'pre-understanding' and 'prejudices' into account at all.

Third, the capitulation of self-consistent argumentation, which makes a virtue of the aporia of historicism-relativism and gives up all claims of philosophical arguments to universal validity, in that *logos* itself is understood as a contingent product of the history of Being.

The following will be an attempt to show that these three positions do not exhaust the possibilities of determination (or abandonment) of the *logos* of philosophy and especially of hermeneutics; rather, that it is possible to do justice to the historicity of understanding without giving up the universal claim to validity of knowledge in general and especially the claim to a progressively better or deeper understanding in the sense of a normative hermeneutic. Thereby it would also be shown – at least sketchily – that only a normatively oriented hermeneutic, one which holds a progress of understanding and judgements of claims to validity to be possible, can do justice – as Gadamer, among others, has maintained – to the internal relationship of hermeneutics with practical philosophy.

The *logos* of hermeneutics in the light of a transformed transcendental philosophy

Before undertaking to answer the questions which have been raised by these theses, I will make a few remarks about what should now be seen as uncontestable insights of the hermeneutic turn in contemporary philosophy, and about the transcendental-philosophical limitation of its scope. To this end a quasi-autobiographical retrospective will be offered as a beginning.

The insights of the 'hermeneutic turn' of contemporary philosophy and the transcendental-philosophical limitation of hermeneuticism

Since my dissertation on Heidegger I have followed the programme of a transformation of transcendental philosophy in the sense of an anthropology of knowledge and, soon thereafter, in the sense of a 'transcendental hermeneutic'.[13] In the beginning the emphasis on historicity, and in this sense the concrete dependence of thought on language, was entirely in the foreground, as for example in my book *The Concept of Language in the Humanist Tradition from Dante to Vico*.[14] After reading Gadamer's *Truth and Method*, however, I underwent a gradual shift of emphasis in favour of the transcendental-philosophical theme. And since the encounter with postmodernism, and especially with Rorty's programme of 'detranscendentalization',[15] I have been convinced of the necessity of a 'retranscendentalization'.

That does not mean, however, that the insights connected with post-Heideggerian hermeneutic thinking ought to or could be abandoned. I would like to refer to these insights here at least in outline, for I would like to make as clear as possible what need not be contentious in a dispute between the defenders of a 'retranscendentalization' and those of 'detranscendentalization'.

First, as has already been indicated, the insistence on consistently indisputable and therefore indispensable universal claims to the validity of argumentation does not mean that one must deny that the content of our knowledge – and thus also for example the hermeneutic understanding of texts – is always already predicated upon a 'pre-understanding', in which the historical embeddedness and the 'event' character of the understanding is manifested. Here it is rather the question about the methodologically relevant relationship of two moments which both determine the *logos* of hermeneutics: the historical conditioning on the one side and the claim to truth as a claim of universal validity on the other.

Second, the first to recognize this relationship and the necessity of a mediation of both moments was, in my view, Hegel. Yet he wanted to offer the concrete mediation as 'absolute'; that is, as a definitive mediation of the transcendental form and the historically conditioned content of understanding from the standpoint, as it were, of the '*ex-post*-reflection' at the end of all history: that is, as a systematic comprehension within the framework of speculative philosophy, and not merely as a philosophical grounding of a possible co-operation and complementing of philosophy and the specialized sciences of historical hermeneutics. In contrast to this, in my view, a philosophical hermeneutic must realize – and this, of course, with a universal claim to philosophical validity – that the concrete hermeneutic understanding, all empirical knowledge, must take its standpoint in the historical situation; and that means under the presupposition of the *a priori*s of facticity and of historicity (Heidegger).

Third, from this arises an alternative to the Hegelian mediation of form and content by speculative thought, namely the 'hermeneutic circle' as the basic model of all concrete, situation-dependent understanding. With Heidegger I can accept and even emphasize that no concrete understanding of the world can depend upon 'avoiding' this circle – the circle between the historically conditioned pre-understanding of the world and the corrective recoil function of the *interpretandum* – but that such understanding rather depends upon correctly 'entering into' the circle.[16] However, this knowledge of the philosophical hermeneutic can itself be expressed with a universal, that is transcendental, claim to validity. And it allows still another question to be added, which is to be answered at least partially in philosophically valid terms: how does one correctly enter the circle in the case of the critical-hermeneutical sciences?

Fourth, the addenda thus far articulated, aimed towards the recognition of the hermeneutic circle, indicate the central problem of transcendental hermeneutics or of a mediation between philosophical hermeneutics and concrete hermeneutical understanding. In the post-Heideggerian philosophy it appears that the virtually unreflective opinion has been formed that the affirmation of a hermeneutic circle, and on the other side the reliance on the universal validity of the transcendental presuppositions of argumentation, that is, of all thought, present irreconcilable paradigms of philosophy between which a choice must be made. But this can hardly be correct, if only because in that case one could not even refer to the insight into the unavoidability of the hermeneutic circle as a valid philosophical insight. But above and beyond that it is also possible to say something universally valid about the methodologically correct way to enter the hermeneutic circle. And it is only in this answer to a question dear to Heidegger's heart, yet not posed by him, that in the spirit of a transcendental hermeneutic the possibility of an alternative to Hegel's total mediation of the form and content of understanding must be demonstrated. I will return to this point below.

Fifth, if one were to acknowledge the programme of a co-operation and mutual complementarity of the (transcendental-) philosophical hermeneutic and the empirical-hermeneutical sciences, then disagreement should no longer be necessary about the fact that hermeneutical understanding – like all empirical knowledge – is incomplete and always falsifiable, thus fallible and open to revision. This is not to admit, contrary to current opinion, that there can be no infallible insights of a transcendental-philosophical hermeneutic. A fact that challenges this is that concepts like empirical testing, falsification, fallibility etc. are understandable to us *only* so long as certain implied presuppositions are held to be universally valid: for example, that there is truth and that we, on the path of the elimination of the false, can get closer to the universal consensual (*konsensfähigen*) truth.

Sixth, more interesting than the general, epistemological admission of the incompletability and fallibility of all empirical knowledge would, naturally, be an answer to the question of the relationship of the hermeneutical methods of the humanities and social sciences to the methods of the so-called exact sciences – thus the mathematical natural sciences and also the quasi-nomological, technologically relevant social sciences. Unfortunately, here I cannot speak in detail about this large area of inquiry, to which I have devoted many works,[17] but would like to permit myself a few appropriate comments.

A noteworthy and regrettable consequence of the post-Heideggerian hermeneutic seems to lie in the fact that in recent times all interest seems to have been lost in the decades-long efforts at detailed distinctions and mediations between the possible methods of knowledge as well as between their fundamental questions and knowledge-determining interests. On the one hand there is a tendency to lump the hermeneutic methods together with all other scientific methods of the Cartesian '*logos* of the frame (*Gestell*)' and, together with the 'logocentric metaphysics', subject them to deconstruction. However, particularly as a result of the Anglo-Saxon appropriation of Heidegger, Gadamer and the post-Kuhnian 'new philosophy of science', theorists often apply the concept 'hermeneutics' in a positive sense to the methodology of all sciences. This creates a tendency, just as once happened in the programme of the nomological unified sciences, to overlook the decisive difference between a scientific form of knowledge, of which the hermeneutic presuppositions involve only the side of the subject, and the truly hermeneutical sciences, which presuppose a communicative relationship to their object and therefore must also on the side of the object – or, better expressed, the subject–object – presuppose and understand speech, intentions, conventions, traditions, understanding, pre-understanding etc.[18]

Today there is for the most part agreement only that one simply must assume for all sciences those restrictions on the older ideal of objectivity, of capacity for progress, and even of the capacity for truth, which one earlier, in any case, held to be unavoidable only in the case(s) of the 'soft', art-related *Geisteswissenschaften* or 'humanities'. But little of value appears in the contemporary tendency toward the de-differentiation, if not the obsolence, of epistemology and scientific theory under the sign of the pan-hermeneutic. It would be much better to hold fast to the results of the older differentiations, above all those of the anthropology of knowledge and (of) the transcendental-pragmatic appeal (*Rekurs*) to different human questions and fundamental knowledge-guiding interests.[19]

Seventh, in this connection only a brief comment will be offered about that unique type of social-psychological science in which the hermeneutical methods are mediated with causal or functional explanatory methods: not however, as in the case of the technologically relevant social sciences, in the sense that the understanding enters the service of nomological explanation and prediction. Rather it involves the reverse process, in that the causal and functional explanation of more or less unconscious or forced relationships of determination finally enters into the service of the deepening of the hermeneutic understanding (and therewith human communication and self-understanding): namely, those which have taken the model of psychoanalysis and the critical emancipatory social sciences oriented towards the critique of ideology.[20]

Doubtless the methodological difficulties in these areas are still much greater than in the classical domains of the natural sciences or humanities respectively. In addition, the models currently available for the mediation of understanding and explanation previously referred to – psychoanalysis and Marxist or neo-Marxist ideology critique – are anything but unproblematic. This has led, on the one hand, to a weariness with or a discrediting of the entire project; on the other hand, to a broadening and subsequent differentiation in the sense, for example, of the critical-hermeneutic-oriented sciences of the rational reconstruction of human competences on the one side, and functional system theories on the other.[21] However, as involved and complex as the relationships in the human sciences have become, it still appears established that it must lie in the interests of practical reason to make the complex relationships of social integration and social evolution, in so far as they are not transparent for communication, as understandable as possible. Human beings then retain a chance to come to agreement about their social systems and institutions and retain, relative to them, the initiative, as it were, in the sense of responsible political action. This does not imply that human beings could ever be able to expect the total transparency of human relationships from the sciences which can be put in the service of hermeneutic understanding. But this in no way implies that the methodological approaches to be mediated could not stand under the regulative idea of the deepening of human self-understanding and therewith the possibility of responsible action.

Eighth, the former observation is valid in particular for the remarkably ambivalent achievements of structuralist and post-structuralist semiotics if observed from the viewpoint of a transcendental-hermeneutic semiotics.[22] Here also the concern is with insights into anonymous – and to that extent not immediately intentionally understandable – structures and processes, which *prima facie* define a limit to the possibility of the transparency of human self-understanding and communicative understanding. Yet the provocative talk of 'the end of humanity' employed by those who thematize the anonymous structures and processes as determinants of human relationships must, particularly coming from them, sound *a priori* paradoxical. For in so far as their investigations achieve valid results at all, the same must also be said about the results of psychoanalysis and systems theory: the valid results can have meaning at all only as an indirect broadening and deepening of human self-understanding and communicative agreement on responsible action.

In this sense one can, for example – with Peirce and with Derrida – gladly admit that the processes of human knowledge, as processes of the sign-mediated interpretation of signs, are as such empirically incomplete and, because of the sense-constitutive difference between the singular act of sign use and the repeatable model of significant form, are subject to an infinite game occurrence (*Spiel-Geschehen*) of differential sense shifting (*différance*) and of dissemination. Still it does not follow from this that the hermeneutically relevant processes of sign interpretation are not, each according to its methodological approach, capable of being subsumed under the 'regulative idea' of a 'transcendental *significatum*' (an ultimate logical interpretant, as Peirce would say).[23] Moreover: contrary to the – in a certain respect semiotistical – claim of Derrida, an inter-subjectively valid agreement about meaning must be not only possible but rather also already actual. For without this transcendental-hermeneutical presupposition the insight claimed by Derrida with respect to difference and dissemination of *signifiants* would of course also not be thinkable. At least the difference of the *signifiants* must also be thematized by Derrida as *signifié* and to that extent brought to a 'logocentric presence'.

With these last remarks I would like to indicate – just as in my quarrel with Gadamer's unargumentative critique of reflective philosophy – that I, to a certain extent as a pedantic philosopher, wish to hold fast to the principle of avoiding performative self-contradiction as the limit of all possible critique of reason or *logos* – or of 'deconstruction', as the case may be. The starting point of an attempt to determine the *logos* of hermeneutics is now revealed to derive from this principle.

Attempt to determine the *logos* of a normative critically-oriented hermeneutic

The following attempt, which is limited to the exposition of seven theses, begins from a presupposition taken to be, within the limits of a transformed semiotic of speech-pragmatic transcendental philosophy, not surpassable (*hintergehbar*) through the appeal to a reflexive final ground.[24] In the present connection this can be advanced only as a claim and presented as a starting point over against relativistic-historicistic hermeneuticism, not to speak of deconstructive semioticism.

Thesis (1): *Logos*, within the limits of a semiotically transformed transcendental philosophy, should not be understood as the *logos* of the 'frame' (*Gestell*) which was, to some extent, correctly relativized by Heidegger and Derrida. That is, we are not speaking of the mind-set of the subject–object relation of the technical-scientific accessibility of the world, but rather of that wider *logos* of the inter-subjective, speech-communicative agreement concerning validity claims,[25] which is always already presupposed in this concretization. It must be assumed concerning this speech-*logos* that it cannot be reduced to a contingent result of the temporalization of Being and thus to the history of Being, since it is that which makes valid statements about the history of Being possible in the first place. (To this extent it is possible to criticize Heidegger's reproach of the forgetting of Being by reproaching it in turn for the forgetting of *logos*.)

Thesis (2): As to presuppositions of the speech-*logos* that are not disputable without performative self-contradiction and therefore must be always already pragmatically implied on the level of argumentative discourse, exactly four universal claims to validity and the presupposition of their redeemability in principle can be established:[26]

(i) the claim to verbally expressible and to that extent inter-subjectively communicable sense;

(ii) for prepositional statements, the assertorically raised claim to inter-subjectively consensual truth;

(iii) for the verbal expression of intentional states of subjects, the claim to truthfulness or sincerity (which cannot be assured through arguments, but only through behavioural *praxis*);

(iv) for speech acts as communicative acts with appellative force, the claim – which is also always already implicitly raised for the assertive acts – to normative, finally ethically justifiable correctness or rightness.

Thesis (3): With regard to the necessary acknowledgement of these universal presuppositions of argumentative discourse – and not only as concerns the factual 'agreement' with regard to contingent background presuppositions with respect to pre-reflexive 'being-in-the-world' or the lifeworld[27] respectively – there can and must exist in a philosophical hermeneutic an ultimate 'agreement' (Gadamer).

This thesis contains the decisive step of a 'retranscendentalization' of the philosophical hermeneutic which can protect it against falling prey to the historicism-relativism of the post-Heideggerian hermeneuticism. In this connection it must be recognized that the famous Heideggerian analysis of the 'fore-structure' of *Dasein* that in 'being-with' the others 'already' understands itself as being-in-the-world, which makes our understanding *a priori* dependent on the 'thrownness' in the 'there' and to that extent (also) on the historically contingent *Seinsgeschick*, has from the beginning neglected an essential aspect of the fore-structure. It has forgotten to take account of the presuppositions of argumentation, presented in theses (1) and (2), which make a philosophical analysis of the existential structure of being-in-the-world – an analysis with a claim to universal truth – possible at all in the first place. In this side-stepping of the conditions for the validity of one's own analysis lies the *logos*-forgetfulness of the Heideggerian philosophy. Since then it has become customary to trivialize the *a priori* of reflection on validity in favour of the supposedly in every respect deeper *a priori*s of the pre-reflective sense-constitution of the lifeworld.

Were the *a priori* of the speech-*logos* in the sense of theses (1) to (3) acknowledged, then it would become possible to introduce a methodologically relevant principle of philosophical hermeneutics, one that shows that the pedantic respect for the formal-reflexive, undebatable presuppositions of argumentation need not, as Gadamer suggests, remain without consequence and unfruitful. In one sense, perhaps intended by Gadamer, this would indeed be the case, if on the level of philosophical discourse one could recognize the presuppositions as undebatable, but at the same time and in spite of that, would have to recognize on the level of the concrete interpretation of texts the total dependency of understanding on the always historically conditioned pre-understanding, and to that extent must acknowledge only an 'other (or different) understanding' without a view toward a normatively regulated progress as truth in the sense of historicism-relativism. As will now be shown, however, this is precisely not the case.

Thesis (4): If the introduced presuppositions of all philosophical argumentation must be acknowledged as an ultimate *logos-a priori*, then this means at the same time that this *logos-a priori* must also be recognized as a part of that *a priori* of facticity of being-in-the-world (Heidegger) which today is always presupposed by us. However, that means that every attempt at a critical hermeneutic reconstruction of the evolution of culture or of social or spiritual history, as the case may be, stands *a priori* under the regulative principle of having to understand its own presuppositions in the sense of the *logos-a priori* as a possible and factual result of evolution or of history respectively. This I have called the self-recuperative principle (*Selbsteinholungsprinzip*) of the critical-hermeneutic, or, to speak with Habermas, of the reconstructive sciences. A little explanation is necessary in order to clarify the methodological scope of this principle.

My appeal to the four validity claims of argumentation and also my application of these argumentative *a prioris* to the reconstruction of the evolution of culture is deeply indebted, as can easily be seen, to the Habermasian conception of a universal speech-pragmatic or the reconstruction of human competences.[28] On the other hand, I have from the very beginning protested against Habermas's devaluation of his own philosophical insights, in that in his concept of reconstructive sciences he did not wish to make a disctintion between the transcendental-pragmatic reconstruction of the ultimate presuppositions of argumentation – thus of the philosophical *logos* – on the one hand and an empirical-hypothetical reconstruction of cultural evolution or concrete history on the other.[29] Habermas here still seems to share with Gadamer and the older Frankfurt School the assumption of the young Hegelians that after Hegel's completion of theoretical metaphysics something like the self-suspension of philosophy – for example in the sense of a fusion with the critical and interpretative social sciences – is at hand. I hold this view to be untenable, for a variety of reasons of which only a few can be presented here.

(i) If one shares with Habermas the view that in the post-Hegelian age it is essential to establish a co-operation between philosophy and the individual sciences, which also foresees mutual support and correction of results in terms of a coherence principle, then one must insist that the validity claims and the related testing methods of philosophy and the individual sciences – for example, the critical-reconstructive social sciences – be carefully distinguished. For only on this precondition is it possible that the convergences and the divergences of the complementary approaches may be methodologically relevant.[30] This means, among other things, the following. Mutual corrections of philosophy and the critical social sciences can never take place directly – that is, through confrontation of results on the same level of discourse – but rather only in such a way that the divergent results stimulate each other to correction with their own methodological means. Philosophy must therefore – especially when it wants to co-operate with the individual sciences – hold fast to its own unique final grounding function, not in order to practise a hierarchical patronage (such rhetorical appeals to modesty rest, in my view, on an ideological confusion of methodological and sociological or psychological categories) but rather in order to retain its worth as a conversational partner for the individual sciences.

This can be illustrated with an example: it makes no sense and is precisely what cannot be of help to the special sciences if, like Habermas, one suggests that the necessary presuppositions of argumentation mentioned above are to be empirically tested by the questioning of competent speakers, analogous to the method of linguistics. For in order even to understand what 'empirical testing' is supposed to mean, one must at least presuppose the validity of those presuppositions of argumentation. And it is this transcendental-pragmatic proof of the function of presuppositions – and not an empirical confirmation – that is capable of distinguishing the universally valid pronouncements of philosophy from the hypothetical universals of empirical science: for example, Chomsky's universals pertaining to the inborn language-learning capacity of human beings.

(ii) If it is supposed to be possible to discover a normative standard of measure for the grounding of critical-reconstructive social sciences from the universal validity claims of human discourse –

something that I along with Habermas hold to be possible and necessary – then it is not enough to take the empirically resonstructible validity claims of the communication found in the lifeworld of human beings as a point of departure. For these, because of their relativity to historically conditioned forms of life, are not non-circumventible (*nichthintergehbar*). They can even, as Max Weber has shown, be called into question in the post-Enlightenment age as non-redeemable (*uneinlosbar*) in principle. Rather it is far more imperative to take recourse to the consistently undebatable presuppositions of discourse qua argumentatation, which are upheld even by the sceptic and relativist as long as he or she argues, and to 'reconstruct' these as the transcendental-pragmatic ultimate presuppositions of every empirical-hermeneutic reconstruction of social and spiritual history. When this is done one can, as was maintained in thesis (4), presuppose the transcendental-pragmatic reconstructed *logos-a priori* as a whole, as well as in the sense of the self-recuperative principle, as a quasi-teleological presupposition of an empirical-hermeneutic reconstruction of social and spiritual history. And therein lies the then methodologically relevant bridge from the transcendental-pragmatic reconstruction of human competences to critical-hermeneutical, empirically testable reconstructions of social and spiritual history.

Thesis (5): The self-recuperative principle of the critical-hermeneutic or reconstructive sciences provides a post-Hegelian substitute, so to speak, for the metaphysically presupposed and to that extent dogmatic (and that means not finally groundable via a transcendental-pragmatic) teleology of the speculative philosophy of history of Hegelian or orthodox Marxist origin. The methodologically relevant difference between the speculative-metaphysical presupposition of a teleology of history and the minimal teleology of those reconstructive sciences grounded through the self-recuperative principle lies in the following: the former presupposes a causal and/or teleological determinism with respect to the empirically discoverable path of history; the latter, on the other hand, presupposes only that an incontestable condition of arguing, from which we can and must today take our point of departure, has factually been reached through the course of history, and that over and above this the necessarily postulated and contrafactually anticipated ideal relations of communication in discourse can and should be a goal toward which we aim. With respect to the causally conditioned dynamic of the historical process, no necessity will be presupposed. It ought to be obvious that thereby Kant's ethically grounded postulate of progress receives its transcendental-philosophical grounding.

Thesis (6): The self-recuperative principle of the critical-hermeneutic or reconstructive sciences contains the transcendental-hermeneutic answer to the question raised, but not made explicit, by Heidegger: how one properly enters into the 'hermeneutic circle' of understanding of the historically conditioned situation of being-in-the-world.

The principle implies, for example, among other things, the following methodological postulate: the 'preconcept of perfection' (Gadamer) with respect to the evaluative judgement of the *interpretandum* is valid as long as the interpreter finds grounds for being able to understand the validity claims of the *interpretandum* in the sense of the differentiating claims to universal validity of human speech as well grounded. Thus, these claims could be taken as possible contributions to an internal progressive history of the knowledge of scientific truth in the widest possible sense, or as possible contributions to the internal progressive history of the judgement of normative correctness in the sense of the evolution of legal or moral consciousness, or as possible contributions to the internal progressive history of the truthful or authentic self-expression of human subjectivity – in particular, in works of art. In all three dimensions of possible historical reconstruction, in the sense of rational reconstruction, the interpreter is compelled and justified, precisely in the sense of the 'preconcept of perfection', in understanding the *interpretandum*. And that means to understand it in certain respects better than it, or its author as the case may be, is capable of understanding itself. That does not rule out the possibility that the *interpretandum* may be superior to the interpreter as a source of possible information. It has rather to be postulated that the tentative exchange between the reflexive, superseding understanding and the readiness to learn is itself an aspect of the hermeneutic circle, which on the whole already received its formal *a priori* regulation through the self-recuperative principle.

However, to the degree that the interpreter is not capable of understanding the *interpretandum* in terms of the internal reconstruction of the evolution of culture in the sense of the three aforementioned dimensions of progress, but rather has good reason for the assumption that the limit of such understanding is conditioned through external causes, to that extent there arises from the self-recuperative principle the licence and even the methodological impetus for the transition to causal and functional (for example systems-theoretical) methods of explanation. Under certain circumstances this amounts to the attempt at analysing pathological cases of cultural decline or regression.[31] Even in these cases, however, the 'preconcept of perfection' as it is characteristic for the hermeneutical sciences remains valid in such a form as that in which it is employed for example by Imre Lakatos for the reconstruction of the history of science.[32] This means that reconstruction must preserve the advantage, in the hermeneutical sense, to be in the position to maximize the amount of internally understandable, rational reconstruction and minimize the element of external explanation.

Thesis (7): The self-recuperative principle of a critical-normative hermeneutic is thoroughly compatible with the presupposition – with Heidegger – that the possibility of true and false assertions has a pre-condition in the 'revealing–concealing' world-sense disclosure in language – or more precisely in the various languages. With Gadamer one could further illuminate the scope of this conditional relationship through the following suggestion. Since every proposition could be seen as an answer to a possible question, the issue arises for a hermeneutical reconstruction of the evolution of culture, about which questions can be asked in this culture and which cannot. About this, however, it appears that the world-sense disclosure is *a priori* decisive. By the same token, the self-recuperative principle is not compatible with taking the history of the world-sense disclosure and the history of the knowledge of truth which is in a certain sense dependent upon it, as an a-rational temporal happening, that is, as exclusive of a rationally reconstrucible progress. It rather forces the conclusion that there are long-term self-sustaining processes of learning – in all three dimensions of the possible rational reconstruction of cultural evolution – that play a decisive role in determining which world-sense disclosures come into being in the history of language.[33]

Hence, we are led finally to the following conclusion: even if the actual insights of the post-Heideggerian hermeneutic are taken as seriously as possible, there is no reason to call into question the specific presuppositions of the *logos* of understanding, or to 'deconstruct' them along with the technical-scientific *logos* of the 'frame'. Even if the greatest possible realm of application is permitted to the temporal and historically conditioned 'play' of sense-differentiation in the area of the interpretation of texts and we are clear about the fact that we will never achieve full self-transparency through critical hermeneutics, still there is no reason to ignore the regulative ideas of a normatively conditioned progress. These already pre-configure all understanding in that it must correspond to a practical need of communicative understanding and the judgement of claims to validity. Also, in the final analysis, through these validity claims are grounded – as demonstrated – the regulative principles of possible progress in understanding, and among them that of a progress in the rational reconstruction of a moral competence in 'judgement'. Therein, and not in the supposedly mere 'happening' or 'event' character of understanding, lies the internal connection between hermeneutics and practical philosophy.

Notes

First published in T.J. Stapleton (ed.), *The Question of Hermeneutics* (Dordrecht: Kluwer, 1994), 37–60.

1 To this point – and that means in the rejection of the attempt at a scientific reduction of understanding to a heuristic moment of the context of the nomological (causal or statistical) explanation of acts as events – there is certainly agreement between H.-G. Gadamer, J. Habermas and myself.

2 H.-G. Gadamer, *Wahrheit und Methode* (Tübingen: Mohr, 1960); critical discussion in Apel, *Transformation der Philosophie* (Frankfurt a. M.: Suhrkamp, 1973), vol. 1, Introduction, note 70.

3 Lyotard, 'Histoire universelle et différences culturelles', *Critique*, 456 (1985), 559 ff., where the paradigm of the superseded historical-philosophical idea of progress is even traced directly to Kant. Hans Jonas also detects – unjustly in my view – in Kant's ethically grounded regulative idea of possible progress a mere preparatory stage of the Hegelian and Marxist conception of the intelligibly necessary (progressive) course of history. See Jonas, *Prinzip Verantwortung* (Frankfurt a. M.: Insel, 1980), 227 ff.

4 I. Kant, 'Das mag im das Theorie richtig sein, taugt aber nicht für die Praxis', Akademie Edition (Berlin: de Gruyter), vol. 8, 308 ff.

5 See, for example, R. Rorty, *Philosophy and the Mirror of Nature* (Princeton: Princeton University Press, 1979), and *Consequences of Pragmatism* (Minneapolis: University of Minnesota Press, 1982).

6 See P. Forget (ed.), *Text und Interpretation* (Munich: Wilhelm Fink, 1984).

7 On Heidegger and Derrida see J. Habermas, *The Philosophical Discourse of Modernity* (Frankfurt a. M.: Suhrkamp, 1985), chapters 6 and 7, as well as Apel, 'Die Herausforderung der totalen Vernunftkritik und das Programm einer philosophischen Theorie der Rationalistätstypen', *Concordia*, 11 (1987), 2–23.

8 See Derrida's contributions in P. Forget (ed.), *Text und Interpretation*.

9 See Gadamer, *Wahrheit und Methode*, 218 ff.

10 *Ibid.*, 326 f.

11 *Ibid.*, 327.

12 *Ibid.*, 3.

13 See for instance Apel, 'Szientismus oder transzendentale Hermeneutik?', in *Transformation der Philosophie* (Frankfurt a. M.: Suhrkamp, 1973), vol. 2, 178–219.

14 Apel, *Die Idee der Sprache in der Tradition des Humanismus von Dante bis Vico* (Bonn: Bouvier, 1963, 1980).

15 See note 5.

16 M. Heidegger, *Sein und Zeit* (Halle: Niemeyer, 1941), 153 and 314 f.

17 See especially Apel, *Die Erklären/Verstehen-Kontroverse in transzendentalpragmatischer Sicht* (Frankfurt a. M.: Suhrkamp, 1979); English translation: *Understanding and Explanation: A Transcendental-pragmatic Perspective* (Cambridge, Mass.: MIT Press, 1984).

18 See in this connection most recently Apel, 'The "Erklären/Verstehen"-controversy in the Philosophy of the Human and Natural Sciences', in G. Floisstad (ed.), *Contemporary Philsoophy: A New Survey*, vol. 2 (The Hague, Boston and London: Martinus Nijhoff, 1982); Apel, 'Diltheys Unterscheidung von "Erklären" und "Verstehen" im Lichte der Ergebnisse der modernen Wissenschaftstheorie', in E.W. Orth (ed.), *Dilthey und die Philosophie der Gegenwart* (Freiburg im Breisgau: Alber, 1985), 285–347.

19 J. Habermas, *Erkenntnis und Interesse* (Frankfurt a. M.: Suhrkamp, 1968), English translation: *Knowledge and Human Interests* (Boston: Beacon Press, 1971); as well as Apel, 'Szientistik, Hermeneutik, Ideologiekritik', in Apel, *Transformation der Philosophie* (Frankfurt a. M.: Suhrkamp, 1973), vol. 2, 96–127, English translation: *Towards a Transformation of Philosophy* (London: Routledge & Kegan Paul, 1980). Also Apel, 'Types of Social Science in the Light of Human Cognitive Interests', *Social Research*, 44, 3 (1977), 425–70, repr. in S. Brown (ed.), *Philosophical Disputes in the Social Sciences* (Brighton: Harvester Press, 1979), 3–50, as well as *Die Erklären/Verstehen-Kontroverse in transzendentalpragmatischer Sicht*.

20 See the discussion volume *Hermeneutik und Ideologie-Kritik*, ed. R. Bubner (Frankfurt a. M.: Suhrkamp, 1971).

21 See J. Habermas and N. Luhmann, *Theorie der Gesellschaft oder Sozialtechnologie?* (Frankfurt a. M.: Suhrkamp, 1971); further Habermas, *Theorie des kommunikativen Handelns* (Frankfurt a. M.: Suhrkamp, 1981), vol. 2: 'Zur Kritik der funktionalistischen Vernunft', English translation: *Theory of Communicative Action*, vol. 2 (Boston: Beacon Press, 1984).

22 Concerning the following, see note 7.

23 On Peirce's philosophy see Apel, *Der Denkweg von Charles Sanders Peirce: eine Einführung in den amerikanischen Pragmatismus* (Frankfurt a. M.: Suhrkamp, 1975), and 'Peirce and Post-Kantian Truth', in E. Freeman (ed.), *The Relevance of Charles Peirce* (La Salle, Ill.: Hegeler Institute, 1983), 189–223; also 'Linguistic Meaning and Intentionality: the Compatibility of the "Linguistic Turn" and the "Pragmatic Turn" of Meaning-theory within the Framework of a Transcendental Semiotics', in H.J. Silverman and D. Welton (eds), *Critical and Dialectical Phenomenology* (Albany: State University of New York Press, 1987), 2–53.

24 Apel, 'Das Problem der Philosophischen Letztbegründung im Lichte einer

transzendentalen Sprachpragmatik: Versuch einer Metakritik des "Kritischen Rationalismus"', in B. Kanitschneider (ed.), *Sprache und Erkenntnis* (Innsbruck, 1976), 550–82; English translation in *Man and World*, 8 (1975), 238–75, reprinted in K. Baynes, J. Bohman and T.A. McCarthy (eds), *After Philosophy: End or Transformation?* (Cambridge, Mass.: MIT Press, 1987), 250–90. See further W. Kuhlmann, *Reflexive Letztbegründung: Untersuchungen zur Transzendentalpragmatik* (Freiburg and Munich: Alber, 1985); D. Bohler, *Rekonstruktive Pragmatik: Von der Bewusstseinsphilosophie zur Kommunikationsreflexion* (Frankfurt a. M.: Suhrkamp, 1985), as well as most recently: Apel, 'Fallibilismus, Konsenstheorie der Wahrheit und Letztbegründung', in Forum für Philosophie Bad Hamburg (ed.), *Philosophie und Begründung* (Frankfurt a. M.: Suhrkamp, 1987), 116–277.

25 Apel, 'Die Logosauszeichnung der menschlichen Sprache: die philosophische Tragweite der Sprechakttheorie', in H.-G. Bosshardt (ed.), *Sprache Interdisziplinär* (Berlin and New York: W. de Gruyter, 1986), 45–87.

26 J. Habermas, 'Vorbereitende Bemerkungen zu einer Theorie der kommunikativen Kompetenz', in J. Habermas and N. Luhmann, *Theorie der Gesellschaft oder Sozialtechnologie?*, 101–41; Habermas, 'Was heisst Universalpragmatik?', in Apel (ed.), *Sprachpragmatik und Philosophie* (Frankfurt a. M.: Suhrkamp, 1976), 174–272, and *Theorie des communikativen Handelns*, vol. 1, chapter 3; as well as my work cited in note 25.

27 Concerning the necessary assumption of contingent psychic and in particular historical presuppositions of world understanding there is at present a widespread consensus among philosophers, originating from Collingwood, Wittgenstein, Searle, Heidegger and Gadamer. That there are also noncontingent – that is, argumentatively indisputable and to that extent universally valid – presuppositions of sensible argumentation seems to most something easy to question – although every questioning as argumentation must obviously involve validity claims.

28 See note 26.

29 See the contributions by Apel and Habermas in Apel (ed.), *Sprachpragmatik und Philosophie*; further Apel, 'Fallibilismus, Konsenstheorie der Wahrheit und Letztbegründung', as well as W. Kuhlmann, 'Philosophie und rekonstruktive Wissenschaft', *Zeitschrift für Philosophische Forschung*, 40 (1986), 224–334.

30 Apel, 'Die transzendentalpragmatische Begründung der Kommunikationsethik und das Problem der höchsten Stufe einer Entwicklungslogik des moralischen Bewusstseins', in Apel, *Diskurs und Verantwortung* (Frankfurt a. M.: Suhrkamp, 1988), 306 ff.

31 Apel, *Die Erklären/Verstehen-Kontroverse in transzendentalpragmatischer Sicht*.

32 See I. Lakatos, 'Zur Geschichte der Wissenschaft und ihrer rationalen Nachkonstruktionen', in W. Diederich (ed.), *Theorien der Wissenschaftsgeschichte* (Frankfurt a. M.: Suhrkamp, 1974), 55–119.

33 Apel, 'Die Herausforderung der totalen Vernunftkritik'.

8

Regulative ideas or truth happening? An attempt to answer the question of the conditions of the possibility of valid understanding

translated by ROLF SOMMERMEIER

Introduction: the quasi-Kantian reservation about the 'hermeneutical ontology' of truth happening

Since the author of the present discussion of Gadamer's ideas is no longer a youngster himself and since he – like the author of *Truth and Method* – has always regarded the solution to the problem mentioned in the above subtitle as the central matter of concern of his philosophy, he may be permitted to introduce the subject matter with the help of an autobiographical retrospective.

Inspired by Heidegger, I arrived in my 1963 thesis, *The Concept of Language in the Humanistic Tradition from Dante to Vico*,[1] at a philosophical position which was very similar to the one which I discovered later in Gadamer's *opus magnum*. However, I named it 'transcendental hermeneutics' in order to express my intention to hold to Kant's basic question. But I still believed at that time that I could comprehend Heidegger's hermeneutics of *Dasein* as the necessary and sufficient transformation of the transcendental philosophy of Kant and Husserl which took into account the linguistic and historical character of our being-in-the-world. I am inclined to think that Gadamer, while he elaborated his 'philosophical hermeneutics', had a notion of Heidegger's position very similar to mine.

However, I changed my idea about Heidegger in the years following, mainly, I think I can say today, as the result of reading *Truth and Method* (*Wahrheit und Methode*).

I now had to recognize with some consternation that Heidegger's assumptions of the hermeneutics of *Dasein*[2] presupposed by Gadamer in *Truth and Method* made something like a normatively controlled progress in understanding appear totally inconceivable. The reason for this was not that the methodologically narrow problem of traditional hermeneutics had been extended in *Truth and*

Method with the help of a radically philosophical (transcendental) question, as Gadamer kept insisting.[3] The actual reason was that Gadamer did not hesitate to equate the conditions of the possibility of meaning understanding (that is of the 'thrown projection' of a world of manifest meaning, one which goes along with a corresponding hiding of possible meaning) with the conditions of the possibility of the inter-subjective validity of understanding, in fact of any knowledge.[4] In this respect he followed the line of the transformation of Kant's transcendental question as it had been suggested by Heidegger in *Being and Time* and in the latter's first book on Kant.[5]

I think that the idea which Heidegger supported until 1964, namely the replacing of the traditional binary correctness concept of truth with the 'more original' concept of *aletheia*,[6] led Heidegger and Gadamer to replace the counterfactual and, therefore, *per se* inter-subjective validity of truth (this validity had been taken for granted by Kant) with the facticity of meaning as it becomes manifest to us in the particular historical situation. (I must come back to this point later.) In the years following, Gadamer could in this way replace the normatively oriented, and hence also epistemologically and methodologically relevant, conceptions of traditional hermeneutics (for example, Schleiermacher's and Dilthey's) with the temporal-ontological, and that is to say, happening-theoretical ones. Examples of such conceptions were understanding as 'moving into the happening of handing down', 'application of understanding as continued forming [*Bildung*] of tradition', 'hermeneutic circle' as 'bringing into play' and 'putting prejudices at risk' in the form of the 'fusion of horizons', and finally, in a unique conjunction of a methodologically relevant conception of reflection with a conception of happening, 'effective-historical consciousness'.

Remarkably, though, Gadamer's notion contrasts with Heidegger's – even after the latter's turn – to the effect that that moment of sense happening and truth happening, which must, as it were, replace the normative control of understanding, is located in the past, but not in the future. In other words, it is not located in the onto-historical 'event' of the 'opening' qua an 'act of mission' of Being. In the history of metaphysics this opening, according to Heidegger, has underlain not only the epochal uncovering of beingness, or of the essence of beings (*ousia*), but also the corresponding withdrawal of Being itself already since Plato; and, in fact, it could once again be imminent today after the 'destruction', or the 'getting over', of this history. Instead, for Gadamer it is located in the validity authority of the contents of cultural tradition that needs further continued formation (*Bildung*) by means of applicative interpretation. Evidently, this is connected with the characteristic presumption of the fundamental superiority of the objective validity claims of the *interpretandum* over the interpreter's adoption and assessment. The latter are in fact always already taken to advantage by applying further continued forming (*Bildung*) of tradition.[7] Of course this presumption is hard to accept from a post-Enlightenment viewpoint.

This strange primacy of the past (that is what was thought to be the handing over of contents) is what first provoked my opposition. Or to be precise, it was this primacy together with the following central thesis of Gadamer's, which was directed against Kant, Fichte and Schleiermacher: 'Understanding is in truth not understanding better, neither in the sense of objectively understanding better through clearer concepts, nor in the sense of the fundamental superiority of the conscious over the unconscious moment of production. It suffices to say that *one understands differently if one understands at all*.'[8]

Here I do not dispute the thesis that we, as finite and historical creatures, *de facto* understand the *interpretandum* differently in each situational context – which also implies differently than it was meant. I was, and am, quite ready to make this concession to the temporal ontology of understanding, that is, the temporal ontology of the accompanying 'fusion of horizons' and the effective-historically conditioned context-dependence. However, it appears to me that this concession does not indicate anything relevant about the correctness, or depth, of understanding. In my view the inevitability of a situation-dependent understanding differently owing to the 'fusion of horizons' trivially also applies to superficial or even false understanding. It simply applies – today I prefer to put it this way – as temporal-ontological determination to preconditions of any human attempt to understand, but not yet, however, to the transcendental conditions of the possibility of valid or non-valid understanding. Like the binary concept of truth itself, these conditions relate by their very nature counterfactually and time-independently to all imaginable interpreters' universal capacity for consensus.

Now, if this determination is understood as 'regulative idea' in the sense of Kant, Peirce and Royce,[9] then it may not follow that, in a transcendental hermeneutics, the always understanding only differently could ever be replaced by an understanding totally correctly.[10] But it does appear as thinkable, in fact even as a necessary postulate of a normatively oriented hermeneutics, that, inasmuch as we understand correctly at all, we understand not only in a different way – owing to the 'fusion of horizons' – but thereby at the same time in a better, or deeper, way. Put more correctly, hermeneutic understanding is superior not only in comparison with former hermeneutic understanding,[11] but even with the *interpretanda*, or their authors.

This postulate seems to me to take into account the factor of reflection (more about this later), which is implied in any creative understanding and thus in any knowledge. This integrating factor of all understanding should be more important for the 'productivity of the temporal distance'[12] than the sheer-temporal-process nature of the effective history of the *interpretandum*. Exactly this seems to me to be the basis of the superiority, emphasized by Gadamer,[13] of Hegel's theory of the 'self-penetration of mind' over Schleiermacher's and Dilthey's theory of the 'identical after-understanding'. This is true at least in so far as understanding in the humanities and the arts is not comprehended in the sense of 'hermeneutic abstraction' from the judging assessment (I must come back to this point as well). The history of the sciences and of philosophy, then, seems to suggest that understanding always already reflectively outstrips understanding in the respect in which it happens. I should like to cite such examples as the relativization of Euclidean geometry by non-Euclidean geometries and its rehabilitation as 'protophysics' by Hugo Dingler or Paul Lorenzen; and also the corresponding relativizations and rehabilitations of the validity of Newtonian physics as physics of the 'mesocosmos'. In philosophy, one could, for example, think of the dehypostatizing reinterpretations of the Platonic doctrine of Ideas; or of the critical and fallibilistic transformations of Kant's unkowable 'things-in-themselves' through Peirce's concept of the 'knowable' which can never be 'known'. Finally, I should like to cite Gadamer's own reference to Heidegger's demonstration that the Greek substance-ontology continues in Descartes's concept of consciousness as well as in Hegel's concept of mind, and that this insight '[goes] beyond the

self-understanding of modern metaphysics'.[14] But how is this assertion of Gadamer's consistent with his fundamental rejection of
'better understanding'?

From the things said it does not at all follow, I think, that
creative understanding must outstrip the meaning of the *interpretandum* in every aspect; this is virtually impossible in the case of the
great works of poetry and philosophy. And in this respect the postulate (*Resultat*) [translator's note: Apel suggests that his word
'Resultat' should be translated in each instance as 'postulate' or
'hypothesis'] of better understanding does not contradict Gadamer's
postulate that all understanding must presuppose the 'fore-
conception of perfection' of the *interpretandum*;[15] this is also relevant
from the point of view of methodology. Hermeneutic understanding
should presuppose the heuristic assumption of the superior validity
authority of the *interpretandum* as well as – on account of the interpreter's autonomy of reason – the likewise necessary reservation of
critical-reflective critique of the understood validity claims. I believe
that this double presumption alone is in general accordance with the
fundamental symmetry of a situation of dialogical understanding.
This, in fact, also forms a basic premise of Gadamer's philosophical
hermeneutics (along or in tension with the paradigm of meaning –
and truth happening?). This has been a first lead-in to a possible
debate between the 'philosophical hermeneutics', as represented by
Gadamer, and a 'transcendental hermeneutics' which was initially
characterized in a similar way, but then returned to a more Kantian
approach. 'Transcendental hermeneutics' is a conception which
cannot find the answer to the question of the validity of understanding in a temporal ontology of understanding as of a truth happening,
but one which looks for regulative ideas for a normative orientation
of understanding.

Two problematic presuppositions of Gadamer's 'philosophical hermeneutics': the *aletheia* theory of truth and the equation of the claim of the inter-subjective validity of 'better understanding' with the objectivity ideal of science

None the less, serious objections might be raised against the truth-
theoretical presuppositions of the just-sketched argumentation that
favours a regulative idea of better understanding. These objections
favour Gadamer's concept of the historical dependence of context

and position of any understanding, in particular historical-hermeneutic understanding. How should it be possible, one could ask, to think a regulative idea of better understanding in the sense indicated if it has to be presupposed, along with Heidegger and Gadamer, that all correctness of knowledge depends on truth qua *aletheia*? (This is to say, if it depends on a linguistically disclosed meaning world and, hence, on a historically determined meaning-uncovering, which implies a simultaneous hiding of possible other meanings.) Is not especially the claim to universality of Gadamer's 'philosophical hermeneutics'[16] well founded on the assumption of the onto-historical uncovering/hiding theory of truth? On the other hand, this claim is also supposed to be founded on the presumptions of understanding of something through correct or false arguments, or arguments that prove to be tenable or untenable in discourse. These presuppositions, I think, cannot be circumvented by philosophers. How is all this to go together?

In my view discussion of the questions raised at this point requires, first of all, the clarification of two central assumptions in Gadamer's work and in the discussion related to it that have so far remained unclarified. The first clarification concerns the already mentioned concept of truth which goes back to Heidegger.[17] The second one concerns Gadamer's presupposed relationship of the idea of a 'philosophical hermeneutics' (which is held with the claim to universality), first to the idea of science qua natural science; and secondly to the idea of hermeneutics in the sense of the humanities and the arts (*Geisteswissenschaften*), as it has been held with the claim to methodological autonomy since Droysen and Dilthey. In what follows I would like to discuss in more detail these two presuppositions of Gadamer's conception of a 'philosophical hermeneutics'.

Problematization of the *aletheia* theory of truth as initiated by Heidegger himself, and its consequences

I should like first of all to call into question or at least relativize the scope of Gadamer's concept of truth (which was inspired by Heidegger) with the help of Heidegger's revocation of the truth-theoretical claim of the theory of *aletheia*. Actually, this revocation has received little attention so far.[18] In his February 1964 lecture 'Heideggers Idee von Wahrheit' ('Heidegger's Idea of Truth') Ernst Tugendhat formulated his criticism of Heidegger's adoption and development of Husserl's concept of truth, in the sense of Heidegger's *aletheia* concept of truth, for the first time.[19] Two months later Heidegger implicitly confirmed Tugendhat's criticism[20] in his lecture 'Das Ende der Philosophie und die Aufgabe des Denkens' ('The End of Philosophy and the Task of Thinking'), by noting:

> Insofar as truth is understood in the traditional 'natural' sense as the correspondence of knowledge with beings demonstrated in beings, but also insofar as truth is interpreted as the certainty of the knowledge of Being, *aletheia*, unconcealment in the sense of the opening may not be equated with truth. Rather, *aletheia*, unconcealment thought as opening, first grants the possibility of truth. For truth itself, just as Being and thinking, can only be what it is in the element of the opening. Evidence, certainty in every degree, every kind of verification of *veritas* already move with that *veritas* in the realm of the prevalent opening. *Aletheia*, unconcealment thought as the opening of presence, is not yet truth.[21]

At this point Heidegger does nothing less than revoke that thesis which he had held with growing determination since *Being and Time*: namely, that the more original and the only significant concept of truth is the unconcealment of beings on the ground of the disclosedness of being-there, that is, the opening of Being. He sees himself forced to revoke this thesis owing to his insight that the unconcealment of meaning[22] is indeed a necessary, but not a sufficient, condition of correctness – that is, it does not operate as the only determining standard. This is the reason why he has to concede that unconcealment is '*not yet* truth' (my emphasis). He is hence explicitly self-critical when he explains: 'To raise the question of *aletheia*, of unconcealment as such, is not the same thing as raising the question of truth. For this reason, it was inadequate and misleading to call *aletheia* in the sense of the opening, truth.'[23]

Of equal importance to this systematically relevant self-correction is Heidegger's revocation of his thesis of the 'essential change' of truth in the sense of a Platonic transformation of the *aletheia* concept of truth into the traditional metaphysical concept of correctness or correspondence. This thesis lies at the basis of his reconstruction of the history of metaphysics. In factorial agreement with Tugendhat's criticism, Heidegger explains:

> The natural concept of truth does not mean unconcealment, not in the philosophy of the Greeks either. It is often and justifiably

pointed out that the word *aletheia* is already used by Homer only in the *verba dicendi*, in statement and thus in the sense of correctness and reliability, not in the sense of unconcealment[24] . . . In the scope of this question, we must acknowledge the fact that *aletheia*, unconcealment in the sense of the opening of presence, was originally only experienced as *orthotes*, as the correctness of representations and statements. But then, the assertion of a change of the essence of truth, that is from unconcealment to correctness, is not tenable, either.[25]

What, now, is the significance of Heidegger's self-criticism for the concept of truth in Gadamer's 'philosophical hermeneutics', which is dependent on the concept of *aletheia*?

First of all, it needs to be pointed out that Heidegger's self-correction does not at all mean that he also intended to discredit his discovery of the necessity of a meaning-disclosedness of the world as the condition of the possibility of truth qua correctness (and incorrectness) of statements. This follows from the text quoted and is emphatically confirmed by Heidegger subsequent to the self-correction cited. After Heidegger's self-corrections, it certainly needs to be asked with more emphasis what the scope of the discovery of the not-sufficient but yet necessary condition of the meaning-disclosedness (which is always already linguistically articulated) consists in. Could it perhaps consist in having provided a conception of truth adequate to a 'philosophical hermeneutics'? This thesis seems to be supported by the fact that a philosophical hermeneutics does not at all deal with the correct knowledge of innerworldly things when it reflects upon the correctness of understanding. Instead, it deals only either with the manifestness of meaning, that is the manifestness of linguistic meaning as such in the pre-scientific, lifeworldly experience, or with the disclosure of the meaning of works of art or texts on the level of interpretation as made in the humanities and arts. If this interpretation is correct, Gadamer understood with safe instinct the plausibility about Heidegger's theory of *aletheia* and used it to make his conception of a 'philosophical hermeneutics' fruitful.

I confess that an argument of this sort was plausible to me not only when originally conceiving a 'transcendental hermeneutics', but also afterwards. However, at the time I conceived a transcendental pragmatics of language or semiotics,[26] which was mainly inspired by Peirce, I was unclear about how a hermeneutics which was one-sidedly related to comprehensible meaning could at the same time be awarded the status of a transcendental hermeneutics that was relevant for theories of knowledge and science. Briefly put, I was unclear about how it could be awarded the status of a universal (and thus methodologically non-circumventible) philosophy of inter-subjective understanding about the world and the knowability of all innerworldly beings. As a matter of fact, it appears to me that Gadamer could claim Heidegger's corrected theory of *aletheia* as a sufficient truth theory of his philosophical hermeneutics then, and only then, if he could disregard the validity claims of the *interpretanda* which transcend the claim to meaning and which need to be assessed or judged: in a word, if he were allowed to separate analytically pure meaning understanding from the evaluative understanding of the factual problems in the sense of the 'hermeneutical abstraction' of traditional, objectivistic hermeneutics.

This is precisely what Gadamer does not want. Rather, if I comprehend his conception of hermeneutics aright, it is one of its chief matters of concern to get beyond the value-neutral objectivism of nineteenth-century hermeneutics, which was modelled after the natural sciences. In this way, he stresses the lifeworldly unity of meaning understanding and coming-to-agreement-about-something,[27] in the sense of the dialectical ambiguity of the German expression *Verständigung über etwas* [translator's note: this phrase signifies (1) communication, (2) coming to agreement about something, or, more clearly, about theoretical and/or practical validity claims]. As I comprehend it, it is this unity on which hermeneutics grounds its philosophical claim to universality and its relevance for theoretical and practical philosophy. And I would like to add at once that, as far as this approach is concerned, understanding about something constitutes the common matter of concern of Gadamer's, Habermas's and my attempts at an up-to-date 'founding' of philosophy in the *a priori* of communicative understanding.

However, if this is so, then the claim to universality of 'philosophical heremeneutics' seems to me incompatible with the restriction of its factual reference to the meaning-disclosedness of the world, or even to the linguistically defined meaning of texts. Instead, that factual reference which is tied in with the validity claims of the *interpretanda* needs to be taken into consideration from the beginning too, both in the epistemologically and the ethically relevant senses of correctness; and this necessity is already based on the semantic reference of language. It needs to be pointed out here that the semantic investigations by, in particular, Kripke, Donellan and Putnam have recently shown that the thesis which Heidegger put forward as early as in *Being and Time* – that is, the thesis that all cognition of innerworldly beings requires an *a priori* understanding of something as something – is not valid without qualification. Heidegger's insight into the 'as' structure of the identification of objects (which is fundamental to the speech-hermeneutic turn of phenomenology and has its equivalent in the Fregian/Russellian conception of names as 'descriptions')[28] finds its corrective in the very possibility of using names as rigid designators which relate in 'as' – free, direct reference to the given that is baptized with the label of deistic or indexical.

In this respect, the given is not yet known – hence, not understood – 'as something' (in the sense of an attributive or predicative modifier). It is, nevertheless, defined by virtue of a direct linguistic reference to its reality which is independent of the conceptual intentions of the factually used language. It is defined in a manner which provides evidence criteria, for example, by means of indexical definitions of 'natural kinds' which are complemented by visual patterns. It is on the basis of these criteria that the conceptual intentions of the factually used language can be corrected by the expert by pointing out deviant extensions. In this way Heidegger's thesis of the rigid ontical-ontological difference (put differently, of the preliminary opening of scope for optical-empirical knowledge through the understanding of Being) is corrected in the sense of a meaning-holism which is yet conditioned also linguistically.

The epistemological importance of this speech-analytical insight seems to lie in the untenability of the currently influential presumptions of a one-sided predetermination of the scope for scientific discoveries by 'epochal openings of the meaning of Being' (according to Heidegger) or by 'incommensurable paradigms' (according to Thomas Kuhn) of the pre-understanding of problems and their possible solutions. They have to be corrected at least in the sense that, especially in the sciences, empirical learning processes are possible; these, in turn, influence the epochal openings of the meaning of Being, or of the paradigms of 'normal science'.

What, now, is the significance of the recent insights outlined so far for the assessment of Gadamer's conception of the claim to universality of philosophical hermeneutics?

So much seems to be clear to me: the recent insights into meaning-holism (roughly put, into the possible correction of the meaning of language by reference of language) elucidate and increase the significance of the insight that a 'philosophical hermeneutics' deals not only with intentional, speech-immanent meaning, but also with the fact-related validity claims of human utterances. This insight was implicitly confirmed by Gadamer himself. But if this is so, then Gadamer's previously criticized thesis, according to which our understanding cannot in principle transcend the 'always understanding differently' of the *interpretanda* (that is, on account of its dependence on the historically determined situational context of the manifestation of meaning in language), appears hardly tenable.

For even if the factual manifestation of meaning (*aletheia* in Heidegger's sense) is always context-relative, it has in the meantime become obvious that the fact-related truth of validity claims is not yet sufficiently determined by the factual manifestation of meaning. Rather, it requires some additional fact-related insight to assess it, and this insight needs to be counterfactually valid at any time, namely for an infinite community of interpreters. If now this explication of the meaning of truth is to have any pragmatic meaning whatsoever, then it must in principle be possible to presuppose the possibility of progress in knowledge, first of all in the dimension of fact-related correctness. Under the condition of meaning-holism, however, such progress cannot in fact be totally relative to a previously determined scope for the factual-historical meaning openings, as Heidegger suggested. It must rather, for its part, be able to influence possible meaning openings (for instance, the intensions of our linguistic terms). But this implies that the consideration of possible progress in knowledge must be constitutive of the speech-mediated understanding of the lifeworld, and beyond that also of understanding in the narrower, methodological sense of the hermeneutics of the humanities and arts. Hence also in this area, meaning understanding must be able to turn into 'understanding better and better' on the basis of progress in the research on things. Apparently, this is exactly what is testified by the previously cited examples from the history of philosophy and science.

All this, I think, is true under Gadamer's assumption – which I share – that understanding in the sense of philosophical hermeneutics must have, and maintain, its place in the context of the communicative understanding about things.

However, the consequences we have just drawn from the problematization of the theory of truth (and meaning) which Gadamer presupposed, still require a more detailed elucidation and substantiation in the context of the previously indicated question of the relationship of 'philosophical hermeneutics' to a differentiated theory of knowledge and science. For from Gadamer's perspective, it could immediately be objected that all consequences which have so far been drawn from the theory of truth are still oriented toward the model of the factual reference of the progressive natural sciences. But it is precisely this model which Gadamer's conception of 'philosophical hermeneutics' called into question.

Problematization of the equation of the inter-subjective validity of progress in understanding with the objectivity of progressive natural science

The crucial difference between Gadamer's assessment of the relationship of hermeneutics to the sciences (wherein he follows Heidegger) and the dichotomy between 'understanding' and 'explaining',[29] which became popular through Dilthey, can, it seems to me, be explicated in our problem context as follows. It is true that Dilthey – like Droysen before him – was interested in working out the epistemological and methodological difference between the factual conditions and the cognitive accessibility of the 'objects' of the nomologically explaining natural sciences, on the one hand, and, on the other hand, the 'historical-social reality', which can be relived and comprehended as an expression of life. At any rate, he was intent to do so more radically than the neo-Kantians, who did not want to let a differentiation occur until the 'concept formation', and certainly not during the constitution of the empirical data. But Dilthey – along with modern, in particular nineteenth-century, epistemology – held to the notion that the understanding humanities and arts (*Geisteswissenschaften*) dealt with a progressively explorable object of knowledge. He did so in spite of his comprehension of the historical dependence of understanding. Since Dilthey held to the objectivity ideal of the *Geisteswissenschaften*, on the one hand, but was, on the other hand, willing to reduce philosophy's claim to truth (namely of the 'absolute spirit' as such in Hegel's sense) to that of the 'objective spirit' (namely of a true expression of the diversity of life), he simply had to become hopelessly entangled in the 'aporias of historicism'.[30]

Now, Gadamer believes these aporias can be resolved by giving up as inadequate the subject–object relation – which was still presupposed by Dilthey as well as the entire epistemological tradition – and the accompanying objectivity ideal of progressive science for 'hermeneutical experience' and the understanding of the humanities and arts;[31] or by relativizing the two in the sense of treating them as at times useful methodical fictions.[32] According to Gadamer, understanding must be comprehended on the level of reflection of a 'philosophical hermeneutics', that is, of a 'hermeneutic ontology', as a factor in the onto-historical happening of the mediation of tradition. Put differently, it must be comprehended not so much as an understanding subject's methodical way of behaving but rather as a way of experiencing the world that is conscious of its effective historical determinedness and that obtains its potential depth and strength as a response to being addressed by the tradition. For Gadamer, this implies that, all in all, there can be no progressive 'better understanding' – since there actually is no progressively explorable object of exploration – but only the context-dependent self-mediation with tradition, namely a meaning happening and a truth happening.

Accordingly, the above-sketched correction of the *aletheia* theory of truth can apparently have no consequences for hermeneutics in the sense of a rehabilitation of understanding's capacity for progress. For even if the difference between meaning manifestation and fact-related correctness is conceded, unlike for natural science, there simply can be no factual reference for hermeneutic understanding which allows progress in knowledge. It may be added in specific accord with Gadamer's spirit that this is true also if understanding is comprehended as being embedded in the structural context of communicative understanding about something (the *thing*!). For even then, in the end it remains a meaning happening and a truth happening which is determined by the 'fusion of horizons' between the respective situation-dependent perspectives of the interpreter and of the *interpretandum*. What can be said about this?

First of all, I should like to make clear that I indeed do not consider the objectivity ideal of natural science (which is based upon the assumption of a homogeneous object of knowledge that is, so to speak, finished and only to be explored progressively) as a possible paradigm for the factual reference of hermeneutic understanding. This goes even for the hermeneutic reconstruction of the history of the natural sciences, which is, after all, also based on historical understanding of the matter of the natural sciences. I think that for all historical humanities and arts (which includes 'understanding sociology', in the sense it was given by Max Weber), factual reference is determined not by an object which is finished and only to be explored progressively but by history's irreversible happening, which these disciplines themselves constitute by way of 'further continued shaping of tradition'.

But does it really follow from these 'concessions' that one has to agree to Gadamer's notion that, by and large, the possibility of – a normatively regulated! – progress in understanding in the humanities and arts does not make sense?

This would, in my view, be unavoidable if the concept of inter-subjective validity – which corresponds with the notion of truth in the humanities and arts – had to be equated with the concept of objectivity in the sense of the objectivity ideal of the value-free natural sciences. As a matter of fact, this widely presupposed equation was suggested by Kant. But could one not also talk of the inter-subjective validity of norms – norms of ethics and norms that guide the evaluative understanding of critical-hermeneutic social sciences, humanities and arts? It would, however, be imperative to justify philosophically the inter-subjective validity of norms which are required in this matter. And this justification would not, for its part, have to return to historically determined contents of tradition, such as the handed-down *ethos* in the sense of Aristotle or the authoritative concept of the 'classic'.[33] For what really is at stake here is the provision of normative standards even for the critical assessment of the validity claims of tradition. And it needs to be pointed out that today, for the first time, we live in a multicultural world civilization that requires interculturally valid basic norms for the various tradition-dependent life forms to live and responsibly work together.[34]

However, not only Gadamer but all present philosophers who see themselves as post-Nietzschean, post-Heideggerian or post-Wittgensteinian seem to be totally confused on the question of the justification of inter-subjectively valid norms, if the question is recognized as a meaningful one at all. On the whole, the justification is regarded as an impossible task, if one wishes to avoid returning to religious or metaphysical dogmas.

At this point I should like to go back to the structure of communicative understanding of something, which even Gadamer recognizes as the condition of understanding along with the happening of tradition. Put differently, I should like to go back to the structure of argumentative discourse. This represents that form of reflection of communicative understanding which philosophy – including philosophical hermeneutics – takes for granted in the context of the justification of validity. Should this form of reflection, in turn, be only conceivable as an instance of a historically located meaning happening and truth happening? Or should it, as the condition of the possibility and validity of its philosophical function of reflection, imply an inter-subjective, and hence historically independent, validity claim *per se*? And if the latter proves to be the case, what are the consequences for the possibility of a normative justification of understanding in general?

The *a priori* of the argumentative discourse as historically non-circumventible form of reflection of understanding on something, and as normative condition of critical-hermeneutic understanding

In the 1971 discussion volume *Hermeneutics and Ideology Criticism*[35] Jürgen Habermas and I gave the impression – today I would say, wrongly so – that the 'claim to universality' of Gadamer's 'philosophical hermeneutics' could be called into question by such social scientific approaches as psychoanalysis and ideology criticism. More precisely put, we left the impression that it could be called into question by indicating the possibility and necessity of critical-reflective suspension of the hermeneutic 'fore-conception of perfection' by means of an objectifying 'analysis' of the communicative competence of socialized human beings and, therefore, also of the 'authority' of linguistic tradition; and all this, if possible, within the framework of a philosophy of history as the comprehensively operating discipline. However, both Habermas and I were at that time developing the approach of a discourse philosophy,[36] which proves the above-sketched act of questioning of the claim to universality as impossible. More exactly, it proves it impossible inasmuch as 'philosophical hermeneutics' (for example, 'transcendental hermeneutics', which after all I had previously supported) may take the place of discourse philosophy. What does this mean?

In my opinion it certainly does not mean that it should not

be possible and necessary to analyse the results of – as they are traditionally called – hermeneutic humanities and arts with the help of unmasking social scientific critiques.[37] Not to hold this possible would, I am sure, amount to a hermeneutic idealism of the *Geisteswissenschaften*, which is doubtless incompatible with Gadamer's conviction of the superiority of historical Being over any possible kind of reflective consciousness of Being.

It should also be clear, however, that empirical-self-critical reflection which both psychoanalysis and all forms of ideology criticism have to take for granted in their human 'objects' is not to be confused with transcendental-hermeneutic, or transcendental-pragmatic, reflection. The latter refers to the conditions of the possibility of argumentative discourses and, consequently, also to those of the critical social sciences. It takes place at the level of philosophical discussion and can in no way be replaced, or even in principle be surpassed, by unmasking critique. This is so simply because only this form can reflect on the conditions of the possibility and validity especially of unmasking critiques. As a matter of fact, this constitutes a thesis which currently meets with less popularity than the supposedly more radical, permanently self-contradictory practice of the total critique of reason.[38] The disrespect for my thesis is modelled on Nietzsche and is to be found, for example, in post-structuralism or postmodernism.

I believe that it can now be stated that this non-circumventible claim to universality which Gadamer makes of 'philosophical hermeneutics' is justified also as far as all critical social sciences are concerned – provided that 'philosophical hermeneutics' is so conceived that it can answer the question of the conditions of the possibility of valid understanding. But it is exactly this feature which cannot be expected of Gadamer's 'hermeneutic ontology' of meaning happening and truth happening.

The reflective perspective of philosophy indirectly makes possible critical 'better understanding'

What actually is the perspective of Gadamer's conception of 'hermeneutic ontology'? Put differently, what is the relationship between the discourse of understanding, in which Gadamer participates as a philosopher, and the discourses of understanding of the lifeworld and the humanities and arts, the structure of which he analyses as meaning happening and truth happening? The reader of

Truth and Method receives only an indirect answer to this question, which, I think, is ambiguous. On the one hand, Gadamer himself – just like the later Heidegger – appears not to participate in the discourse of understanding at all, but only to talk about the conditions of understanding as a temporal-historical happening in an unreflected, objectivistic attitude. Heidegger had, in the sense of the ontical/ontological difference, attached importance to distinguishing between the innerworldly/inner-temporal happening in the ordinary sense – that is, empirical happening – and the 'bringing about' and 'making room' of the world itself in an epochal-eventful meta-happening of the history of Being.[39] As far as I can see, Gadamer abandoned this idea completely. This is why there remains the impression of the inner-temporal objectivization of those phenomena which, at least in the classical ontology of the Greeks since Parmenides and Plato, could not have the character of inner-temporal happening: that is meaning that can be comprehended in thinking (namely idea or form and truth, or untruth).

Now, it was Hegel who first objectified the spiritual as something falling into time. It is true that he did so with the intention of simultaneously making it, as 'reflection in itself', nullify time (and history) in its being-in-and-for-itself, which required 'absolute knowledge'. Evidently, Gadamer constantly keeps this quasi-model in mind. But no matter how much he admires it,[40] it is certain from the very beginning that he needs to dissociate himself from it in the name of the finite nature of human *Dasein*. He does so in favour of the objectifying observation of a happening purely within time: that is, of the always only understanding differently of the respective 'view of Being'.

But is this really a legitimate alternative to Hegel's excessive demands on the reflective powers of the philosophical concept? Can the truth claims of the arts and philosophy (which realizes the relativity of the situation) be thought without contradiction after the model of the inner-temporally appearing 'objective spirit' – that is to say, as an 'expression of the diversity of life' (Dilthey) – like perhaps the truth claims of art and religion? Gadamer realizes that Dilthey's total reduction of 'the absolute' to the 'objective spirit' caused Dilthey to become entangled in the 'aporias of historicism'.[41] But, like Heidegger, Gadamer only seemingly manages an 'overcoming' of the relativism of historicism. He believes himself to have managed this overcoming by simply giving up Dilthey's objectivity ideal and historically-contextually relativizing understanding's validity claim right from the start. But is this not making a virtue out of Dilthey's necessity and cutting the gordian knot of the relativism of historicism in two instead of untying it?

Bearing in mind what I said in my introduction, I must at this point qualify my reservations about Gadamer: I am not interested in defending Dilthey's objectivity ideal of 'critical after-understanding' of uttered meaning. Neither am I interested in renewing Hegel's claim to comprehend the reflectively outstripping 'self-penetration of mind' – which is tied with all understanding – in the sense of the possibility of a total mediation of the form of understanding (of the 'concept') and of the contents of history. Instead, I am interested only in being able to think the truth capacity of reflectively outstripping – and hence also potentially critical – understanding in the sense of the regulative idea of inter-subjective validity *per se*, and in this respect of real possible, continuous progress. This is of particular interest to me in view of the fact that understanding which is always already reflective cannot, it is true, be raised to 'absolute knowledge'. However, in transcendental hermeneutics it has always already achieved the level of formal self-reflection with universal validity claim. This means that the discourses of understanding [in the sense of communicative understanding of something – translator], as a factor of which understanding has to be comprehended (also according to Gadamer), cannot simply be objectified inner-temporally as 'happening'. For in philosophical discourse they have always already achieved a form of reflection which can no longer reduce its own truth claim to a historically conditioned perspective among other temporally limited perspectives – as long as one intends to avoid performative self-contradiction.

Of course this observation is valid only in so far as we are really capable of making universally valid formal statements in philosophical discourse on discourses in general, and thereby of relativizing the perspectives of understanding of the individual discourses in the sense of their 'belongingness to history' (Gadamer). But this simultaneously opens the possibility of empirically comparing between different context-related perspectives of understanding, both synchronically and diachronically.[42] Nowadays a number of historical and cultural-anthropological/ethnological sciences take advantage of this. In addition the radicalization of reflective understanding – which has already been achieved in philosophy – makes possible the 'hermeneutics of suspicion' (Ricoeur) which suspends the 'fore-conception of perfection', as well as the corresponding methods of the critical social sciences.[43]

Should it not, consequently, be possible, even absolutely necessary, to comprehend the formal transcending of the viewpoint-dependence of understanding – which has already been achieved in the philosophical form of reflection of discourse – as a condition of the possibility of synthetically gaining new, superior perspectives of understanding? (These are new forms of the fore-conception of the world which make possible deeper understanding and which do not constitute simply 'further continued development' of traditions, but rather achievements of critical reflection.)

It goes without saying that these new perspectives of understanding (meaning-openings, if you will) which are mediated through critical reflection will also differ as perspectives; they open material 'view of the world' from out of the formal independence of the viewpoint of philosophical reflective insights; hence they again are historically situated and finite. This however does not change anything about the fact that these perspectives of philosophical discourse are subject to the regulative idea of better and deeper understanding.

Now Gadamer simply blocks this, so far only indicated, answer of a reflective, transcendental hermeneutics to the question of the conditions of the possibility of valid understanding. He does so by polemicizing against 'reflective philosophy', and his polemics are certainly indications of 'bad prejudices'. Although he clearly recognizes how the total historical relativization of all understanding leads to performative self-contradiction, he is willing to accept it after the model of Nietzsche, Heidegger and many of their successors. This reads as follows:

> However clearly one demonstrates the inner contradictions of all relativist views, it is as Heidegger has said: all these victorious arguments have something about them that suggests they are attempting to bowl one over.[44] However cogent they may seem they still miss the main point. In making use of them one is proved right, and yet they do not express any superior insight of any value. That the thesis of scepticism or relativism refutes itself to the extent that it claims to be true is an irrefutable argument. But what does it achieve? The reflective argument that proves successful here falls back on the arguer, in that it renders the truthfulness of all

reflection suspect. It is not the reality of scepticism or truth dissolving relativism, but the claim to truth of all formal arguments that is
affected.[45]

I must confess that I can regard this plea for the acceptance of
self-contradiction only as a fashionable capitulation of reason and
as the breaking-off of argumentative discourse by means of a word
from him. However, it is not this side of Gadamer's 'argumentation'
which, I think, is interesting, but the question whether this passage
does not express motives which should be comprehended and taken
seriously from a hermeneutic point of view. Should not, for instance,
the indication of the *reality* of scepticism and of all-truth-dissolving
relativism be taken seriously? Gadamer underscores this indication
in the above-quoted passage by remarking that, for example,
'Heinrich Rickert, who outright refuted the "philosophy of life" in
1920 . . . was in no way [able to] match the *influence* of Nietzsche and
Dilthey, which began to spread at that time'.[46]
My answer is, 'Yes and no!' 'No' inasmuch as philosophy is not
allowed to accept the 'actual effect' of arguments as an argument
against their validity. 'Yes' inasmuch as the great actual effect even of
defective arguments might contain some indication of their possible
explication by means of valid arguments. Conversely, valid arguments might be practically irrelevant concerning their significance,
and hence their possible fruitfulness. This appears to be Gadamer's
motive, and one that needs to be taken seriously. The following
passage shows this clearly: 'The consciousness of contingency does
not do away with contingency. It is one of the prejudices of reflective
philosophy that it understands as a relationship of propositions that
which is not at all on the same logical level.'[47]
This observation obviously affects the previously indicated circumstance: the formal-reflective discourse on discourses – which in
fact 'does not lie on the same logical level' as those discourses that
disclose the contents of the world and about which it makes statements – cannot directly open any new fact-disclosing perspectives
for the time being. Therefore, it seemingly leaves everything
the way it is (as Wittgenstein claimed of philosophy in general).
However, I have already attempted to show that, and for what
reason, this impression of fruitlessness turns out to be erroneous, if
one considers the at first only formal-general reflection with its
logically possible consequences (namely the new and superior fac-

tual perspectives of understanding that were mediated through reflection).

In the following, I should like to enforce this, in Hegel's sense dialectical, aspect in more depth. I shall attempt to show that the (certainly not fruitless) reflection on the presuppositions of the philosophical form of reflection of the discourse of understanding is able to uncover precisely those inter-subjectively valid norms of practical reason and of the critical-hermeneutic reconstruction of history which hermeneutic reflection, in Gadamer's sense, on the meaning happening and truth happening of historically situated understanding cannot discover.

The self-recuperative principle of the reconstruction of history as the normative basis of critical understanding

In contemporary philosophy – for example, hermeneutic phenomenology and Anglo-Saxon philosophy as it is influenced by Collingwood, Wittgenstein and American pragmatism[48] – there is broad agreement on the notion that our understanding and judging are dependent on the historical-contingent background preconditions of the lifeworld or the socio-cultural life forms. They are considered to be dependent on preconditions which in principle cannot totally be brought under the objectifying control of consciousness. It goes without saying that this demonstrates a far-reaching and multifold confirmation of the 'fore-structure' of the 'disclosedness' of 'being-in-the-world' as it was worked out by Heidegger and Gadamer – that is to say, of the 'a priori perfect of facticity' and of the 'thrownness' of our understanding of the world.

The consequences of this epochal insight apply both to theoretical philosophy (including philosophy of science) and practical philosophy. They lie almost without exception in the direction of a historical-relativistic approach, even if this is frequently concealed by a strategy which is inspired by Wittgenstein or philosophical pragmatism. This strategy consists in making the problem of universally valid norms and regulative ideas in theoretical and practical philosophy appear to be an obsolete, wrongly dramatized legacy of traditional metaphysics. In any event there is general consent that such things as universally valid norms or regulative ideas could be generated only by a metaphysical-fundamentalistic position. Also in my view, however, such an approach does not lie within the sphere of critical philosophical thought. Is there no other way out of this dilemma but to make a virtue out of necessity and see precisely in our insight into the dependence of our thinking on contingent tradition the sufficient solution to all normative problems of ethics and of the hermeneutic humanities and arts? In this respect Gadamer seems to propose an answer which demonstrates likemindedness with such thinkers as Rorty and MacIntyre![49]

I have already indicated that I do not regard the above-suggested answer as a plausible one. I do not understand why for the various cultures which today need to live and work together in the one lifeworld of humankind (and at many places already do so in the form of multicultural societies) a solution to the normative problem could be achieved if every culture, every socio-cultural life form, merely 'continued' its tradition or, in Rortyan diction, showed it off 'persuasively' in each particular context. (Particular attention should be paid to the way Rorty uses the words 'persuasive' and 'persuasion' in their ambiguous meaning between *überzeugen* (to convince) and *überreden* (to talk into). This ambiguity is characteristic of the entire history of these words in the occidental tradition of rhetoric. Owing to his denial of the existence of universally valid criteria for convincing by means of arguments, Rorty could not even welcome the possibility of dissolving this ambiguity with the help of speech-act theory. For instance, I am inclined to think that Gadamer's position is fairly close to Rorty's, certainly closer than to Kant's brusque condemnation of *überreden*. Kant regarded this notion as a method of robbing the partners in the discourse of their 'autonomy'.

But what is the point of these critical remarks, if in fact there is no way of justifying universal norms of critically understanding and judging traditions independently of these very traditions? Or should the reflective viewpoint of philosophical discourse on the diversity of traditions open up a solution? In the following I intend to show exactly this in defiance of all the prejudices against the fruitfulness of the reflective viewpoint. However, I believe it is necessary to make a few preliminary remarks on a post-linguistic-turn theory of philosophical reflection, which, in my view, is urgently needed these days.

First of all, it needs to be pointed out that philosophical discourse alone is capable of reflecting on itself and its presuppositions. Herein it is only in accordance with the specific validity claim of philosophical statements, for example, of statements on discourses in general:

it is universal and hence also self-reflective. I think that through this 'self-reflection', philosophical discourse finishes the reflective 'self-upgrading' of discourses, and hence of language.[50] This self-upgrading process leads from the thematization of the 'universality of facts' of natural laws to the empirical-hermeneutic thematization of the 'universality of meaning' of language or texts to the self-reflective thematization of the formal, but absolutely universal, validity claims of philosophy. In this respect the 'self-reflection' of philosophical discourse also completes the reflective certainty of the non-circumventibility of argumentation for reflection: this reflective certainty performatively accompanies all acts of argumentation. Any further self-reflection on the part of the participants in the discourse could have only psychological significance, but certainly no validity-theoretical relevance.

This clearly shows that this reflective self-upgrading of discursive understanding (which can be carried out in discourse by any partici-pant at any time) has to be distinguished from self-reflection in the sense of traditional philosophy of consciousness. As is commonly known, the latter leads either to paradoxes or infinite regress, which corresponds to the regress of the meta-languages (or the meta-theories) in meta-logic.

Such reflection on the necessary (that is, under pain of perfor-mative self-contradiction, non-disputable) existential and rule pre-suppositions of philosophical discourse, is, I believe, suitable for bringing to light the always already recognized norms (in the broad-est sense); this reflection has to be carried out in philosophical discourse itself. These norms are definitely different from those which – along with the tradition-dependent 'preconception of the world' and social 'consent' – are always already recognized by any finite human being as contingent *a priori* of facticity. They are pre-cisely part not of the 'fore-structure' of 'everyday being-in-the-world' (the lifeworld) in the sense of Heidegger and Gadamer (and the later Wittgenstein's life forms) but of the fore-structure of that reflection on the fore-structure of everyday being-in-the-world which people have tended to pursue since its origin in the 'axis age' (Karl Jaspers) of the high cultures of the classical world. Neither Heidegger nor Wittgenstein ever attempted to analyse the 'fore-structure' of their analyses of everyday behaviour and its accompa-nying language games. Had they done so, Heidegger would not have been able to put down the *logos* of occidental philosophy together with the 'thrownness' of all understanding of the world to an onto-historical 'event'. And Wittgenstein would have had to answer the question how – that is to say, by virtue of what 'healthy' philosophical language game – he would be able 'to bring to rest' the disease of 'empty' philosophical language games.)[51]

But what, now, are the normative presuppositions of philosophical discourse, and how are they different from those of the contingent preconception of the world? I would like to cite the experience of the Sixth East–West Philosophers' Conference in Hawaii (1989) on Culture and Modernity.[52] For in this conference all currently relevant requirements for a self-reflective discussion of the problem taken up in this paper were met: an encounter between philosophers and scholars in the humanities and arts from Europe, North America and the Asian countries; the thematization of the problems of universalism, pluralism and relativism; and, last but not least, the confrontation between representatives of the various positions I have mentioned (for example Rorty, Bernstein and MacIntyre). But most of all I would like to emphasize, as I did in the paper which I gave at this conference,[53] that the conference as such offered the opportunity of laying open the – usually not re-flected upon – normative presuppositions of current philosophical discourse. For our topic, this could be spelled out as the presuppositions of an attempted understanding between members or representatives of the most diverse cultural traditions and philosophical positions.

I think that I can now honour the following normative presuppositions as being of such a nature that none of the participants would have been able to contest them without simultaneously committing a performative contradiction.[54]

First, philosophers strive to achieve consensus on the validity of their own validity claims in principle with all (ideally, with all possible) partners in the discourse. They do so with the help of arguments, that is to say, by way of convincing, but not persuading, not to speak of such other strategic ways of using language as bribing or threatening. (They may no doubt expect and accept in the interest of their practical arguments that there will be actual dissent. But, in spite of Lyotard, they cannot strive for dissent by way of arguing.[55] Rather, in the case of dissent, they at least have to strive for a consensus on the reasons for the dissent, provided they continue to argue at all.)

Second, when arguing, philosophers necessarily have at least the following four validity claims (they always need to presuppose them at the same time, but they can individually emphasize them by the choice of their speech acts).

(i) Philosophers must have a claim on the inter-subjectively sharable meaning of their speech acts as a precondition of all further validity claims. (They must presuppose this claim as sufficiently fulfillable even in case they argue – for example, as linguists or speech psychologists – that, empirically speaking, we can never associate precisely identical meanings with our utterances; or in case they are of the opinion – along with Derrida – that *dissémination* (dissemination) or *différance* (difference) as fundamental happening of any semiotic process makes impossible the present of a sharable *signifié*. Derrida, of course, is able to bear the ensuing performative self-contradiction.) I believe it is possible to call into question even the claim to meaning of arguments, especially of philosophical questions, in the sense that the claim to meaning has to be explicitly defended. (It is true that comprehensibility that cannot be problematized any further needs to be presupposed also for the problematizable claims to meaning on the levels of linguistic syntax and semantics.)

(ii) In theoretical discourse the claim to truth or the claim to the unlimited capacity for consensus of assertions must be at the forefront. The claim to truth includes no claim to certainty: it is rather compatible with the explicit support of the reservation of fallibility, except in those cases where the presuppositions of the meaning of the thesis of fallibility are concerned. Examples of such presuppositions are those of the binary concept of truth and of the possibility of discourses for the forming of consensus.[56]

(iii) A precondition of any further validity claims – along with the claim to meaning – is the claim to truthfulness, which refers to subjective intentions. If it is called into question it can of course not be proved by arguments, but only be declared by means of speech acts or be realized practically.

(iv) A precondition of the exposition of the claims to truth as claims that can be accepted or rejected in an – in principle unlimited – community of communication is an ethically relevant claim to rightness in every argument. This fundamental claim to ethical rightness[57] can be explicated in a foundation of ethics which is reflective of its arguments in the following manner. The solidarity of an ideal community of communication, which follows the tightly interwoven basic norms of equality and of equal responsibility for the raising and solving of problems in the mutual recognition of the partners in discourse, has to be presupposed, and even be counterfactually anticipated, as every serious act of argumentation demonstrates. (From this, there instantly follows the demand that all moral problems which the participants in the discourse could raise – for example, conflicts of interests in the lifeworld, which otherwise could not be solved without the use of violence – should be solved by means of practical discourses by those who are affected.)

What now is the significance of the normative presuppositions of the philosophical discourse of understanding for our debate on Gadamer?[58] More precisely, in what way do we deal with a non-metaphysical, but transcendental-hermeneutic, or transcendental-pragmatic, basis for the normative control of all evaluative understanding? In other words, in what way do we deal with an authority which is independent of the validity claim of tradition (or more exactly, independent of the claims of the various, at least partly, incompatible cultural traditions) inasmuch as it is capable of justifying universally valid standards and, hence, also restricting conditions for the recognition of the responsibility of the validity claims of tradition(s)?

In the following I cannot attempt to unfold the relevance of the transcendental-reflective justification of a discourse ethics in the current situation of the world by, for instance, discussing a 'neo-Aristotelian' or 'communitarian' ethics that refers only to particular traditions (for example, those of a 'good *polis*' or a certain life form).[59] I would like only to stress the following central thesis: the formal-procedural basic norms of a discourse ethics relate to the evaluations of the contents of a substantial morality in the Hegelian sense, or of an *ethos* in the Aristotelian sense, the same way as the universally valid presuppositions of philosophical discourse relate to the historical-contingent presuppositions of the various life forms. These basic norms of a discourse ethics are not able, and are not supposed, to replace those evaluations or make them superfluous. However, they subject them to the restricting conditions and regulative principles of practical discourses in which those norms are to be justified which all people affected (including the next generations) could consent to. Such norms include human rights as well as currently pressing norms of an ecological ethics of global responsibility for the consequences of collective activities in the fields of science, technology, economics and politics. No doubt the difficulties involved in this programme of a macroethics of a thousand talks and conferences are large.[60] But the fact that this programme has long been recognized and followed, at least by public pretension, shows that the contemporary world knows no alternative to it.

In what follows I should like to put forward another argument which is able to demonstrate the possibility of justifying the regulative principles for a critical-reconstructive understanding of all human cultural traditions (or of the cultural evolution of humankind) on the basis of the universally valid presuppositions of philosophical discourse. In fact this argument does so more clearly than all so-far indicated arguments for the possibility of new, reflection-dependent perspectives of understanding. I am talking about what I named the self-recuperative principle of all critical-reconstructive social sciences, humanities and arts.[61]

The point of departure for the following thoughts is reflection on the fact that the recognition of the non-contingent presuppositions which form the 'fore-structure' of philosophical discourse today also is part of the *a priori* of facticity of our being-in-the-world.[62] In other words the recognition of the intended presuppositions is not only a noncontestable *a priori* of argumentation for all critical-reconstructive sciences. For them it also constitutes a fact of history that needs to be reconstructed – that is, a fact that needs, in a manner of speaking, to be caught up in its capacity and its actuality through understanding the reconstruction of history. Hence, the point of departure for the reconstruction of history, which is presupposed to be transcendental-hermeneutic, functions as the *telos* of this reconstruction. The function of this *telos* as a regulative principle of reconstruction cannot really be contested, provided that one intends to avoid reconstruction which contradicts performatively its own validity conditions. I think that this fore-structure of the reconstruction of history forms the alternative both to speculative philosophy of history (which must dogmatically-metaphysically presuppose the *telos* of history) and to Gadamer's hermeneutics of meaning happening and truth happening, which is unable to justify a regulative principle of possible progress.

The significance of the self-recuperative principle of the reconstruction of history can best be demonstrated by confronting it with attempts of a (metaphysical-anti-metaphysical) naturalistic-reductionist explanation of the history of mind from external causal motives. These attempts are characteristic of the modern era in general and, ironically, also of postmodernism's total critique of reason. For instance, it could be confronted with Nietzsche's attempts to call into question absolutely all validity claims of human reason from a genealogical point of view; examples would be truth, moral rightness and, in the end, also truthfulness – Nietzsche's *Redlichkeit* or honesty – which he had claimed for himself for so long. In the face of such attempts to replace understanding with explaining (they are condemned to be performatively contradictory), the self-recuperative principle of the reconstruction does not at all demand the abandonment of all external explanation. It does, however, demand a – at least validity-theoretical – subordination of the latter to (the act of) understanding in the sense of a rationally evaluating reconstruction.

In my view Imre Lakatos, in his discussion of Thomas Kuhn's conception of the history of science, provides a model for the relation that I demand here.[63] He postulates the general priority of the attempt to reconstruct an internal history of progress in natural science (in the sense of the understanding of sound scientific reasons) over any attempt to provide external explanations of the history of science by returning to psychological and social causes. On top of that he demands striving for a maximization of the 'internal history' compared with the 'external history'. (This caused Feyerabend to draw the problem-annihilating and consequently absurd conclusion that, in that case, it would be best to assume that 'anything goes'.)

Now, I think that Lakatos's model of the reconstruction of the history of science can be generalized in the sense of a principle of the reconstruction of the history of mind, or of cultural evolution altogether. (For what has to be regarded as an external motive from the point of view of the history of science could certainly be comprehended and appreciated as an internal one from the perspective of a hermeneutic reconstruction of the history of mind in general. One example would be Newton's theological, or theosophical, speculations, which motivated him to presuppose the existence of 'absolute space'.) This way it becomes evident that, basically, Lakatos's postulate constitutes nothing but an analogue of Gadamer's principle of the 'fore-conception of perfection', which is applied to history in general. However, this application to history in general also shows, I believe, that this principle in its heuristic-methodological function rather goes with the self-recuperative principle of transcendental hermeneutics (as supported here) than with a hermeneutics of the always only understanding differently. For the latter can just not comprehend the 'fore-conception of perfection' as a postulate of progress, but can only relate to it particular texts, or contexts.

The same, I think, is true with regard to the 'hermeneutic circle', if it is applied to the reconstruction of history. In this case the self-recuperative principle again needs to be presupposed in order to 'get into it [the circle] in the proper way'.[64] But this clashes with the later Heidegger's idea that the history of Being has to be comprehend as a – in this respect irrational – succession of 'epochal uncoverings-hidings' of the meaning of beings. In the end an antithetical conflict becomes apparent which I should like to comprehend as one between the *logos* of understanding (which can be caught up through reflection and hence be recognized) and temporal Being (that is, the happening of the manifestations of meaning). Gadamer's 'philosophical hermeneutics' has devoted itself to an ontology of temporal Being. In my view this contradicts its referral to the Socratic–Platonic dialectics of dialogue – that is to say of argumentative discourse, which is capable of catching up its assumptions maieutically. This is what I attempted to correct.

Notes

First published in L.E. Hahn (ed.), *The Philosophy of Hans-Georg Gadamer* (Chicago and La Salle, Ill.: Open Court, 1997), 67–94.

1 K.-O. Apel, *Die Idee der Sprache in der Tradition des Humanismus von Dante bis Vico* (Bonn: Bouvier, 1963; third edition 1980).
2 Gadamer called it 'philosophical hermeneutics', and he strove to substantiate it in later-Heideggerian terms of a meaning happening and truth happening of the 'mediation of tradition'.
3 See e.g. the preface to the second edition of *Wahrheit und Methode* (Tübingen: Mohr, 1965), xv f. and 483. On this point see Apel, *Transformation der Philosophie* (*Towards a Transformation of Philosophy*) (Frankfurt a. M.: Suhrkamp, 1973), 34 f.
4 See in particular Gadamer, *Wahrheit und Methode*, 249.
5 See M. Heidegger, *Kant und das Problem der Metaphysik* (*Kant and the Problem of Metaphysics*) (Frankfurt a. M.: Klostermann, 1951). On this point see Apel, 'Sinnkonstitution und Geltungsrechtfertigung: Heidegger und das Problem der "Transzendentalphilosophie"', in Forum für Philosophie Bad Homburg (ed.), *Martin Heidegger: Innen- und Aussenansichten* (Frankfurt a. M.: Suhrkamp, 1989), 131–75; abridged English translation: 'Meaning Constitu-

tion and Justification of Validity: Has Heidegger Overcome Transcendental Philosophy by History of Being?', Chapter 5 above.

6 *Aletheia* is rendered by Heidegger as 'disclosure' of the 'being-there' or, in his later terminology, 'unveiling' or 'opening' of Being. In ancient Greek it signifies truth and its personification.

7 Gadamer, *Wahrheit und Methode*, 261 ff.

8 *Ibid.*, 280; cf. Apel, *Transformation der Philosophie*, 46, n. 70. Emphasis by Apel.

9 Apel, 'Szientismus oder transzendentale Hermeneutik?', in *Transformation der Philosophie*, vol. 2, 178–219.

10 I am not talking about the idealistic utopia of complete transparency, contrary to the suspicion frequently voiced by Gadamer.

11 This was and is even today the methodological precondition of the practising humanities and arts (*Geisteswissenschaften*), and of linguistics in particular.

12 Gadamer, *Wahrheit und Methode*, 279 ff.

13 *Ibid.*, 161.

14 This proof is mentioned by Gadamer. See *Wahrheit und Methode*, 254.

15 Gadamer, *Wahrheit und Methode*, 277 f.

16 This affects, in particular, its claim to superiority over modern, especially positivist and Kantian, epistemology and philosophy of science.

17 See on this issue J. Grondin, *Hermeneutische Wahrheit? Zum Wahrheitsbegriff Hans-Georg Gadamers* (*Hermeneutical Truth? On Hans-Georg Gadamer's Conception of Truth*) (Königstein: Forum Academicum, 1982).

18 Compare, however, the thorough revolutionizing of the common Heidegger interpretation by Cristina Lafont-Hurtado's excellent dissertation, *Sprache und Welterschliessung: Zur linguistischen Wende der Hermeneutik Heideggers* (*Speech or Language and Disclosure of the World: The Linguistic Turn of Heidegger's Hermeneutics*) (Frankfurt a. M., doctoral dissertation, 1992). The dissertation was published under the same title by Suhrkamp in Frankfurt in 1994; an English translation, *Language and World Disclosure*, is forthcoming from Sage Publications.

19 E. Tugendhat, 'Heideggers Idee von Wahrheit', presented in 1964, published in O. Poggeler (ed.), *Heidegger* (Berlin: De Gruyter, 1969). See also E. Tugendhat, *Der Wahrheitsbegriff bei Husserl und Heidegger* (Berlin: De Gruyter, 1967). See also Tugendhat's Habilitationsschrift, in which he elaborated his criticism of 1964.

20 It is not certain but highly probable that Heidegger was familiar with Tugendhat's criticism.

21 M. Heidegger, *Zur Sache des Denkens* (Tübingen: Mohr, 1969), 76. Translation quoted from M. Heidegger, 'The End of Philosophy and the Task of Thinking', in M. Heidegger, *On Time and Being*, ed. and trans. Joan Stanbaugh (New York: Harper and Row, 1972), 69.

22 See M. Heidegger, *Vom Wesen der Wahrheit* (Frankfurt a. M., 1968), 97, where that equation which is 'decisive' for *Sein and Zeit* (*Being and Time*) is stressed, that is the equation of the 'question of meaning, for example, of the scope of projection, i.e., of openness, i.e., of the truth of Being'.

23 Heidegger, *Zur Sache des Denkens*, 77; 'The End of Philosophy and the Task of Thinking', 70. See note 21.

24 *Ibid.*, 70.

25 *Ibid.*

26 Apel, *Transformation der Philosophie*, vol. 2, part 2.

27 Gadamer, *Walrheit und Methode*, 278.
28 Lafont-Hurtado, *Sprache und Welterschliessung*, 241 ff. See also Apel, 'Linguistic Meaning and Intentionality: the Compatibility of the "Linguistic Turn" and the "Pragmatic Turn" of Meaning-theory within the Framework of a Transcendental Semiotics', in H.J. Silverman and D. Welton (eds), *Critical and Dialectical Phenomenology* (Albany: State University of New York Press, 1987), 2–53; also in G. Deledalle (ed.), *Semiotics and Pragmatics* (Amsterdam and Philadelphia: John Benjamins, 1989), 19–70; and in Apel, *Towards a Transcendental Semiotics* (Atlantic Highlands, N.J.: Humanities Press, 1994), 132–75.
29 Or between the *Geisteswissenschaften* and the 'natural sciences'. See Apel, *Die Erklären/Verstehen-Kontroverse in transzendentalpragmatischer Sicht* (Frankfurt a. M.: Suhrkamp, 1979). Also Apel, 'Diltheys Unterscheidung von 'Erklären' und 'Verstehen' im Lichte der Ergebnisse der modernen Wissenschaftstheorie', in E.W. Orth (ed.), *Dilthey und die Philosophie der Gegenwart* (Freiberg im Breisgau: Alber, 1985), 285–347; abridged English translation: 'Dilthey's Distinction between "Explanation" and "Understanding" and the Possibility of its "Mediation"', *Journal of the History of Philosophy*, 25 (1987), 131–50.
30 Gadamer, *Wahrheit und Methode*, 205 ff.
31 *Ibid.*, 437.
32 This is how I understand Gadamer's repeated explanations that, because of the point of view of 'philosophical hermeneutics', the objectivistic and progressive conditions of methodologically oriented hermeneutics do not become totally invalidated.
33 Gadamer, *Wahrheit und Methode*, 279 ff., 269 ff.
34 Apel, *Diskurs und Verantwortung: Das Problem des Übergangs zur postkonventionellen Moral* (*Discourse and Responsibility: The Problem of the Transition to Postconventional Morality*) (Frankfurt a. M.: Suhrkamp, 1988), in particular index, 'Neoaristotelismus'. In addition, see Apel, 'A Planetary Marcroethics for Humankind: the Need, the Apparent Difficulty, and the Eventual Possibility', in E. Deutsch (ed.), *Culture and Modernity: East–West Philosophical Perspectives* (Honolulu: University of Hawaii Press, 1990), 261–78.
35 Apel, Bormann, Bubner, Gadamer, Giegel, Habermas, *Hermeneutik und Ideologiekritik* (Frankfurt a. M.: Suhrkamp, 1971).
36 Habermas, 'Vorbereitende Bemerkungen zu einer Theorie der kommunikativen Kompetenz' ('Preliminary Remarks on a Theory of Communicative Competence'), in J. Habermas and N. Luhmann (eds), *Theorie der Gesellschaft oder Sozialtechnologie?* (*Social Theory or Social Technology?*) (Frankfurt a. M.: Suhrkamp, 1971), 101–41; 'Was heisst Universalpragmatik?' ('What Is Universal Pragmatics?'), in Apel (ed.), *Sprachpragmatik und Philosophie* (Frankfurt a. M.: Suhrkamp, 1976), 174–272: see also Apel, 'Sprechakttheorie und transzendentale Sprachpragmatik zur Frage ethischer Normen' ('Pragmatics of Language and Transcendental Pragmatics of Language on the Question of Ethical Norms'), in Apel (ed.), *Sprachpragmatik und Philosophie*, 10–173. See also Apel, 'Die Logosauszeichnung der menschlichen Sprache', in H.-G. Bosshardt (ed.), *Perspektiven auf Sprache* (Berlin and New York: W. de Gruyter, 1986), 45–87.
37 These are meant to include not only those of Freud or Marx, but also of Nietzsche, Foucault, and of Derrida's deconstructionism.

38 Apel, 'Die Herausforderung der totalen Vernunftkritik und das Programm einer philosophischen Theorie der Rationalitätstypen' ('The Challenge of the Total Critique of Reason and the Program of a Philosophical Theory of the Types of Rationality'), *Concordia*, 11 (1987), 2–23; English translation in D. Freundlieb and W. Hudson (eds), *Reason and its Other: Rationality in Modern German Philosophy and Culture* (Providence and Oxford: Berg, 1993).

39 Apel, 'Sinnkonstitution und Geltungsrechtfertigung'.

40 Compare the numerous references to Hegel in *Wahrheit und Methode*.

41 Gadamer, *Wahrheit und Methode*, 205 ff.

42 Gadamer, however, placed very little value on this. Compare *Wahrheit und Methode*, 220 and 380.

43 These are methods that employ external explanations of motives. Not included, though, are the quasi-nomological behavioural sciences, which stand in the service of social technology. See Apel, 'Types of Social Science in the Light of Human Cognitive Interests', *Social Research*, 44, 3 (1977), 425–70; repr. in S. Brown (ed.), *Philosophical Disputes in the Social Sciences* (Brighton: Harvester Press, 1979), 3–50.

44 M. Heidegger, *Sein und Zeit* (Halle: Niemeyer, 1941), 229.

45 Gadamer, *Wahrheit und Methode*, 327; English translation from *Truth and Method*, second edition (New York: Continuum Publishing Corporation, 1975), 308–9.

46 *Wahrheit und Methode*, 327; *Truth and Method*, 308; emphasis by Apel.

47 *Ibid.*, 424; *ibid.*, 405–6.

48 Examples are Searle's theory of the background and ethical-political 'communitarianism'.

49 A. MacIntyre, *After Virtue* (London: Duckworth, 1985); also *Whose Justice? Which Rationality?* (London: Duckworth, 1988); R. Rorty, *Contingency, Irony and Solidarity* (Cambridge: Cambridge University Press, 1989); *Objectivity, Relativism and Truth* (Cambridge: Cambridge University Press, 1991); J. Habermas, *Erläuterungen zur Diskursethik* (Frankfurt a. M.: Suhrkamp, 1991); Apel, *Diskurs und Verantwortung* and 'Das Anliegen des anglo-amerikanischen "Kommunitarismus" in der Sicht der (transzendentalpragmatischen) Diskursethik' ('The Matter of Concern of Communitarianism from the Point of View of Transcendental-pragmatic Discourse Ethics'), in M. Brumlik and H. Brunkhorst (eds), *Gemeinschaft und Gerechtigkeit (Community and Justice)* (Frankfurt a. M.: Fischer, 1992), 149–72.

50 See T. Litt, *Mensch und Welt: Grundlegung einer Philosophie des Geistes (Man and World: Foundations of a Philosophy of Mind)* (Munich: E. Reinhardt, 1948), 214 ff.

51 Apel, 'Wittgenstein und Heidegger: die Frage nach dem Sinn von Sein und der Sinnlosigkeitsverdacht gegen alle Metaphysik' ('Wittgenstein and Heidegger: the Question of the Meaning of Being and the Charge of Meaninglessness against All Metaphysics'), in *Transformation der Philosophie*, vol. 1, 225–75: in particular see 272 ff.; 'Wittgenstein und Heidegger: kritische Wiederholung eines Vergleiches' ('Wittgenstein and Heidegger: Critical Repetition of a Comparison'), in J. Habermas (ed.), *Der Löwe spricht . . . und wir können ihn nicht verstehen (The Lion Is Speaking . . . and We Cannot Understand Him)* (Frankfurt a. M.: Suhrkamp, 1991), 27–68, in particular 28 f., 53 ff. and 65 ff.; English version in C. Macann (ed.), *Martin Heidegger: Critical Assessments*

(London and New York: Routledge, 1992), vol. 3, 341–437; repr. in C. Macann (ed.), *Critical Heidegger* (London: Routledge, 1996).

52 See E. Deutsch (ed.), *Culture and Modernity*.

53 *Ibid.*

54 See the cited works by Habermas and Apel in note 36.

55 J.-F. Lyotard, *La condition postmoderne* (Paris: Minuit, 1979), 66.

56 Apel, *Diskurs und Verantwortung*; also *Ethics and the Theory of Rationality* (Atlantic Highlands, N.J.: Humanities Press, 1996).

57 This claim should not be confused with the claims to rightness produced in practical discourses, in the form of demands, for example.

58 In fact the presuppositions sketched here are without any pretensions to completeness.

59 Apel, *Diskurs und Verantwortung*; also *Community, Language and Ethics.*

60 Apel, 'The Ecological Crisis as a Problem for Discourse Ethics', in A. Ofsti (ed.), *Ecology and Ethics* (Trondheim: Nordland Akademi for Kunst og Vitenskap, 1992), 219–60; 'Discourse Ethics as a Response to the Novel Challenges of Today's Reality to Co-responsibility', *Journal of Religion*, 73, 4 (1993), 496–513.

61 Apel, 'Regulative Ideas or Sense Events? An Attempt to Determine the *Logos* of Hermeneutics', Chapter 7 above; also 'The Hermeneutic Dimension of Social Science and its Normative Foundation', *Man and World*, 25, 3/4 (1992), 247–70.

62 This was overlooked by Heidegger.

63 See I. Lakatos, 'History of Science and its Rational Reconstructions', *Boston Studies in the History of Science*, 8 (1971), 91–136; German translation in W. Diedrich (ed.), *Theorien der Wissenschaftsgeschichte* (Frankfurt a. M.: Suhrkamp, 1974), 55–119.

64 M. Heidegger, *Sein und Zeit*, 153, n. 35.

9

History of science as a problem of hermeneutics: an argument with Karl Popper's third-world hermeneutics

The problem

The original challenge and motive for my present inquiry was provided by a puzzling problem, which may be phrased as follows: assuming the usual distinction between empirical questions of description and explanation, on the one hand, and logical or normative questions of justification, on the other, how can it be understood that Thomas Kuhn's book *The Structure of Scientific Revolutions* could become a challenge to the 'logic of science'? How can we explain that the ensuing debate between historians and logicians has led to serious attempts on the logicians' part to modify their conceptions of good science (and possibly even to admit the alleged irrationality of scientific progress, in the case of Paul Feyerabend's anarchistic theory of knowledge)? This whole development is unintelligible on the classical presuppositions of the logic of science: for how should it be possible that facts about history could entail a modification of the norms of good science, since norms cannot be derived from facts if the 'naturalistic fallacy' is to be avoided? Indeed, to suggest an analogous problem: is there any good reason to modify Christian or Kantian ethics simply because people have usually failed to conform to them?

One might, of course, argue that norms of good science may be derived not simply from the historical facts as empirical facts but from the facts and the assumption that the behaviour of the historical agents – in this case, the behaviour of the great scientists – was following better norms than those of our proposed methodology. But this raises another question: how can we know that the great scientists were following better norms, without already presupposing the norms of our methodology of logic of science? Or, to put the same question more radically, how can we identify great scientists, or even just select scientists among other people in history, without already presupposing a normative logic of science?

The normative claims of empirical historiography necessarily seem to involve a vicious circle. I think that criticisms of the latter type were rightly directed by Popper and Lakatos[1] against Kuhn's initial claim that he was just relating the empirical facts; but, as at least Lakatos clearly realized, this argument in favour of a normative logic of science does not refute the suggestion that we might have good reasons to modify our methodological norms (and, incidentally, even our norms in general after confronting them with better ones), in short, that we may have to learn from history. The usual application of the 'naturalistic fallacy' argument does not take into account the emphatic meaning of the latter phrase, which does not simply say that we can learn from history about empirical facts (such as the fact that certain norms and not others were followed by people), but that we can learn about norms that are better than ours.

But if this explication of the problem situation is correct, then it becomes clear that the classical dichotomy between empirical science and (normative) logic (of justification), or, more precisely, the *tertium non datur* implied by this dichotomy, must be deficient. For it is on this understanding of the epistemological situation, and only on this understanding, that learning from history, in the emphatic sense of learning about better rules or norms of action, must lead to a vicious circle. What does this mean?

If, outside the normative logic of justification, only a value-neutral type of cognition, in the sense of empirical science, were possible, the claim to discover better norms of methodology (or, for that matter, ethics) by inquiring into the facts of history must lead to a vicious circle; for this claim obviously presupposes the validity of those better norms, which it can describe as empirical facts only. In that event however it may never become intelligible how we can find out something new about norms as well as historical experience.

In fact, even Kuhn himself, contrary to his empiricist claim, selects and evaluates scientists' behaviour in the light of a tacitly presupposed rational norm of progressive science. Indeed, in the course of his argument with the logicians it becomes quite clear that he is telling them not just facts about everything that has been called, or pretended to be, science in the course of history but rather facts about the structure of, say, real progressive science. Thus he makes the following statement (which, incidentally, shows how he distances himself from Feyerabend's view of the conclusions to be drawn from his work):

> As I have said before, both here and elsewhere, I do not for a moment believe that science is an intrinsically irrational enterprise. Scientific behavior, taken as a whole, is the best example we have of rationality. Our view of what it is to be rational depends in significant ways, though of course not exclusively, on what we take to be the essential aspects of scientific behavior. That is not to say that any scientist behaves rationally at all times, or even that many behave rationally very much of the time. What it does assert is that, if history or any other empirical discipline leads us to believe that the development of science depends essentially on behavior that we have previously thought to be irrational, then we should conclude not that science is irrational but that our notion of rationality needs adjustment here and there.[2]

The last-quoted sentences show Kuhn implicitly claiming that we can learn the truth about the structure of progressive science (or the progress of science as a whole) from history, and that this knowledge can be used in order to modify our concept of methodological rationality. Now this claim brings us back to our puzzling problem and may in fact help us to state it more clearly.

Our problem, I believe, is not only to understand how a non-value-neutral understanding of the history of science is possible; say, a reconstruction of history in light of the presupposed value or normative nature of scientific progress towards the truth. Our problem is, additionally, to understand how we can find out by understanding, or, say, reconstructing the history of science as a whole, that certain particular methodological rules, or norms, followed by scientists were better than those known to us thus far. The point is here that history must be able to teach us something new about norms as such; something that is not *a priori* implied by the norm of scientific progress towards truth, which must in any event be presupposed if we are to be able to select and understand the relevant facts of history.

At this point, I suggest, we can no longer avoid the conclusion that some kind of circular argument must be characteristic for the methodological structure of the historiography of science. However, since we may no longer take it for granted that historiography must be just a value-neutral, empirical (descriptive and possibly explanatory) science, we must no longer conclude that the 'circle' involved in our learning from history is necessarily a vicious one. In fact the hermeneutic tradition of the philosophy of the *Geisteswissenschaften* has always recognized more or less clearly that learning from history by understanding other people, foreign cultures and earlier periods of history involves a non-vicious but fruitful circle of understanding: the so called 'hermeneutic circle'. And our problem of productive mediation between empirical and normative reconstruction in historiography might suggest that the hermeneutic circle is, in fact, a specific methodological structure characteristic of a type of human cognition which presents a third dimension, so to speak, between value-neutral empirical description and explanation, on the one hand, and logical (or ethical) justification, on the other.

In the following two sections I shall try to bring to bear and eventually explicate and qualify my conjectures about the hermeneutic structure of historiography by analysing in its light the pertinent conceptions of Karl Popper (and Imre Lakatos).

Some critical remarks on Karl Popper's contribution to hermeneutics

I must confess from the start that I have some difficulties in dealing fairly and adequately with Popper's conceptions of the structure of historiography. In my opinion these difficulties stem from the following situational facts.

Viewed from the standpoint of the explanation–understanding controversy,[3] one point seems clear to me. In Popper's last writings, especially in his theory of 'situational analysis' in the light of 'third-world' structures[4] (and in Lakatos's theory of 'internal' versus 'external' history),[5] we no longer find any attempt to reduce the problems of understanding people's reasons (i.e. aims, beliefs and followed rules, norms or maxims) to those of nomological, causal (or statistical) explanations. On the contrary we are faced rather with a new tendency, to understand as much as possible from good reasons (i.e. as belonging to an 'internal' history of human rational action) and to leave only the unintelligible remainder to external explanations, which appeal to causes in the sense of the original naturalism of the covering-law schema of explanation.

Thus far, I can – and I shall in this chapter – appreciate Popper's and Lakatos's theories of historiography as a contribution to hermeneutics.[6] On the other hand, however, Karl Popper was himself one of the protagonists of the deductive-nomological model of explanation and of the conception of unified methodology based on that model; and it does not become completely clear, even in his last writings, to what extent he became conscious of the radical methodological difference between nomological explanation and, on the other hand, understanding human reasons in history (in order possibly to discover something new about rationality principles or norms as such).

There are in fact good reasons for the assumption that Popper, in his essay 'On the Theory of Objective Mind',[7] clearly recognizes the special features of understanding people's acting from reasons, in contradistinction to explaining the determination of an event by laws and antecedent conditions. (In addition Popper's plea for indeterminism, in the sense of the freedom of the will from physical determination, seems to me to be of crucial importance in this context.) In the present context the following of Popper's insights is especially significant. As early as in *The Poverty of Historicism* Popper realized that interpretations of history are not theories, properly speaking, since they 'cannot be tested'; that is to say: 'they cannot be refuted, and apparent confirmations are therefore of no value, even if they are as numerous as the stars in the sky'.[8] However, in contradistinction to his earlier treatment of Marxism and psychoanalysis, Popper later no longer seems to consider this fact the sign of a 'pseudoscience'. Rather he recognizes that the non-testability of historical interpretations is bound up with the fact that problems of understanding and interpretation are 'meta-problems' (i.e. problems on a higher level of epistemological reflection) in comparison with problems of natural science;[9] moreover, he even seems to see that, on the level of understanding how other people understand their situations, the problem of the 'hermeneutic circle' replaces, so to speak, the problem of testing theories due to the non-falsifiability of *a priori* principles of rationality.[10] Thus the structure of the hermeneutic circle is acknowledged, so it seems, as a feature unique to understanding and interpretation in the *Geisteswissenschaften*.

It is in full accord with these insights that Popper, in his own hermeneutic conception of 'situational analysis', seems to keep clear of two polar pitfalls or zones of failure. On the one hand, he rejects all psychological (e.g. behaviourist) interpretations of hermeneutic problems (which would reduce rational principles to dispositions); but, on the other, he also seems to steer clear of the danger of confusing the (empirical) problem of understanding with that of logical justification (i.e. with the problem of subsuming the agent's situation and his or her reaction to it under fixed normative criteria). He also seems to sail clear of the latter danger zone when he realizes that in order to understand the intentions of some agent (or author) we must first understand his or her situation, that is the situation as he or she saw it. It is this goal, of understanding something possibly new about people's reasons by understanding their situations and their intentions, that finds its 'regulative principle' in the following methodological device of Popper:

> We must try to refute our (hermeneutic) conjectures until they fit fully into the context of the problem-situation [namely of the agent or author! – K.-O. Apel], lose arbitrary features, and achieve something like a maximum of explanatory [I should rather replace that term by a hermeneutic one! – K.-O. Apel] power of what the author wanted to say.[11]

Thus far, we seem to be on the right track in our endeavour to discover the specific dimension of hermeneutic understanding which, as I have said, lies between the classical alternatives of the logic of science. But we have not yet considered the new approach by which Popper intended to overthrow the methodology of classical hermeneutics, say of Schleiermacher, Dilthey, Collingwood and Emilio Betti (not to speak of post-Heideggerian hermeneutics).

There are two main features to be considered in this context, neither of which is quite new, as both were anticipated to a certain degree by the neo-Kantians, especially by Heinrich Rickert.[12] I am referring, on the one hand, to the Platonistic theory of the 'third world' and, on the other, to the contraposition of 'objective understanding' as against 'subjective' or 'psychological' understanding. The latter point may itself be expressed more precisely in terms of Popper's three-worlds theory, as follows.

Traditional hermeneutics is, in Popper's view, a world-two method about world-two objects; that is to say, it is directed at the subjective thoughts, experiences or feelings of other persons and relies on empathy, intuitive identification or imaginative re-enactment. The main methodical device in this context is the postulate of putting oneself into the actor's situation and trying to imagine what thoughts or feelings one would have in this case. As against this device, Popper – like Rickert in his argument against Dilthey – claims that understanding, if it is to be an objectively valid method of cognition, must be directed at third-world entities or third-world structures. For, as Plato first realized, there is no intelligible meaning of whatever we may think of that may not be conceived as a structural unit in such a world outside, as it were, the world of experience, that is outside genesis and vanishing in space and time. Popper draws all the conclusions from this Platonic conception; for he postulates as the structural units of the third world not only ideas or concepts but also propositions, even false propositions, and moreover theories and even problems and problem-situations (i.e. problems together with their historical backgrounds). And he claims as the fundamental thesis of hermeneutics that it is only in the light of the objective structures of the third world that one can even understand the subjective intentions of actors or, for that matter, of authors of texts.

At this point, however, the old Leibniz–Kant–Reichenbach distinction between the context of justification and the context of discovery comes into Popper's argument, for he is prepared to admit that the second-world method of intuitively reliving some personal experience may have a 'limited and subjective yet at the same time indispensably suggestive' value in the context of discovery[13] and, even more important, he considers it an original feature of his own theory that it can combine the Platonic assumption of the superhuman autonomy of the third world (of virtual objects of thought) with the idea that this world originates and grows by means of an interaction of human creativity – say, of theory information – with the pre-existing structures of the third world.

On the basis of these assumptions Popper reaches the conclusion that our understanding should be directed not at human acts as psychical processes but at the products of human acts, that is at third-world objects, whose meaning may be progressively understood by studying the structural relations between the structural units of the third world. He contrasts this method of progressively deepening and logically justifying our understanding of an objective meaning with the implausible suggestion, due to the subjective method of empathy, that the historian should 'revive' or 're-enact' psychical states or acts which are 'far beyond the historian's capacity', say, acts of 'unbearable cruelty', of 'supreme heroism' or 'artistic or literary or scientific or philosophical achievement'.[14]

Now, in trying to examine critically this 'objective' approach to hermeneutics, I can agree from the outset that understanding as a justifiable achievement of cognition cannot consist in reviving the real psychical process of another person; in this sense, any suggestion that a historian becomes, so to speak, a Nero, a Caesar or a Rembrandt is of course nonsense (although there are phenomena of play-acting, magical reliving of the deeds of deceased tribal chiefs by shamans and suchlike, which have at least some affinity to understanding other persons). However, even if one focuses on the problem of justifiable understanding of meaning, there is, it seems to me, a weak point in Popper's approach.

It is not true, I believe, that the Popperian dichotomy between world-two understanding and world-three understanding can be unambiguously paralleled or co-ordinated with the distinction between the context of discovery and the context of justification. One might just as well go the other way around. Thus, it is even the greatest merit of Popper's approach that it provides a heuristic horizon for possible understanding within the context of discovery of historiography, especially with regard to the history of science.[15] It seems quite clear to me that it is this heuristic function of world-three structures of possible meaning that must be exploited primarily in the method of reconstructing an 'internal' history of science, as proposed by Lakatos.[16]

But, if this is true, we are left with the problem of how to check that our heuristic projects (designs, blueprints) of the possible meaning of a text (or action) will fit the meaning intentions of the author (or actor). Of course this is the task of 'situational analysis', but, on Popper's account, this analysis must proceed also by understanding in the light of the third world, that is in the light of ideal structures of possible meaning. Of course even the unique meaning of the individual meaning intention of a historical person, say a creative scientist, is a possible item and structural unit in the third world; and thus it indeed becomes intelligible how, in Popper's view, objective understanding of the subjective intention of an author (or actor) should be possible. Still, at this point an aporia emerges.

In fact hermeneutic understanding is not only an attempt to imagine, or conceive of, a possible meaning that might possibly be justified by a reasonable structural context; it is at least also an empirically relevant attempt to grasp the factual meaning intention of a human individual. Thus far it needs also an empirical justification of its own correctness. Now this empirical justification cannot be provided by one's understanding of possible meanings in the light of third-world structures; for in the third world there is only a possible equivalent or counterpart of the unique meaning of the author's intention, not an index to a meaning that can be grasped as empirical evidence to support our conjectured understanding.

At this point it becomes doubtful whether Popper, unlike Hempel, has actually recognized the difference between justifying the correctness of a human belief or action and, on the other hand, justifying the correctness of our understanding of a person's belief or action. This latter problem is an empirical one concerning hermeneutic experience. If we ignore this problem, any project of understanding the meaning of a text or action would run the risk of falling into albeit productive error; that is to say, it might very well produce a marvellous systematic account of a possible problem situation and a possible problem solution, without hitting or touching the actual meaning intention of the author of the text that is to be interpreted. Now, if our problem is to learn something new about rules or norms from history (and not from speculation), then the flaw in making exclusive use of the third-world method of understanding is a matter not only of bad philology but also of failing to learn something new about possible meanings of the third world via historical understanding. This aporia is, I believe, precisely what characterizes the unsolved problem of Popper's approach to hermeneutics.[17]

What we need in order to provide empirical evidence for the correctness of understanding is obviously something like hermeneutic experience. To my mind this was already Dilthey's problem. The real reason why he rejected the neo-Kantian third-world theory of understanding was not that he should have identified understanding with 'empathy' or 'reviving'. (This is rather a myth that was produced by the neo-positivists.) The proper reason was rather that Dilthey postulated, in addition to the traditional rules of hermeneutics, 'empathy' (*Einfühlung*) or 'reviving' (*Nacherleben*) as a special type of sensory experience with reference to (pre-linguistic and linguistic) expressions of meaning. Thus, with regard to the hermeneutic experience of meaning, the Kantian synthesis of cognition (i.e. the synthesis of understanding and sensation) was to be different from that of the natural sciences as Dilthey saw them. It was different in that it presupposed a peculiar type of sense data: those which are in themselves expressive vehicles of meaning intentions.

The neo-Kantians, on the other hand, adhered to the orthodox Kantian version of the cognitive synthesis of experience, according to which the sense data in all kinds of experience are the same. Thus, the neo-Kantians, unlike Dilthey, did not revise the epistemological basic conception of a unitary human experience in the case of grasping non-real (valid or non-valid) meanings of a third world (of values), in the light of which the individual meaning intentions of persons were to be understood.

However, as we have seen, this neo-Kantian conception, which was renewed in a sense by Popper, is not adequate for an exact solution of the problem of justification in hermeneutics. It simply cannot account for the specific dimension of empirical justification of understanding other persons' meaning intentions, because it cannot consider the specific function of sensation in hermeneutic experience as an ingredient of synthetic cognition, and hence as a non-psychological topic of transcendental epistemology.[18]

In order to deal adequately with the problem of the synthetic achievements of cognition, such as causal explanation, on the one hand, and, on the other, hermeneutic understanding, it is in fact necessary, in my opinion, to transcend the abstract context of 'logical semantics' (in the sense of Tarski and Carnap) and to reintroduce the explication context of a Kantian-type epistemology, or rather of a transcendental pragmatics or transcendental semiotics of cognition.[19] Within the context of transcendental semiotics, for example, it becomes quite clear that hermeneutic experience is a kind of communicative experience. As such it has, even on the level of its sensory 'faculty', a semiotic referential object other than perception in natural science: it is not directed at symptoms or 'indices' (in the sense of Peirce's semiotics), but at 'symbols' or, at least, symbol-like expressions of meaning, especially of meaning intentions.

Hence, what we have to do in order to approach a solution to the problem of hermeneutic understanding is somehow to combine the Popperian third-world method with a non-psychological account of how individual (subjective) meaning intentions are understood. The epistemological (transcendental-semiotic) possibility, however, of such a combination is provided, I believe, by the horizon of transcendental pragmatics of language communication. For it is within this horizon that the reciprocity of placing oneself in someone else's position and re-enacting his or her thought perspective and meaning intention can be mediated (and always has been mediated) with the objective structures of the 'third world'. This mediation is due to the public or inter-subjective meaning that we humans can share thanks to the so-called meaning conventions of language.[20]

In this context I must emphasize, to avoid being misunderstood by Popperians, that to my mind the possible sharing of inter-subjective meaning is not restricted *a priori* to the factual usage of particular languages or language games, say, in the sense of an incommensurability thesis with regard to frameworks of meaning. As against this fashionable post-Wittgensteinian paradigm-relativism I should rather postulate that each natural language – and hence also the philosophical or scientific language game of argumentative discourse that is carried through in a natural language – is open to the whole Platonic dimension of the third world, that is to the regulative idea of having its meanings progressively widened and/or refined towards an ideal limit of interlingual translatability.[21]

I do not think that this regulative idea – which matches the human 'communicative competence' which *a priori* (by a counterfactual anticipation, so to speak) refers to an indefinite communication community – contradicts the well-understood Quinean thesis of the 'indeterminacy' of interlingual meaning translation: for the latter thesis refers to the possible facts of translation which, according to Kant, can indeed never correspond precisely to the regulative idea of inter-subjective sharing of the meanings of (even different systems of) language. But I think that there are two different, but complementary, ways of widening and refining one's understanding of meaning, that is of progressively approximating the limit of ideal inter-subjectivity. Both ways are made possible by language as a medium of common or public meaning; but one is the way of the Platonic 'voiceless dialogue of the soul with itself', in the light of third-world structures, such as possible systems of thought or theories. This way, which is indeed also an indispensable aid to hermeneutic understanding, is the typical method of pure philosophy, from Plato to Popper. The other way is that of public communication, especially of the 'great dialogue of the spirits' beyond the limits of time[22] which has been made possible by written texts and has found its specific methodical *organon* in the humanistic *ars interpretandi* (translated by the Greek term *hermeneutics* in the seventeenth century).

This latter way is the specific method of the 'humanities' or *Geisteswissenschaften*, although it, too, is of course an indispensable aid to pure philosophy. But its methodological point is not constituted so much by the Platonic light of the third world, which, so to speak, shines also on solitary thinkers and in fact provides a horizon of theoretical structures for all scientific disciplines. The specific methodological point of hermeneutic understanding consists, rather, in a beneficial compulsion, or pressure, to overcome through communication the difference between the individual perspectives of subjective meaning intentions and hence also between idiosyncratic personal views of the third world.[23] This is another way of widening one's subjectivity towards inter-subjectivity; it supplements our solitary interaction with the structures of the third world, and is of course the specific method of learning from history even about principles of rationality and methodological norms.

This brings us back to our special problem and reminds me that I have still to show how the proposed method of hermeneutic understanding may eventually supplement Popper's (and Lakatos's) conception of a historiography of science.

In order to pinpoint, so to speak, the real problem of rational understanding beyond the limits of any quasi-theoretical heuristics, let us consider an example of rational understanding presented by Karl Popper himself. I refer to his attempt to understand Galileo's rejection of Kepler's theory of the tides, which was later justified by Newton as being approximately true. To my mind, Popper's account of Galileo's good reasons for adhering to the hypothesis of the circular motion of the planets, as against Kepler's introduction of elliptical orbits, and his denial of any influence of the moon, is in fact an admirable hermeneutic hypothesis, based on 'situational analysis'. Moreover, it marks, I believe, a considerable step forward in the historiography of science compared with the traditional interpretations, which attributed Galileo's adherence to the false theory solely to his dogmatism and other personal deficiencies.

Nevertheless, two points may be made to show up the intrinsic limits of the third-world method in Popper's account and the necessity of having it combined with, and counter-checked by, a method of hermeneutic experience, within the context of quasi-communication with the authors of the pertinent texts.

The first point is simply the following argument. Popper's analysis of Galileo's historical situation does not rest solely on the third-world method, imagining the relevant structures of Galileo's supposed problem situation; Popper always tacitly supplements and probably corrects it by registering empirical evidence for Galileo's thoughts or meaning intentions, as represented by the symbolic meaning expressions of the texts. Thus, for example, Popper supports his important argument that 'Galileo rejected the lunar influence because he was an opponent to astrology' by pointing to the last passage in Galileo's *Dialogue Concerning the Two Chief World Systems*.[24] Popper would admit this point as being a matter of course, but, since he opposes his new method to the traditional hermeneutics, one must reflect upon the fact that, within the context of his communication with the text, Popper must also try to re-enact the thoughts of Galileo as a historical individual as they are expressed by the text. And it was, I suggest, through the 'hermeneutic circle' which is permanently and continuously mediating between the poles of the third-world method and the registration of empirical evidence about thoughts or meaning intentions that Popper in fact arrived at his interpretation.

Second, if this is true, however, a further problem arises with regard to the possible limits of the heuristics provided by Popper's special version of the third-world method of historiography: that is to say, by the falsification methodology which is the hard core of his quasi-theory of an ideal history of science. In his account of Galileo's good reasons for adhering to Copernicus's simple theory of circular planetary orbits, Popper argues that 'from the point of view of method Galileo was perfectly right in attempting to explain everything on this narrow basis; for only if we try to exploit and test our fallible theories to the limit can we hope to learn from their failure'.[25]

Now, I readily admit that this argument provides a possible justification of the possible good reasons for Galileo's attitude, but it nevertheless remains doubtful whether his actual reasons for spurning Kepler's friendly advances are in fact sufficiently well explained by Popper's 'good-reasons essay'. For it is not very plausible to suppose that Galileo actually understood his problem situation in the light of Popper's methodology of falsification. (In fact, his writings sometimes contain hints of a certain naive empiricism.) At the very least the third-world method here leaves us some latitude, in principle, for further attempts at precisely understanding Galileo's individual motives. This argument is reinforced by the fact that, in the light of a methodology of proliferating competing theories, Kepler's adoption of a more complicated theory of the orbits of the planets could also be justified for objectively good reasons.

These considerations imply, to my mind, that third-world methods of ideal-typical reconstruction of a supposed problem situation can and must, in principle, be supplemented and also counter-checked by other methods, of a more socio-historical and even psychological orientation. Thus a biographer of Galileo might have recourse to special institutions, conventions and customs of the society and/or community of scholars that might have determined Galileo's behaviour; and, in the case of his attitude to Kepler, he or she might at least be justified in also registering and considering symptoms of ambition, jealousy or aggressiveness that could be found in the available documents.

Of course one could argue, along with Lakatos, that such sociological and psychological accounts would at least provide external explanations of Galileo's behaviour, and in that sense are even foreseen by the third-world method as a supplementation of the internal reconstructions of history. But this argument does not do justice to the hermeneutic argument which implies that there is no guarantee that a special third-world quasi-theory of the internal history could ever exhaust the possibilities (and thus satisfy the regulative idea) of optimizing our understanding of individual (unique) historical actions for good reasons. Therefore, we must always reckon with the possibility that our good reasons will need enrichment by subjective reasons of the actors (or the authors), which may seem to be external only from the perspective of a special, ideal-typical conception of internal history. We arrive, it seems, at the following conclusions. In the methodology of historiography it is indeed not only possible but even necessary to introduce the distinction between internal and external history, and an understanding of the former must certainly have priority over a causal explanation of the latter. Nevertheless, if we wish to understand and interpret individual actions or texts, we must grant the ultimate methodological priority to the hermeneutic circle over every special third-world quasi-theory of internal history, for the following reason. The hermeneutic circle is simply the methodological device for mediating between heuristic third-world projects of possible meaning and hermeneutic experience of the symbolic expression of individual meaning intentions. By contrast, all possible quasi-theories of internal history – although they may be more or less adequate for an understanding of individual meaning intentions rooted in good reasons – are only, albeit coherent, ideal-typical heuristic devices of what, in the light of our conception of the third world, could belong to the internal history of science. This being the general result of our considerations with regard to hermeneutics, there is also a conclusion to be drawn with regard to the debate on the relationship between methodology and history of science. The ultimate priority of the hermeneutic circle over ideal-typical quasi-theories of internal history which may be inspired by the 'third world' implies that the philosophical methodology of science cannot prescribe to creative scientists in advance a method of good science. But this does not mean that there is no point in a constant attempt to justify good science by reconstructing the internal history of science (in the light of third-world-projection) and the results of these attempts should not be irrelevant even for the methodological strategies of the creative scientists.

Notes

1 See I. Lakatos and A. Musgrave (eds), *Criticism and the Growth of Knowledge* (Cambridge: Cambridge University Press, 1971).

2 T. Kuhn, 'Notes on Lakatos', in R.C. Buck and R.S. Cohen (eds), *Boston Studies in the History of Science*, vol. 8 (Dordrecht: Reidel, 1971), 143 ff.

3 K.-O. Apel, *Die Erklären/Verstehen-Kontroverse in transzendentalpragmatischer Sicht* (Frankfurt a. M.: Suhrkamp, 1979); English translation: *Understanding and Explanation: A Transcendental-pragmatic Perspective* (Cambridge, Mass.: MIT Press, 1984).

4 K.R. Popper, *Objective Knowledge: An Evolutionary Approach* (Oxford: Clarendon Press, 1972).

5 I. Lakatos, 'History of Science and its Rational Reconstruction', in R.C. Buck and R.S. Cohen (eds), *Boston Studies in the History of Science*, vol. 8 (Dordrecht: Reidel, 1971), 91–136.

6 See the interesting paper by Farr (1983), to which I am very indebted in my own statement of Popper's position, although I shall deviate from Farr's general tendency in two respects. First, I shall insist on a certain dramatization of Popper's shift from the deductive-nomological model of explanation to the new model of rational understanding by 'situational analysis'. (Viewed from the standpoint of the *Erklären–Verstehen* controversy, this is clearly a step from one side to the other, for example from Hempel's to Dray's position. This should not be disguised.) Secondly, I shall try to show that Popper does not yet do full justice to traditional hermeneutics since he

overlooks in a sense the special problem of hermeneutic experience and hence of empirical corroboration of the conjectures toward understanding human meaning intentions in the light of the 'third world'.

7 K.R. Popper, 'On the Theory of Objective Mind' (1968), in *Conjectures and Refutations* (London: Routledge & Kegan Paul, 1972).

8 K.R. Popper, *The Poverty of Historicism* (London: Routledge & Kegan Paul, 1967), 151.

9 K.R. Popper, 'On the Theory of Objective Mind', 177.

10 *Ibid.*, 187, n. 39.

11 *Ibid.*, 190, n. 41.

12 See H. Rickert, *Die Grenzen der naturwissenschaftlichen Begriffsbildung* (Tübingen: Mohr, 1921, 1930).

13 K.R. Popper, 'On the Theory of Objective Mind', 170, n. 18; 188.

14 *Ibid.*, 188.

15 The most impressive example of this thesis known to me is the Renaissance reconstruction of Archimedes' work on hydrostatics. As shown by L. Olschki (*Geschichte der neusprachlichen wissenschaftlichen Literatur* (Leipzig, 1922), vol. 2, 200 ff.; vol. 3, 71 ff.), this task of hermeneutic understanding could not be carried out by the humanist scholars of Greek, but only by a mathematician-engineer like Nicola Tartaglia, who knew little Greek but was so proficient in problems of technical hydrostatics that he could imagine what Archimedes must have meant.

16 I. Lakatos, 'History of Science'.

17 It also hints at a difficulty in Lakatos's method of reconstructing the 'internal history' of science.

18 The modern 'logic of science' is in a sense a successor to neo-Kantianism's logicist approach to the problems of synthetic cognition; and it suffers even more than neo-Kantianism did from the 'abstractive fallacy' of banishing all problems of sensory experience – and of cognitive interests – into the wastepaper basket of psychology or 'empirical pragmatics'. This also applies to Popper's 'logic of scientific discovery', especially to this treatment of the empirical evidence of 'basic sentences' and of logic explications of 'explanations'.

19 Apel, *Die Erklären/Verstehen-Kontroverse*; Apel, 'C.S. Peirce and Post-Tarskian Truth', *The Monist*, 63 (1980).

20 Apel, 'Intentions, Conventions, and References to Things: Dimensions of Understanding Meaning in Hermeneutics and in Analytic Philosophy of Language', in H. Parret and J. Bouveresse (eds), *Meaning and Understanding* (Berlin and New York: W. de Gruyter, 1981), 79–111.

21 Apel, 'Linguistic Meaning and Intentionality: the Compatibility of the "Linguistic Turn" and the "Pragmatic Turn" of Meaning-theory within the Framework of a Transcendental Semiotics', in H.J. Silverman and D. Welton (eds), *Critical and Dialectical Phenomenology* (Albany: State University of New York Press, 1987), 2–53.

22 Apel, *Die Idee der Sprache in der Tradition des Humanismus von Dante bis Vico* (Bonn: Bouvier, third edition 1980).

23 D. Böhler, *Rekonstruktive Pragmatik* (Frankfurt a. M.: Suhrkamp, 1985).

24 K.R. Popper, 'On the Theory of Objective Mind', 176, n. 24; *Objective Knowledge*, 38, n. 4; 118, n. 4.

25 K.R. Popper, 'On the Theory of Objective Mind', 173.

10

The self-recuperative principle of a critical-hermeneutic reconstruction of history

History of science as a paradigm of hermeneutic reconstruction of history

In what follows my objective is to contribute to a normative-methodological foundation for the hermeneutic reconstruction of history by the humanities (*Geisteswissenschaften*). In order to elucidate these concepts I will start out from an example. Let us consider the difference between the following two 'why' questions which may be asked in different scientific contexts.

The first 'why' question, which could be posed by an institute for economic research, may read: 'Why, during recent years, has the demand of a certain group of consumers – for example male students – for cigarettes decreased, whereas that of another group – for example female students – has increased?' The second 'why' question, which could be posed by a historian of science, may read: 'Why did Isaac Newton, in the context of his *Philosophiae Naturalis Principia Mathematica*, introduce the idea of "absolute space"?'

Are these two 'why' questions to be considered questions for causes of the occurrence of an event as in the case of natural science, that is questions to be answered through a nomological-causal explanation that would have recourse to laws or at least regularities and antecedent – or marginal – conditions?

Prima facie one might be inclined to understand the two 'why' questions in this way. Advocates of the neo-positivist methodology of unified science are even committed to such an understanding. I think, however, that only – perhaps – in the first case, which concerns the question of the institute for economic research, can the 'why' question be understood as a nomological-causal question but by no means in the second case, which concerns the question posed by the historian of science. In what respect exists here a difference? My answer would run as follows.

Already in the first case the 'why' question is not a question of the natural sciences but of the social sciences. That means that, even in this case, it is not necessary to conceive of the 'why' question primarily as a nomological-causal question. One could rather understand it primarily as a question about the consumers' good or bad reasons for smoking. Thus far it would not be at all a question for a nomological-causal explanation but rather one of hermeneutic understanding and eventually one of evaluating people's reasons for action. (After all, it could be the case that the female students for reasons of prestige, or demonstrating equal status, are at present less accessible to warnings against damage to health than male students are. In this case the understandable reasons would not be very good ones.)

If however the 'why' question was posed by an institute of economic research, it would not be very probable that the cognitive interest underlying the 'why' question was primarily directed towards understanding or even evaluating the good or bad reasons of the male and female students for smoking. In this case the understanding of reasons might rather have only a heuristic function in order to find out the causes of the behaviour that can regularly be expected. This means that the reasons for action are not interesting here as good or bad reasons but as causally effective reasons which may be put into the value-neutral scheme of a quasi-nomological – for example statistical – explanation of the behaviour; and this (value-neutral) causal explanation would stand in the service of prediction.

In brief: we would be confronted in this case with an example of that type of social science – often called behavioural science – which indeed to a large extent represents a methodological analogy to nomological-explanatory natural science. Hermeneutic understanding here has indeed only a heuristic function in the vanguard of science, as C.G. Hempel has asserted with regard to hermeneutic *Verstehen* in general;[1] for what matters in this case is value-neutral causal explanation in the service of prediction.

But let us now consider the question of the historian of science: 'Why did Newton introduce the concept of "absolute space"?' Would it be possible in this case also to understand the 'why' question, along with Hempel, as being only a question for a nomological-causal explanation in the sense of the unified science methodology and answer it correspondingly?

My answer would be: this would be impossible (in this case), on principle. The 'why' question must in this case be understood as a question for the – good or bad – reasons for Newton's acting as he did. For – as Karl Popper has rightly maintained[2] – any attempt at nomologically explaining and predicting the creative and innovative achievements of science would be paradoxical. For, if it were possible, this would mean that it would be possible to explain the creative achievements of natural science by the methods of a social science that could causally explain the behaviour of natural scientists and hence, in principle, could predict the achievements of natural science. This would obviously be absurd. In other words: the 'why' question of the historian of science cannot fall within the scope of a behavioural science as quasi-natural science. In this case the meaning of the 'why' question must aim at the hermeneutic understanding and even evaluating of the good and bad reasons for action. Thereby it becomes clear that history of science – and precisely history of natural science – is a paradigmatic case of what has been called *Geisteswissenschaft*.

It is interesting in this context that Karl Popper, whose position first was close to Hempel's unified methodology of nomological-causal explanation by the example of history of science, was motivated to dissociate himself from naturalistic reductionism and finally to develop for himself a conception of hermeneutics.[3] Even more interesting in our problem context is the following fact: Popper and his disciple Imre Lakatos, who first – like Hans Albert – understood historical sociology as value-neutral science in the sense of Max Weber, saw themselves compelled, at least in the case of history of science, to defend a non-value-neutral reconstruction of history.[4]

How did this turn come about? Considered historically, the reason seemed to be that the Popperians wanted to show – as against Thomas Kuhn's theory of (mere) paradigm change – that history of natural science can be understood as a process of internal progress, which means that it can be reconstructed by critical evaluation. The same motive was brought to the fore even more sharply by Lakatos in his confrontation with empirical sociology of science. There he formulated his notable distinction between internal and external history of science. First – according to Lakatos's thesis – the historian of science has to construct an 'internal history' of the progress of good science in order to understand the facts of science; for without this heuristic construction he or she could not even identify the subject matter, that is select the relevant achievements of scientists from non-scientific achievements of human culture and other irrelevant facts of human behaviour. The aim of the historian of science, according to Lakatos, must moreover be to maximize the extent of the 'internal history' by his repeated hypothetical reconstructions of the history of science, and this means that he or she should try to understand as much of 'good' science as possible as rationally justified in this internalist sense.

Only if this attempt at an affirmative understanding and evaluation arrives at its limit is it meaningful, according to Lakatos, to try to understand and causally explain the scientists' motives in the light of empirical psychology or sociology. By this conception Lakatos has in fact, at least for the history of science, claimed the methodological priority of hermeneutic understanding over causal explanation; and moreover, going beyond Max Weber, he has in fact even claimed the priority of critical-reconstructive, that is non-value-neutral, understanding of reasons. Was thereby the priority of a conception of critical-reconstructive non-value-neutral social science or *Geisteswissenschaft* proclaimed, in general, on the level of philosophy of science? In my opinion this assumption would go too far, and this holds, as far as I can see, for the following reason.

Is history of science an exceptional case of *Geisteswissenschaft*, such that by its critical evaluation of good (or bad) science the Weberian principle of value-freeness is not refuted?

At least according to Hans Albert, Gerhard Radnitzky and Herbert Keuth,[5] Popper and Lakatos are not committed to consider the case of reconstructive history of science as a paradigm case of non-value-free cultural science or *Geisteswissenschaft* in general. They would rather consider it as an exceptional case, which is very well compatible with Weber's thesis of the value-freeness of social and cultural sciences. In general how can this be understood? One could argue as follows.

The reason for the fact that history of science, in contradistinction to all other cultural sciences or *Geisteswissenschaften*, must not be value-neutral is simply constituted by the circumstance that it can presuppose a standard or yardstick or evaluation that is itself science-immanent, namely that of progress in searching for the truth. Evaluation of scientific achievements according to this yardstick may be considered to be scientifically legitimate, in contradistinction to any evaluation of other cultural achievements according to extra-scientific yardsticks, for example those of morality. On Weber's account, understanding and evaluation of human cultural achievements in light of moral, religious or aesthetic measures would presuppose subjective and thus far irrational ultimate axioms of evaluation as measures. Only in the case of critical history of science – so one could argue along with Weber – is it objectivity itself, for the sake of which science has to be value-neutral, that provides (also) the ultimate yardstick of evaluation. Therefore – one could conclude – only evaluation in critical-reconstructive history of science can itself be objective and to that extent scientific.

(In all other cases it is possible, according to Max Weber, to understand cultural achievements only in the light of 'value-relations' that have to be supposed hypothetically. It is in this way that Weber obviously understood his own evaluations in his sociology of religion and in his reconstruction of the 'occidental process of rationalization'. These are cases, so to speak, of conditional evaluations since they are dependent on hypothetically and heuristically supposed ultimate yardsticks of evaluation such as, for example, occidental rationality in the sense of objective and means–ends rationality of action.)

Somehow in this way one could try to prove that the turn of the Popperians to critical-reconstructive history of science is compatible with Max Weber's general thesis of the necessary value-freeness of the social and cultural sciences. And thereby a widely held standard position of modern philosophy of science would be maintained. However, would this solution be satisfactory? In a first move one could argue as follows.

Precisely on Weberian premises, one could – and in a sense should – call into question even the exceptional status of history of science. It is true indeed that, on the presupposition of the 'value-axiom' of objectivity of science, the critically evaluative reconstruction of the 'internal history of science', that is the reconstruction of the progress of good science towards the truth, must itself appear to be objective and scientific. But, according to Max Weber, even the 'value-axiom' of scientific rationality and hence objectivity is a hypothetical supposition. This means that, on Weber's account, it cannot itself be grounded as being necessarily true but is based on a subjective, that is, ultimately irrational, positing of values by human beings. With this a characteristic ultimate position of contemporary philosophy is reached, which is held for example by Nietzsche, Max Weber and the existentialists. It could be expressed by the proposition: there are no ultimate, inter-subjectively valid yardsticks of evaluation (valuing); there are only ultimate subjective value decisions.

At this point I want to challenge the spirit of our time by a quite different strategy of argumentation, which I would call transcendental-pragmatic. I want to defend the thesis that there are indisputable ultimate yardsticks of evaluation not only for critical-reconstructive history of science but, beyond that level, for critical reconstruction of history in general, hence for all hermeneutic *Geisteswissenschaften*.

The indisputability of the normative presuppositions of argumentation

If I propose – as I do – a defence of the thesis that the normative presuppositions of argumentation are indisputable by rational arguments, I could immediately be confronted with the objection that I am going to commit a *petitio principii*. For exactly my talk of indisputability by rational arguments seems to show that I indeed presuppose a subjective ultimate decision in favour of the occidental value-axiom of rationality.

This objection is based on the supposition that, in our thinking, we could even step behind the rationality of argumentation and could first decide in favour of it from a vantage point outside of reason, so to speak. This again is a conception shared by many modern thinkers, for example by Nietzsche, Kierkegaard, Max Weber and especially by Karl Popper.[6] (The origin of this conception may be traced back to the voluntaristic scholastic theologians, for example Duns Scotus and William of Ockham, who defended the priority of God's will over any kind of knowledge.)

I would however claim that whoever argues in favour of this preparational decision must show that it is untenable; for by his or her very arguing he or she necessarily already lays claim on the inter-subjective validity of argumentative rationality. Thus for example by his or her directing against me the objection of my committing a *petitio principii* he or she lays claim on the inter-subjective validity of (the laws of) logic. In short: it turns out that, while arguing, one cannot, in principle, get behind the rationality of arguing: this rationality is non-circumventible (*nichthintergehbar*). And this means: there is no philosophical standpoint of pure subjectivity that would be situated even prior to the inter-subjective validity of argumentative rationality. Any attempt at disputing this must lead into a performative self-contradiction.

But what has been reached by this transcendental-pragmatic argument with regard to our problem concerning the ultimate yardstick or normative foundations of valuing? Here the next step of argumentation is the following.

We can recognize through transcendental-pragmatic reflection that at least the following claims to inter-subjective validity belong to the indisputable presuppositions of arguing.[7]

First, a claim to linguistically articulated meaning, about which it must be possible, in principle, to reach a consensus between all possible discourse partners.

Second, a claim to truth, about which it must be possible as well to reach a consensus, in principle.

Third, a claim to veracity which also must be capable of consensus, in principle.

Fourth, a claim to moral rightness capable of consensus of the acts of arguing as acts of communication and interaction in an ideal argumentation community.

The claim which corresponds to the transcendental-pragmatic fact that thinking is arguing with universal inter-subjective validity claims, implies at least the recognition of the following fundamental moral norms of an ideal communication community: equal rights of all possible communication partners and equal co-responsibility of all partners for the posing and solving of problems.[8]

Through these presuppositions of argument, which – I would claim – cannot be denied without committing a performative self-contradiction, a normative foundation for the critical-hermeneutic reconstruction of human history in general is provided.

It now turns out that there is not only a normative foundation for the truth claim of science – one that cannot be relativized to the occidental rationalization process – but, bound up with the truth claim of arguing qua communication, there is also an ultimate normative foundation for moral validity claims. It would be impossible for us to argue – and hence to think with a claim to inter-subjective validity and hence to consensus – if we could not presuppose and anticipate – of course counterfactually – an ideal communication community, and, together with this, the inter-subjective validity of certain fundamental norms of morality.

Thereby we have already proved the possibility of an ultimate foundation not only for the evaluation of scientific truth claims but also for the possible inter-subjective validity of evaluating moral rightness claims. Thereby the exceptional position of evaluation in the context of history of science has already been called in question – in favour of a certain parallelism of the ultimate yardsticks of evaluation in theoretical or practical reason. But does from this also follow the possibility of a critical-hermeneutic reconstruction of history in general, in which the paradigm of history of science – that is, the paradigm of a critical reconstruction of progress in the search for truth – would be expanded to other value dimensions – for example to those of morality and/or law? Possibly in such a way that we could postulate – by a certain extrapolation of Lakatos's conception – a priority of the internal history over the external history for the reconstruction of the history of moral consciousness and/or the institutions of law as well?

I would answer this question in the affirmative. But, in order to redeem this claim, I must introduce a new point of view for the normative foundation of the hermeneutic reconstruction of history in general. What I mean is a quasi-teleological vantage point which I would call the 'self-recuperative principle' (*Selbsteinholungsprinzip*).[9] By the predicate 'quasiteleological' I want to point out that I must not, in a dogmatic-metaphysical way, suppose a *telos* of history, as occurs in the speculative philosophy of history of, say, Hegel or Marx. Rather the transcendental-pragmatic, strictly reflexive, recourse to the indisputable presuppositions of argument must suffice, that is the recourse to those four validity claims that, as I suggested, are bound up with the consensus claims of argumentation. But how should it be possible from these presuppositions to derive a quasi-teleological yardstick for the critical evaluations of a hermeneutic reconstruction of history in general?

The self-recuperative principle of hermeneutic reconstruction of history

In this final section I suggest an answer to my question through an explication of the self-recuperative principle of hermeneutic reconstruction of history in five steps.

First, it should be clear that the indisputable presuppositions of arguing are *eo ipso* necessary presuppositions of all sciences and hence of hermeneutic historical sciences as well. Even today all particular sciences and philosophy are tied together through the transcendental-pragmatic presupposition of argumentative discourse and its necessary presuppositions, in short through the *a priori* of discourse.

Second, now it is itself a fact of history that we can recognize today that the discourse-*a priori* is a necessary presupposition of all sciences. For the 'facticity' (Heidegger) of our historical 'being-in-the-world' comprises not only the presuppositions of particular cultural traditions or forms of life, as is often suggested in our day, but also the universally valid presuppositions of the *a priori* of argumentative discourse.

Third, if it is the task of historical social or cultural sciences (*Geisteswissenschaften*) to reconstruct, through hermeneutic understanding and evaluation, the progress of human cultural evolution, then it must also belong to this task to make understandable how the insight into the *a priori* of argumentative discourse could come about and in fact has come about as a fact of history. In other words: the critical-reconstructive social or cultural sciences have got to understand their own presuppositions of rationality as a quasi-*telos* of history and hence as a normative yardstick of their critical evaluations. This I call the self-recuperative principle of hermeneutic reconstruction of history.

It provides a teleological foundation for the reconstruction of history that is not based on the metaphysical assumption that history as such is determined by a *telos* that makes it a necessary process of progress; rather it is based only on the methodological condition that a hermeneutic reconstruction of history must be able to explain itself – that is the historical fact of its own existence and function – as a result of history. Should it dispute or only disregard this methodological necessity, it would be inconsistent with its own conditions of rationality. In short: the self-recuperative principle of hermeneutic reconstruction of history follows from the principle of performative self-contradiction, given the further premise that the reconstructive sciences are themselves a fact of history to be accounted for.

Fourth, if one accepts this argument, then it follows, I suggest, that it must be possible as well to generalize (by extrapolation) the thesis of the priority of internal history over external history that was proposed by Lakatos with regard to history of science. If it is true that striving for consensus by arguments presupposes the recognition of, and compliance with, the fundamental moral norms of an ideal communication community then it is also the case that a critical reconstruction of the history of moral consciousness – and beyond that, of the institutions of law – should be possible: a reconstruction that conceives of the fundamental norms of the ideal communication community as ultimate yardsticks of its positive evaluations. And such a critical reconstruction must then claim priority over all external – merely causal (psychological and sociological) – explanations of the history of morals and law, in the same way that, as in history of science, the reconstruction of the good reasons in the sense of possible progress towards the truth must claim priority over all external explanations.

Fifth, the significance of this normative foundation of the hermeneutic reconstruction of history in general becomes evident from the following consideration: the history of modern science and philosophy is characterized by the thought figure of naturalistic reductionism as an attempt at transferring the successful method of causal and functional explanation in the natural sciences to the problems of the cultural sciences.

In this context I think especially of the numerous variants of the attempt to reduce the normative validity claims of human reason to hidden causes in the background, that is to determining natural factors that make freedom and normative reason appear to be illusions. Thus there is a series of slogans like the following: human motives in history are nothing but material interests, sexual drives, will to power, conditioned reflexes or, recently, constraints of functional social systems.

Now, already these 'nothing but' verdicts themselves share the common logical structure of not being able to take seriously their own validity claims. To this extent they entangle themselves in a performative self-contradiction. But in so far as they claim to provide an explanation of the history of cultural evolution, to that degree they are restrained by the self-recuperative principle. That is: they are refuted *a priori* in so far as they contradict the priority of 'internal history', for then they cannot explain the historical conditions of their own possibility and validity. If, however, they restrict their metaphysical/anti-metaphysical claim of total reductionism – that is the status of 'nothing but' explanations – they may indeed retain a function that is complementary to that of the hermeneutic understanding and evaluating of critical-reconstructive sciences: they may then serve as causal and functional explanations of the 'external history' of humankind which begins precisely at the limit of the 'internal' one. This limit, however, is methodologically determined through the attempt at maximizing the 'internal history', that is the effort to understand hermeneutically and evaluate as much as possible by appeal to good reasons, and that is as a contribution to progress in cultural evolution. As an example for the relationship between the two methodological approaches I would consider the rivalry between a reconstruction of the development of moral consciousness in light of Piaget's and Kohlberg's approach, on the one hand, and Nietzsche's unmasking 'genealogy of morals', on the other.[10] All tenets of the present chapter could be corroborated and illuminated by a confrontation of these two approaches to the origin and history of human morality.

Notes

1 C.G. Hempel, 'Explanation in Science and in History', in R.J. Colodny (ed.), *Frontiers in Science and Philosophy* (1966), repr. in W. Dray (ed.), *Philosophical Analysis and History* (New York: Harper & Row, 1966).

2 K. Popper, *The Poverty of Historicism* (London: Routledge & Kegan Paul, 1967).

3 K. Popper, 'On the Theory of Objective Mind', in *Objective Knowledge* (Oxford: Clarendon Press, 1972), chapter 4. Cf. also K.-O. Apel, 'History of Science as a Problem of Hermeneutics: An Argument with Karl Popper's Third-world Hermeneutics', Chapter 9 above.

4 I. Lakatos, 'Zur Geschichte der Wissenschaft und ihrer rationalen Rekonstruktionen', in W. Diederich (ed.), *Theorien zur Wissenschaftsgeschichte* (Frankfurt a. M.: Suhrkamp, 1974), 55–119.

5 G. Radnitzky, 'Wertfreiheitsthese: Wissenschaft, Ethik und Politik', in G. Anderson (ed.), *Voraussetzungen und Grenzen der Wissenschaft* (Tübingen: Mohr, 1981), 49–128; and H. Keuth, *Wissenschaft und Werturteil* (Tübingen: Mohr, 1989).

6 K. Popper, *The Open Society and its Enemies* (London: Routledge & Kegan Paul, 1966), vol. 2, 231 ff.

7 J. Habermas, 'Was heisst Universalpragmatik?', in Apel (ed.), *Sprachpragmatik und Philosophie* (Frankfurt a. M.: Suhrkamp, 1976), and *Theorie des kommunikativen Handelns* (Frankfurt a. M.: Suhrkamp, 1981), vol. 1, chapter 3.

8 Apel, *Diskurs und Verantwortung* (Frankfurt a. M.: Suhrkamp, 1988), and *Ethics and the Theory of Rationality, Selected Essays*, vol. 2 (Atlantic Highlands, N.J.: Humanities Press, 1994).

9 Apel, 'The Hermeneutic Dimension of Social Science and its Normative Foundation', *Man and World*, 25, 3/4 (1992), 247–70.

10 Apel, *Diskurs und Verantwortung*, especially 306 ff.

INDEX